T0330245

Reputation Risk and Globalisation

This book is dedicated to Natalie and Brian Burgess: two lifelong friends with flawless reputations.

Reputation Risk and Globalisation

Exploring the Idea of a Self-Regulating Corporation

Terry O'Callaghan

Senior Lecturer, The University of South Australia

 Edward Elgar
PUBLISHING

Cheltenham, UK • Northampton, MA, USA

Published by
Edward Elgar Publishing Limited
The Lypiatts
15 Lansdown Road
Cheltenham
Glos GL50 2JA
UK

Edward Elgar Publishing, Inc.
William Pratt House
9 Dewey Court
Northampton
Massachusetts 01060
USA

A catalogue record for this book
is available from the British Library

Library of Congress Control Number: 2009940997

This book is available electronically in the **Elgar**online
Business subject collection
DOI 10.4337/9781786431745

ISBN 978 1 84542 303 2 (cased)
ISBN 978 1 78643 174 5 (eBook)

Typeset by Columns Design XML Ltd, Reading
Printed and bound by CPI Group (UK) Ltd, Croydon, CR0 4YY

Contents

Figures and tables

FIGURES

TABLES

Acknowledgements

This book would not have been completed without the love and support of so many people.

I thank my wife Margherita. She has created a wonderful home environment within which to work and write. Most of all, I acknowledge her support and love over the last 22 years. *Grazie mille Margherita.*

I doubt that this book would have ever been completed without the help of Belinda Spagnoletti. She worked at the Centre for International Risk at the University of South Australia (UniSA) during the time I was writing it. She helped me to get the manuscript into publishable shape. In addition, I modified some of the language in the text as a consequence of our lengthy conversations together. We argued a lot, but the manuscript is better for it. Bel, I cannot thank you enough for your help and insightful comments on the text.

Daniel Feher is a great friend too. He is an immensely interesting person, and a fountain of knowledge on so many subjects. He is especially erudite on the concept of political risk. I have enjoyed many long conversations with him about various aspects of this idea. Our next project together will give us an opportunity, in good Oakeshottian fashion, to keep the conversation going.

Geordan Graetz has recently completed his doctorate at the University of Queensland. He is an expert on uranium mining and community engagement. Geordan is a great friend and colleague. We have been discussing the performance of the global mining sector for the past six years. This book has benefited greatly from these discussions. I look forward to seeing him begin a successful career in the years to come.

Angela Scarino is the Director of the Research Centre for Languages and Culture at UniSA. When I started at the university in 1999, Angela was my first Head of School. She soon became a terrific friend and colleague. I thank her for her support over the last 16 or so years.

The quality of this manuscript has been enhanced by the editing skills of Judith Timoney. Judith is a professional editor in the School of Communication, International Studies and Languages at UniSA. It is wonderful to have had her help towards the end of this project. She was meticulous in her attention to detail. She also gave me an insight into the world of professional editing. I thank her so much for her contribution to the manuscript.

Finally, I want to thank the two external reviewers for their comments. Their insights helped to improve the manuscript considerably.

The book is dedicated to Natalie and Brian Burgess. I would not be where I am today without their love. Brian taught me a trade as a watchmaker when I dropped out of school in the early 1970s. He also taught me how to saw wood, build stuff and be a part-time handyman. He is an extraordinarily gifted individual. It is wonderful here to acknowledge his part in my life. His wife Natalie has been immensely influential as well. She has listened to me, guided me and cared for me for all these years. She is such a wonderful friend.

I have known Natalie and Brian since 1971. It is strange to think that they are still in my life after all these years. Not many marriages last 44 years, let alone friendships. This is testament to the fact that they are such fine people. Their two favourite subjects are politics and religion. So it is even more astonishing that we are still talking! This is especially the case given my Irish heritage. I am sure they will not mind me saying so here, but we have very robust discussions. But that does not matter as much as sitting around their lounge room, chatting about the big issues of the day. They are the most engaged people I know. The wonderful thing about handing the manuscript to Edward Elgar is to thank them for their part in my life's journey. It is a gift I can never repay. But I know that it does not matter.

Abbreviations

AIDS	Acquired Immune Deficiency Syndrome
ASA	Advertising Standards Authority
BHP	Broken Hill Proprietary Company Limited
BoE	Barrel of Oil Equivalent
BP	British Petroleum
CAFE	Corporate Average Fuel Economy
CARE	Carpet America Recovery Effort
CEO	Chief Executive Officer
CIA	Central Intelligence Agency
CMA	Chemical Manufacturers Association
CNOOC	Chinese National Offshore Oil Corporation
COSA	Coalition on South Africa
CSG	Coal Seam Gas
CSR	Corporate Social Responsibility
DAN	Direct Action Network
EITI	Extractive Industries Transparency Initiative
EP	Equator Principles
EPD	Environmental Product Declaration
FOEI	Friends of the Earth International
FRA	Financial Reporting Authority
GATT	General Agreement on Tariffs and Trade
GDP	Gross Domestic Product
GFC	Global Financial Crisis
GHG	Greenhouse Gas
GM	Genetically Modified
GNI	Gross National Income
HSE	Health, Safety and Environment
ICCA	International Council of Chemical Associations
ICMM	International Council on Mining and Metals
IIED	International Institute for Environment and Development
IMF	International Monetary Fund
IOC	International Oil Company
IPCC	Intergovernmental Panel on Climate Change
IR	International Relations

IWT	International Water Tribunal
ITT	International Telephone and Telegraph
LCA	Life-Cycle Assessment
LEED	Leadership in Energy and Environmental Design
LSE	London Stock Exchange
LTO	Licence to Operate
MDG	Millennium Development Goal
MIGA	Multilateral Investment Guarantee Agency
MIT	Massachusetts Institute of Technology
MMS	Minerals Management Service
MMSD	Mining, Minerals and Sustainable Development
MNC	Multinational Corporation
MNE	Multinational Enterprise
MOSOP	Movement for the Survival of the Ogoni People
NASDAQ	National Association of Securities Dealers Automated Quotations
NGO	Non-Governmental Organisation
NHTSA	National Highway Traffic Safety Administration
OB	Obsolescing Bargain
OECD	Organisation for Economic Co-operation and Development
OICA	Organization of Motor Vehicle Manufacturers
OPIC	Overseas Private Investment Corporation
OSPAR	The Convention for the Protection of the Marine Environment of the North-East Atlantic
OTML	Ok Tedi Mining Limited
OWS	Occupy Wall Street
PCB	Polychlorinated Biphenyl
PETA	People for the Ethical Treatment of Animals
PNG	Papua New Guinea
PRI	Political Risk Insurance
PR	Public Relations
PVC	Polyvinyl Chloride
QUEST	Quality Utilizing Employees' Suggestions and Teamwork
RDSL	Royal Dutch Shell Limited
RQ	Reputation Quotient
SARF	Social Amplification of Risk Framework
SDG	Sustainable Development Goals
SG	Secretary-General
SME	Small to Medium Enterprise
SRO	Self-Regulatory Organisation
SUV	Sport Utility Vehicle
TNC	Transnational Corporation

TPS	Toyota Production System
TRIPS	Trade Related Aspects of Intellectual Property Rights
UN	United Nations
UNCTC	United Nations Centre on Transnational Corporations
UniSA	University of South Australia
UNESCO	United Nations Educational, Scientific and Cultural Organization
UNGC	United Nations Global Compact
UNICEF	United Nations International Children's Emergency Fund
Unocal	Union Oil Company of California
US	United States
VOC	Volatile Organic Compound
WBCSD	World Business Council on Sustainable Development
WBG	World Bank Group
WEF	World Economic Forum
WHO	World Health Organization
WSF	World Social Forum
WTO	World Trade Organization
WWW	World Wide Web
ZSL	Zoological Society of London

Introduction

I begin this introduction with a short story about a crisis that happened to Australia's largest mining company. The crisis occurred around the time that globalisation was becoming the subject of intense debate among academics, journalists and social commentators. The company in question is The Broken Hill Proprietary Limited (BHP).[1]

BHP merged with Anglo-Dutch company Billiton in 2001. The merged entity became known as BHP Billiton. At the time, it was the largest in the history of the industry. It capped off a thirty-year plan by BHP to become a global mining giant. The merged company is now the largest diversified mining company in the world. Currently, the company has a market capitalisation of US$176 billion and revenues of US$67.2 billion (BHP, 2014: 4). As of 2014, the company has 31 active mines in 12 countries. These include nine oil and gas operations, five copper mines, two iron ore mines, seven coal mines, and eight aluminium, manganese and nickel mines (BHP, 2014: 6–7).

Until the 1980s, BHP had a predominantly Australian focus, centred on its operations at Broken Hill in New South Wales. After that, it began to globalise. It acquired coal mines in New Mexico and discovered huge reserves of copper in Chile (the Escondida Mine). In 1980, after Kennecott Copper failed to reach an agreement with the government of Papua New Guinea (PNG), BHP stepped in and was able to gain approval to mine gold and copper on Mount Fubilan in the Western Province of the country.

BHP put together an international consortium. This included Amoco and a number of small West German companies. The initial agreement gave both BHP and Amoco a 30 per cent share in the project. The West German companies held a 20 per cent share. The PNG government held the remaining 20 per cent. At the time, it was the PNG government's largest income stream. Ok Tedi Mining Limited (OTML), as the joint venture came to be known, began mining gold in 1984 and copper in 1987 (Thompson and Macklin, 2010: 192). BHP would later buy out its smaller German partners and they ended up with a 60 per cent interest in the mine (Thompson and Macklin, 2010: 196).

The Ok Tedi mine is located in the Star Mountains, close to the headwaters of the Ok Tedi River. The Ok Tedi River runs parallel to the Fly River for about 200 kilometres, before the two systems merge at D'Albertis Junction. The Fly River then continues some 450 kilometres, before empting into the Gulf of Papua. The Fly River flood plain covers an area of about 5800 square kilometres. The terrain is mountainous and prone to seismic activity and landslides. The mine itself is situated some 600 kilometres south of the equator and 1800 metres up Mount Fubilan. The rainfall varies in the area. According to BHP, rainfall could be as high as 10 000 millimetres annually, that is, the equivalent of 400 inches of rain a year.

From the outset, the project was plagued with environmental problems. In June 1984, 2700 60-litre drums of sodium cyanide spilled into the Fly River when the barge carrying the drums overturned. This was the largest loss of cyanide into a watercourse in the world. Only 117 drums were recovered. In addition, when a bypass valve malfunctioned five days later, some 1000 cubic metres of untreated cyanide waste discharged into the Ok Tedi River (King, 1997: 97). Of more significance, however, is an avalanche that destroyed the tailings dam and severely impacted on the surrounding ecosystem. Without the option of a workable tailings dam, the company began to dispose of tailings and other waste directly into the river. This included both solid waste, and a cocktail of sulphur and other heavy metals from the mine. The acid used to separate the ore from the waste rock also found its way into the river system.

The OTML project brought jobs and other benefits to the communities in the region. This included schools, medical facilities and other valuable infrastructure. Indeed, it has been an important agent of development for the poor Western Province. Economically, the mine also provided about 10 per cent of PNG's Gross Domestic Product (GDP). However, the dumping of tailings and other waste into the Ok Tedi River has had a terrible impact on the local region and its inhabitants.

First, waste from the mine has raised the level of the river bed five or six metres and this led to flooding during periods of high rainfall. The flooding also swept away valuable nutrient-rich top soil, making it more difficult for locals to establish gardens and grow food. Periodic flooding has also spread mine waste and other sediment over the nearby forest floor. Second, there has been an estimated 90 per cent reduction in fish stocks and this has led to a shortage of food.[2] Third, the vegetation around the river systems has either died or become severely stressed by the sediment. Some reports suggest that as much as 2725 square kilometres had been affected by it.[3] Fourth, transport on the river is now more difficult because of the increased flow rates. Consequently, dredging is now a daily feature of life on the river.[4] Finally, the cultural impact on the 50 000 or so people living in the area has been profound.

A group of landowners began to express concern about the impact of the tailings and waste disposal on the local ecosystem. In response to the situation, locals did four things. They sent a petition to the PNG government and to OTML. They travelled to the Rio Earth Summit to protest the environmental damage. They filed a claim against the company at the International Water Tribunal (IWT). Finally, they sent protest letters to the PNG Prime Minister and to the Prime Minister of Australia, Paul Keating (Gordon, 1997: 143).

At first, they were unsuccessful in either getting BHP to stop polluting the Ok Tedi, or in gaining compensation. BHP simply did not listen. In May and June 1994, an Australian law firm, acting on behalf of locals living in the affected area, brought a class action against BHP in the Melbourne Supreme Court. According to Gordon (1997: 151), one of the lawyers acting for the plaintiffs, 'Victoria was selected for the four test cases because the plaintiffs wanted Australians to see the damage an Australian company had done to their lands and their lifestyle'.

Right from the start BHP displayed complete indifference to the issue. They failed to lodge their defence on time, and rather than confronting the issue, they tried to get the judge to dismiss the complaints. They also told the plaintiffs that they were happy to fight the case in court, but argued that the plaintiffs had to place AU$2 million dollars into a trust account so that they could pay BHP's legal bills if they lost the case. This was a problematic play, given the high level of poverty among the local villagers.

More serious was their attempt to manipulate the PNG government. The company was found guilty of criminal contempt for its involvement in drafting legislation in PNG that would jail anyone who publicly objected to the mine or sought compensation. To make matters worse, the company spent a large sum of money trying to persuade the Australian public that the tailings waste was not affecting the river; that the local ecosystem was not under stress; and the plaintiffs were simply vexatious litigators. Eventually, BHP agreed to settle with the plaintiffs and instituted a mine waste management plan to reduce the environmental damage. They also paid compensation to the landowners.

To many, BHP's behaviour throughout the case was unconscionable and arrogant. The company was criticised by the Australian government, the media and non-governmental organisations. Even comedy shows and media cartoonists poked fun at the company. One cartoonist in particular noted that they responded to the disaster by launching a 'massive self-promotion campaign' (Banks and Ballard, 1997: 2).

While BHP was forced to take responsibility for the disaster, the government of PNG must also shoulder some of the blame. Interested in bringing development to the Western Province, it allowed the mine to operate without an adequate environmental regime in place. Part of the reason for its laxity was the fact that it derived substantial revenues from the mine. The government decided that the environmental damage was an acceptable price to pay for the lucrative revenue stream. Indeed, as BHP pointed out, even when they wanted to leave the project, the PNG government requested the company continue to manage the mine until its closure date.[5] Eventually, BHP divested itself of the asset and placed the proceeds of the sale in a development fund in the Netherlands.

BHP now admits that it failed to consult with the affected communities. It also decided to end its policy of disposing of tailings into local river systems. However, what lessons have been learned from this debacle is unclear. In 2000, the company was seriously investigating the possibility of mining a large nickel deposit on Gag Island, off the coast of Irian Jaya. They were exploring the possibility of disposing the tailings waste at sea, in an area that the United Nations Educational, Scientific and Cultural Organization (UNESCO) was considering for a world heritage listing. Given concerns about this project from BHP's own shareholders, it is perhaps a blessing that the Indonesian government stepped in and enacted a forestry law, which meant that it prevented any further mining activity on the island. Otherwise, BHP might have found itself at the centre of another environmental disaster and another difficult reputational crisis.

There are a couple of coincidences with the environmental problems BHP experienced at the Ok Tedi mine. First, the Brundtland Report was released in 1987, at a time when BHP began to experience problems. The report argued that contemporary resource usage should not be so aggressive that it compromises the ability of future generations to have access to these same resources. Underlying this message was an environmental one. MNCs could no longer exploit the earth's natural resources with impunity, or leave a terrible environmental legacy for future generations. Unfortunately, BHP had done both. It had destroyed the area surrounding the two river systems in PNG and undermined the capacity of the children of locals to enjoy their traditional lands in the way that their parents and grandparents had done. In essence, the Brundtland Report painted companies like BHP as greedy and rapacious, happy to ignore the needs of future generations in the pursuit of profits today.

Second, the determination of BHP to become a global player in the mining industry dovetailed with the emergence of globalisation. Globalisation is a term used to explain the political, economic, cultural and technical changes that were taking place around the world during the late 1980s and early 1990s. Most definitions revolve around thinking about the world as a single place, and the fact that new communications technologies were beginning to link the distant corners of the earth. Add computer power and access to new sources of information and you have a revolution of historical proportions, Moss Kanter's (cited in Scholte, 1997: 15) playful notion that '[t]he world is becoming a global shopping mall in which ideas and products are available everywhere at the same time...' nicely captures the impact of globalisation on contemporary politics. Also terms like 'globalism', 'global society', global commons' or even 'planetary politics', made their debut during this important period. The collapse of the Soviet Union and the end of communism further heightened the sense that the world had become a very different place than it had been for those who had lived through the 1950s, 1960s and 1970s. BHP's expansion plans ran into the headwinds of globalisation. It was a game-changer for them, as it was for all large multinational corporations (MNCs). Perhaps the best evidence of this is that BHP was the first large MNC to be sued by people living in another sovereign state. This was a sign that globalisation was beginning to undermine the protection that sovereign borders once offered to companies like BHP.

BHP and the OK Tedi disaster is a good example of a company caught between two eras. Drop 80 million tonnes of waste into a river system in the 1940s and nobody would, in all likelihood, have blinked an eye. Do it during the era of globalisation, and the company becomes a pariah, with serious reputational issues to contend with.

Globalisation has profoundly changed the way that MNCs conduct business. In response to it, most companies now have corporate social responsibility (CSR) initiates, work hard to integrate into the communities in which they operate, and are now more aware of the impact of their activities on communities than ever before. BHP Billiton now has part of its website devoted to its social and environmental commitments.

There is now a very large body of literature on various aspects of CSR. Some writers are critical of the concept, while others see a real tangible shift in corporate thinking. Ellis (2012) highlights the extent to which MNCs are now building sustainable business success through innovation and entrepreneurship. She refers to these companies as 'the new pioneers'. These pioneers are 'this century's generation of visionary leaders, social entrepreneurs and social intrapreneurs that are turning the doom and gloom of current global challenges into new business opportunities and sustainable ways of creating value' (Ellis, 2012: xxiv).

Pioneering MNCs are now realising that there are considerable benefits in becoming a self-regulating corporation. These benefits include, among other things, an increase in market share, improved environmental performance and, most importantly of all, a reduction in reputation risk. In the future, those MNCs that do not self-regulate will be left behind by those that do.

The idea that MNCs have a capacity for self-regulation is provocative. Certainly, many non-governmental organisations (NGOs) and activist groups would take issue with this proposition. I examine the arguments of these groups at various points in the first three chapters. I argue that while many of their arguments are problematic, they are a key reason why MNCs are now moving in the direction of corporate self-regulation.

Unfortunately, these NGOs and activist groups are never able to get beyond a negative view of MNCs and, in many ways, have not fully comprehended their success in changing the behaviour of MNCs over time. What they have been extremely effective at doing is politicising the corporate reputations of these large companies. That is, they have had a disciplining effect on MNC behaviour. In effect, activist pressure has caused MNCs to adjust their behaviour to a new commercial and social reality. As a consequence, I argue that corporate self-regulation is the next step in the evolution of business–society relations.

The book is divided into two parts. The first part is largely theoretical. I highlight the shortcomings in the activist understanding of business–society relations and explore how corporate reputation is changing the way that MNCs think about their interactions with society. In addition, I examine various forms of regulation, including command and control, industry self-regulation and corporate self-regulation. I defend the latter notion against its critics.

The second half of the book examines the way three individual MNCs have dealt with the challenge of corporate self-regulation. These are Royal Dutch Shell, the Toyota Motor Corporation and Interface Inc. The choice of cases is important. First, with the exception of perhaps the chemical industry, the oil industry, automotive industry and the carpet industry are the worst polluting industries in the world. For example, the oil industry has the highest level of greenhouse gas, methane and sulphur emissions. In addition, it produces more hazardous waste than most other industries combined. In addition, the automotive industry is linked to high levels of pollution, road deaths, and a high use of raw materials, including steel, iron, rubber, copper and rare earth minerals. Similarly, hundreds of thousands of tonnes of used carpet go to landfill each year.

As a petroleum by-product, it does not begin to break down for decades. Second, each of the companies has a unique story to tell about their efforts to move toward corporate self-regulation. The first two cases faced serious crises along the way. This severely dented their reputations. Their rehabilitation is worth discussing on its own terms. The third case is crisis free, but no less compelling. It is a story of a company that has systematically changed its philosophy, manufacturing processes and relationship to the environment. As a consequence, it has gained unparalleled respect in the business community. The world's largest company, Walmart, has sought inspiration from Interface. This is a company that seeks to have no environment footprint by 2020 and, after that, to become a restorative company, that is, a company that decouples economic activity from nature and begins to heal the earth. Consequently, this book argues that Interface offers the best example of a self-regulating corporation to date. But valuable lessons can also be learned from the experiences of Royal Dutch Shell and the Toyota Motor Corporation. Both these companies became embroiled in terrible corporate crises and had their reputations severely damaged. These crises were both costly and embarrassing. Moreover, neither company reacted to their problems particularly well. So they give us an interesting look at the swings and roundabouts of managing reputational crises.

The conclusion of this book refers to an endangered species of Australian parrot. It is called the night parrot. This little bird is thought to have been extinct since the 1920s. In fact, in a 1970s compendium of Australian birds, it is the only entry without a photograph. The last live capture of the night parrot occurred in 1867 in the Gawler Ranges in South Australia. But it has recently been spotted and photographed by ornithologists in the desert country of Queensland and the Pilbara region in Western Australia. It is a wonderful example of the resilience of nature. But it is also an example of what we owe to the environment. To lose sight of a little bird for almost a century is a great loss. To find this little bird alive and flourishing in the remote parts of Australia is a miracle. I hope that the night parrot becomes an emblem for a new type of company. This is a type of company that many commentators also thought to be extinct, but is re-emerging as a more ethical and responsible organisation.

Finally, corporate self-regulation is a discipline. MNCs are now judged on their capacity to moderate their behaviour in light of community expectations. In the future, MNCs will be more disciplined than they were 20 years ago. The age of MNC profligacy is over. We have anti-corporate activists largely to thank for ushering in a new era of ethical business conduct.

This book is a narrative of change in corporate behaviour over the last twenty years. There is probably no company that will not be challenged in the coming years on social, political and environmental grounds. The lessons from Shell and Toyota offer other companies a blueprint for a shift in thinking. Interface went through tough economic times in trying to realise its environmental vision. That they are now the world's largest carpet tile manufacturer is testament to the fact that the company had a clear vision and was willing to take a risk.

The book presents challenges to two interest groups. First, it challenges anti-corporate activists to hone the quality of their arguments in relation to MNCs and to understand that they are not all the same, and are certainly not all predators. In many cases, the arguments construct a 'straw man'. This is not conducive to a mature debate about the impact and value of MNCs to society. Second, it challenges other MNCs to understand the trials and tribulations of the three companies examined in the case studies. In my view, Interface Inc. is a global lighthouse for other companies to be guided by. The argument of this book is that it offers a path for other companies to follow. Consequently, I hope this book will be read by anti-corporate activists and MNCs alike. The goal of the book is to improve the quality of criticism of MNC behaviour, and hopefully to offer some insights into MNCs seeking to improve their relationship with the communities where they operate and to build strong corporate reputations.

NOTES

1. On the history of BHP see Thompson and Macklin (2010).
2. It is also worth pointing out that prior to the dumping, there were a number of commercial fishers operating along the river. They were forced out of business by the damage to the river system.
3. Mining, Minerals and Sustainable Development (2002: 9).
4. Alex Maun, one of the plaintiffs against BHP, and member of the local Yonggom people, described the impact in the following terms: 'Fish of all species that lived in the river died and floated up to the surface. Now fish are hardly found in the river. The whole ecosystem is completely dead. The Ok Ted river has been polluted with the sediment from the mine. The river bed has filled up with sediment causing the river level to rise. Sediment has also been deposited along the river banks, leaving a muddy effluent of one metre deep. The Ok Tedi river overflows its banks, depositing waste and sediment along what was the most fertile area for gardening. Instead of enriching the soil so that crops can be grown almost continuously along the edge of the river, the sediment from the mine stops crops from growing at all ... The lives of all the people along the Ok Tedi river are a complete disaster' (cited in Banks and Ballard, 1997: 113–14).
5. However, in 2001, the PNG government passed a bill indemnifying BHP from any further liabilities for the environmental damage caused to the OK Tedi and Fly River systems. In return, BHP placed its 52 per cent stake in the mine into a trust fund for the rehabilitation of the devastated area.

1. Towards corporate self-regulation

It is hard to imagine a world without multinational corporations (MNCs).[1] They provide much-needed goods and services, undertake invaluable research and development, and coordinate most of the world's trade and investment. Without them, it would be impossible to telephone family and friends overseas, travel to new and exotic destinations, watch global events on television, or indulge in life's many luxuries. Indeed, if MNCs did not exist, our life experiences would be truncated, localised and, in all probability, quite miserable. But when they spill toxic chemicals into our rivers, pollute the atmosphere, defraud investors, and are linked to mercenary groups and wicked dictatorships, critics are right to question whether they do more harm than good.

When challenged about their activities, MNCs have often claimed that their sole purpose is to maximise shareholder value. They exist to make a profit, and return a portion of that profit to those individuals who have a financial stake in the success of the company. In order to live up to this commitment, it is sometimes necessary for them to engage in socially questionable ventures, such as mining on traditional lands or logging old-growth forests. Friedman (1970: 126) famously articulates this view when he suggests that '[t]here is one and only one social responsibility of business – to use its resources and engage in activities designed to increase its profits so long as it stays within the rules of the game, which is to say, engages in open and free competition without deception or fraud'. But, as Schwartz and Gibb (1999: 59) perceptively point out, many MNCs have sought to maximise shareholder value by playing outside the rules of the game, that is, by operating in what they call the 'gray area'.

Friedman's defence of the function of the corporation in society is no longer convincing, nor is it providing much of a safeguard for MNCs against criticism of their behaviour. Governments are displaying a greater willingness to punish companies for criminal and regulatory breaches. Activist groups are more adept than ever at mounting powerful and embarrassing protest campaigns. The global media have also shown a fondness for highlighting corporate crime, despite themselves being large

MNCs. And, as the experience of *News of the Day* in Great Britain demonstrates, even large media organisations are not immune from crisis.

Members of the general public, too, are standing up to MNCs.[2] In Australia, farmers are protesting against coal seam gas (CSG) exploration on their properties, while a number of coastal communities in Queensland are opposing development projects that may impact on the local marine environment, especially around the Great Barrier Reef.

There are numerous other examples of civil society groups who have 'bested' MNCs. The issue of control over the water supply in Cochabamba, Bolivia, is one of the most recent examples of a successful protest against a large MNC. Dangl's (2007) account of this protest is a powerful reminder that ordinary people can effect meaningful change in the societies in which they live.[3]

Over the last decade, and in response to pressure from activist groups, many MNCs have been reinventing (and rebranding) themselves as socially responsible, environmentally sensitive actors. This has resulted in the emergence of a range of new corporate strategies for addressing community concerns.[4]

Royal Dutch Shell is one of the first MNCs to rethink its business model.[5] Others, like The Body Shop, have been remarkably successful in committing to an ethical approach to business. Even those MNCs with a poor ethical track record in the past have begun to promote themselves as good corporate citizens. Nike, a company associated with sweatshops, exploited labour and human rights violations, has stated that it is working to transform community perception of its business activities as immoral. The company is now a signatory to the United Nations Global Compact (UNGC) (Fisher and Lovell, 2006: 495). It has also founded a not-for-profit foundation to further development goals in the poorer countries of the world. Specifically, the Nike Foundation focuses its attention on improving the welfare of adolescent girls. The programme is called The Girl Effect (n.d.).

The mission statement of the organisation is called the Girl Declaration. It includes five goals and seven principles to improve the lives of young women. As the organisation's website notes:

> Girls were left out of the original Millennium Development Goals. The Girl Declaration has been written to make sure that doesn't happen again. Bringing together the thinking of 508 girls living in poverty across the globe with the expertise of more than 25 of the world's leading development organizations, the Girl Declaration is our tool to stop poverty before it starts.

Given that there are as many as 600 million adolescent girls living in poverty worldwide, Nike's commitment is symbolic, and could easily be read as a cynical attempt to tie the company to an important global social issue. Indeed, it is possible to argue that the company had learnt nothing from its sweatshops crisis. Instead of exploiting young women in its sweatshops in Asia, it is now exploiting 508 girls to demonstrate to the world that it is a responsible, caring company. What the Nike project highlights, though, is the extent to which companies are now seeking to engage with important social issues. This is indeed a revolution in corporate behaviour.

Jackson (2004: 21) argues that we are witnessing the emergence of a new paradigm in international business. At the heart of this paradigm is what he calls the 'business integrity thesis'. This thesis suggests that, while investors want to see financially profitable enterprises, they also want companies to engage in environmentally and socially responsible conduct. According to him, the engine driving this paradigm shift is the corporate reputation. This has become the most prized commodity of MNCs in an era of globalisation.

If a concern with corporate reputation is the engine driving this new business paradigm, it is activist groups that have fanned the flame of change (Nace, 2005: 197–218; Manheim, 2002).[6] Business advocate Peters (1999) observes that these groups have discovered that they could 'name and shame' offending companies and, in so doing, affect their reputations in the marketplace (Skeel, 2005; Bartley and Child, 2010).[7] Peters likens these groups to prehistoric velociraptors. He argues (1999: 1) that '[t]he Velociraptor was among creation's most ferocious predators, and its killer instincts live on in the form of well-intentioned but deadly activist groups ready to shred and devour your company's reputation'.

I call this broad group of dissenters 'anti-corporate activists'. The identifiable characteristics of anti-corporate activists are first, an opposition to what they call 'corporate rule'. By this, they mean that the international community has allowed MNCs to gain control over the political and economic processes of international politics. Anti-corporate activists seek to overturn this state of affairs. As Danaher and Mark (2003: 1) note: '[a]n insurrection against corporate rule is underway'. Second, they are fiercely opposed to capitalism, neoliberalism and globalisation. While these are interwoven concepts, anti-corporate activists see these ideas as the philosophical, political and economic foundation of MNC power. Finally, they are the group most dangerous to the interests of MNCs. Manheim and Holt argue that anti-corporate activists pose an 'existential threat' to MNCs. As they (Manheim and Holt, 2013: 430) note: 'It is anticorporate campaigners, not labor activists, who hang by ropes from bridges and buildings to garner attention, anticorporate campaigners, not activist investors, who challenge legislatures to rescind corporate charters'.

The arguments of anti-corporate activists are most clearly articulated in Mander and Goldsmiths' *The Case Against the Global Economy* (1996); Karliner's *Corporate Planet* (1997); Korten's *When Corporations Rule the World* (2001); Danaher and Mark's *Insurrection* (2003); Bakan's *The Corporation* (2005); Willis and Hardcastle's *The I Hate Corporate America Reader* (2004); and Derber's *Corporation Nation* (2014). The sentiment flowing from these works can be summed up crudely by Willis and Hardcastle (2004: ix–x).

> Corporations exert a troubling influence – make that horrifying – degree of control over every aspect of our lives: our work, our play, our entertainment, our health care, our food supply, our transportation, our environment, our government … Hmmm. You know what? We think we're getting fucked – and so are you.[8]

Other well-known voices in this space include Noam Chomsky, Noreena Hertz, George Monbiot, Gore Vidal, Howard Zinn, Michael Moore, John Pilger, Vandana Shiva, Naomi Klein and Tariq Ali. These are highly politicised opponents of MNCs, and fair and reasoned argument is sometimes less important than the moral rhetoric necessary to get their point across (O'Callaghan, 2007b). We can get some idea of this rhetoric from a passage from Korten's well-known book. He (2001: 22) suggests that globalisation has:

> [t]ransformed once beneficial corporations and financial institutions into instruments of a market tyranny that reaches across the planet like a cancer, colonizing ever more of the planet's living spaces, destroying livelihoods, displacing people, rendering democratic institutions impotent, and feeding on life in an insatiable quest for money.

Whether one agrees with the provocative nature of this sentiment or not, I argue that anti-corporate activists have been instrumental in pushing MNCs to embrace a new and more ethical approach to business.

Their negative critique of MNCs has been very successful – up to a point. Anti-corporate activists have managed to turn the corporate reputations of MNCs into a political issue. At the same time, I argue that their inability to move beyond a negative ideological critique has now blunted much of the force of their attacks. This is not to say that they are irrelevant. They simply do not understand the extent of the shift in MNC behaviour that is taking place today. Nor do they understand how important they have been in driving this agenda.

The chapter is divided into four sections. The first section discusses the four main criticisms that anti-corporate activists level at MNCs. There are other issues, but these dominate the debate. The second section looks at the rise and fall of anti-corporate activist power over the last decade or so. The third section examines how international institutions are adding their voice to this important debate. The final section explores the 'politicisation' of the corporate reputation. It employs the social amplification of risk framework (SARF) to explain theoretically why anti-corporate activists have been so successful in getting their negative message about MNCs across. Put simply, as a consequence of globalisation, anti-corporate activists have become adept at communicating risk to the public. By painting MNCs as a threat, they increase the degree of fear about them in the broader community. This novel tactic has led to MNCs taking the challenge of anti-corporate activists more seriously than ever before. As a result, MNCs are responding in novel ways to this challenge. Some of these strategies I discuss further in the case study chapters. This chapter concludes by suggesting that MNCs are now moving toward corporate self-regulation as a means of dealing with anti-corporate activist pressure, as well as that emanating from international institutions such as the United Nations (UN). In short, corporate reputation is having a disciplining affect on MNC behaviour. As a consequence, we are entering a new period in business–society relations. The corporate reputation is now calling the shots in this debate.

MNCS IN THE CROSS-HAIRS

MNCs are commercial enterprises that carry out profit-making activities in more than one country (Griffiths et al., 2014: 224). The definition of an MNC is contested. O'Brien and Williams (2010: 188) note that '[m]ost writers make no distinction between these terms and have settled for one terminology rather than another without any seeming reflection on the implications of these terms'.[9] They acknowledge, however, that the term 'multinational corporation' (MNC) is most commonly used in the international political economy literature, and that trend is continued here.

The last decade or so has seen a remarkable increase in the number of MNCs. In 1998, the UN estimated that there were over 53 000 MNCs operating around the world. In addition, another 450 000 foreign affiliates had commercial relationships with these companies (Kegley and Wittkopf, 2004: 226). By 2007, that number had increased dramatically. According to the *2007 World Investment Report* (UNCTAD, 2007) that number had increased to 77 175, and these parent companies owned more than 773 000 commercial affiliates (Kegley and Blanton, 2009: 205).

Some MNCs now have larger revenues than many sovereign states. In 2007, ExxonMobil had revenues of US$390.32 billion and the company made a staggering US$40.6 billion profit (ExxonMobil, 2007: 4). In 2010, with a drop in the price of oil, profits fell to a modest US$37.012 billion (ExxonMobil, 2010: 10). In 2013, the company rebounded with US$420.83 billion in revenues and made a profit of US$33.44 billion (ExxonMobil, 2013). This is larger than the gross national income (GNI) of Norway, the Philippines and South Africa. Similarly, according to Walmart's (2014) most recent annual report, the company earned revenues totalling US$476.29 billion and made US$16.022 billion profit.

Anti-corporate activists never tire of highlighting how this wealth is (mis)used to advance the interests of MNCs, at the expense of local communities. They level a number of criticisms at MNCs. While these are expressed in various ways, they can be distilled into four key concerns. First, MNCs have excessive power and influence over national governments. This power undermines democracy. Second, they have a poor human rights record. Third, they pollute the environment. Fourth, they weaken traditional cultures and promote cultural homogenisation.[10] I examine each of these issues in turn.

They Have Excessive Power and Influence

MNCs evaluate political risk as a matter of course. Countries that have a stable political environment are generally more preferable sites for investment than those that are unstable, prone to spontaneous changes of government and policy direction, and where the obsolescing bargain may occur (Vernon, 1971; Vivoda, 2008).[11] However, the type of political system governing the host country is a much less important factor. MNCs can operate as easily in an authoritarian country as they can in a representative democracy. The mining company Freeport McMoRan has had a strong relationship with the Suharto regime in Indonesia (Waldman, 1998). This began in the late 1960s, and continued until Suharto stepped down from power in 1998 (Leith, 2002). In this sense, MNCs are moral relativists; they rarely make ethical judgements about the merits of one political system over another, or the merits of a particular government. They are often on record as stating that, as a matter of corporate policy, they do not interfere in the domestic affairs of the countries in which they operate.[12]

For anti-corporate activists, this is a difficult argument to accept. The moment an MNC begins to negotiate with a host government for a licence to operate (LTO), it enters into a dialogue that has political consequences and outcomes. For example, tax breaks reduce government revenue, which has an impact on the distribution of goods and services to local communities. An agreement between a host country and an MNC to mine a tract of land may infringe on the rights of traditional landowners. Most large MNCs are also members of host country chambers of commerce and various industry groups. The express purpose of these organisations is to lobby governments on behalf of their members. MNCs may not be directly involved in these negotiations, but membership amounts to a de facto involvement in the political process, as these organisations actively seek to influence public policy for the benefit of their members.

Anti-corporate activists, then, argue that MNCs interfere in the political process. But in this, MNCs are no different from non-governmental organisations (NGOs), political parties, elites, and other well-placed individuals. Where anti-corporate activists believe that MNCs are most damaging, however, is as a result of their immense economic and political bargaining power.[13]

Certainly, they have enormous wealth at their disposal, possess superior technology, and are able to utilise the intellectual and legal powers of the best negotiators and lawyers.[14] In addition to this, bilateral and multilateral trade regimes clearly favour MNCs. The Multilateral Investment Guarantee Agency (MIGA) and the Overseas Private Investment Corporation (OPIC) also favour the interests of MNCs. Wells and Ahmed (2007) are forthright in their view that the power of these organisations to support the interests of MNCs is significant. Spagnoletti and O'Callaghan (2011) also note the extent to which the Political Risk Insurance (PRI) industry underpins a great deal of MNC activity in the developing world, albeit at an enormous cost to the insured companies.

One of the most often cited examples of an MNC interfering in the political process of another country is the role that International Telephone and Telegraph (ITT) played in the overthrow of Chilean President Salvador Allende in the 1970s (Sampson, 1973).

Allende was a democratically elected leader who had a socialist agenda for his country. When elected, one of the first political decisions he made was to nationalise the assets of a number of American MNCs, including Kennecott Copper and ITT.[15] The latter pressured the United States (US) government to overthrow Allende and have its assets returned. With support from ITT and Kennecott Copper, the Central Intelligence Agency (CIA) engineered a coup to remove Allende from power. During the coup, Allende reportedly committed suicide, and a fascist military junta came to power that was favourable to US interests.

The Pinochet regime turned out to be one of the most repressive in Latin America. ITT had a direct hand in removing a democratically elected president and, as a consequence, fostered 28 years of tyranny in Chile.[16]

A more recent example is Chevron's lobbying of the American Congress in 2005 to stop the China National Offshore Oil Corporation's (CNOOC) bid to acquire the Union Oil Company of California (Unocal). CNOOC wanted to purchase Unocal because of its large footprint in Asia. Chevron wanted to acquire the company for much the same reasons. Chevron used its influence to persuade the House of Representatives and President George W. Bush Jr that the CNOOC bid threatened America's energy security. The resulting negative press led CNOOC to withdraw its bid for the company and this, then, paved the way for Chevron to buy Unocal for US$18.4 billion in stock and cash (Mouawad and Barboza, 2005). The amount was considerably lower than the CNOOC offer.

Anti-corporate activists often draw a link between MNCs and the subversion of democracy within home countries as well. This is a particularly controversial issue in the US, where the relationship between politicians and MNCs is very close. Bendell and Kearins (2005: 374) highlight the problem of political lobbying by MNCs. According to them, this includes the financing of political campaigns, threats to relocate their industries offshore, contributions and gifts to well-connected public figures, and the provision of funding to peak industry bodies. Toyota's funding of the American Automobile Manufacturers Association's campaign to stop a law requiring all new passenger cars achieve a 35 miles to the gallon efficiency is a good example of this practice. In addition, almost one-third of the members of the US Defense Policy Board are representatives of large American MNCs, such as Lockheed Martin and Gulfstream Aerospace. Given the emphasis that the US places on democracy, anti-corporate activists worry that this close (perhaps cosy) relationship undermines the democratic process. Jewell (2004: 138–9) offers an interesting approach to this question. He has developed a chart he calls 'USA, Inc.' that shows the linkages between defence MNCs and individuals in government. It shows a complex web of linkages and relationships between companies, the White House, Congress, the CIA, the Pentagon and, interestingly, Saudi Arabia. Jewell argues that: 'the threat that corporations pose to our democracy is clear. The tapestry of government/corporate influence illustrated by U.S.A. Inc. is not a democracy of the people. It is not the democracy envisaged by our forefathers' (Jewell, 2004: 137).[17] Bakan (2005: 95) makes the same point in a slightly different way. He argues that '[c]orporate America's long and patient campaign to gain control of government ... is now succeeding'.

They Abuse Human Rights

Anti-corporate activists argue that MNCs are also responsible for significant human rights abuses.[18] Concern about the link between the activities of MNCs and human rights abuse is not new. The early colonial trading companies were notorious for their disregard of human rights, with slavery being the most obvious example.

In recent years, a number of high-profile court cases in the US involving MNCs and human rights abuses have brought the issue to the attention of the public (Muchlinski, 2001: 31). These cases followed a US court decision to allow protest groups to use the Alien Torts Statute to litigate against American companies for their activities in foreign jurisdictions. *Business Week* has called this statute a 'milestone for human rights' (*Business Week*, 2005; Kurlantzick, 2004). The statute allows foreign litigants to seek financial damages in the US courts. A Colombian Labour union brought a lawsuit against Coca-Cola for allegedly employing a paramilitary group that killed union organisers (Leech, 2001).[19] Unocal found itself in a similar position during the construction of a US$1.2 billion pipeline through a remote part of Myanmar (Burma) (Benson, 2000). Opposition from local villagers and a refusal to work on the infrastructure project led to military intervention. Allegations of murder, torture, rape and forced labour surfaced. Human rights groups were continually refused entry into the country to verify the truth of these claims. While Unocal denied any wrongdoing, the statute provided a legal basis for a lawsuit brought against the company by 15 unidentified villagers (Wells, 1998).[20]

A second suit brought against the company by the National Coalition Government of Burma and the Federation of Trade Unions of Burma claimed damages on behalf of all Burmese who had suffered human rights abuses as a consequence of the project. Once again, Unocal denied wrongdoing and stated publicly that it did not know that there were human rights abuses taking place. However, the judge in the case was not convinced by this argument, finding that it was almost inconceivable that the company did not know that human rights abuses were occurring. A number of MNCs had already pulled out of the country, citing human rights abuses as the main reason for leaving.[21] Unocal eventually settled the lawsuit out of court (Eviatar, 2005). Regardless of whether or not the company was unfairly treated by the courts, the case demonstrates how human rights issues have become a major problem for MNCs.

No case has done more to highlight the questionable behaviour of MNCs than Nike's use of sweatshop labour to produce its footwear in the late 1990s (Klein, 2001: 405–21). Investigations carried out at a number of plants in Cambodia, Indonesia and Vietnam revealed that Nike was paying below minimum wages and requiring staff to work long hours under oppressive conditions. In Cambodia, many Nike subcontractors were also found to be employing children. What made the situation worse was that while Nike was paying its workers just a few cents an hour, it was at the same time paying famous athletes millions of dollars to advertise its products. In addition, as Schwartz and Gibb (1999: 51) point out, 'Nike boss Phil Knight's 1994 salary was US$1 500 000. On current wages, a young woman in China churning out his shoes would have to work nine hours a day, six days a week for 15 centuries to match that'. Consequently, Nike became the subject of global protests by human rights and labour organizations. Indeed, for a number of years, protestors conducted an 'International Day of Action Against Nike'.[22] The most visible and lasting memory of these protests is the 'swooshstika', a combination of the Nike swoosh and a swastika. This is meant to demonstrate that Nike acted in a way reminiscent of the Nazis during the 1930s and 1940s, when they press-ganged European Jews, Poles and others into labour camps.[23]

It is probably the case that most MNCs have, at some time or other, violated the human rights of their workers and those of the people living in communities around their operations. This is especially true in the extractive industries (Handelsman, 2002; Orellana, 2002).[24] Sometimes the abuses have stemmed from Western arrogance and a lack of cultural sensitivity for the rights of indigenous peoples. It is only recently that traditional communities have begun to receive compensation for the use of their lands by mining companies. Anti-corporate activists believe that almost all MNCs have a bad record on human rights. Few MNCs have explicit statements about respect for human rights in their codes of conduct. The determination of activist groups like Human Rights Watch and Amnesty International suggests that there will be continued pressure on MNCs to improve their human rights record in the future (Arnold, 2010; MacDonald, 2011; Wettstein, 2010).

They Destroy the Environment

Climate change is the accelerated warming of the Earth as a direct result of human activity. This warming is caused by the release of substantial amounts of carbon dioxide, methane and other greenhouse gases into the atmosphere, as a consequence of industrialisation, fossil fuel use, changing land usage and agricultural practices, and deforestation. If left unchecked, climate change has the potential to impact humankind profoundly on a global scale, exacerbating poverty and underdevelopment, and contributing to the destruction of entire communities. Stern (2007: xv) warns that the basic requirements for life are at risk as the Earth warms. Access to food and water may be affected, negatively impacting health standards. Further, changes in the environment could make parts of the world uninhabitable. As the Earth's temperature increases, glaciers will melt, leading to rising sea levels and a growing incidence of flooding. This is estimated to affect one-sixth of the world's population, particularly those living in the Indian subcontinent, parts of China, and the Andes region of South America. It is also likely to lead to the widespread displacement of communities (Stern, 2007: 65). Droughts in some areas, particularly Africa, will lead to a reduction in crop yields, thus resulting in food shortages and starvation. The economic burdens of inaction against climate change are equally intimidating, with the costs potentially amounting to 5 per cent of GDP annually, or 2 per cent if a broader range of risks are factored in (Stern, 2007: xv). These are just some of the potential adverse impacts of climate change and, consequently, every country stands at a climate change crossroads. Experts warn that this is a time for prompt, calculated decision-making, not bureaucratic inertia (Garnaut, 2008: 20; Flannery, 2009).

Climate change is only one aspect of the problem. Particle pollution cloaks many cities and towns in dense, acrid smog that affects the health and well-being of millions of people.[25] According to the World Health Organization (WHO), as many as 2 million people a year die prematurely as a consequence of air pollution.[26] Acid rain is eating away at historic and architecturally significant buildings and monuments. Reckless and unsustainable agricultural practices are leading to deforestation, habitat loss, and the extinction of animal, insect and plant species. Overfishing is reducing fish stocks, making it difficult for some coastal communities to feed themselves. Equally concerning is the fact that deforestation is also leading to creeping desertification, with around 12 million acres of farmland becoming unproductive deserts annually (Holtz, 2007).

According to anti-corporate activists, the major cause of our environmental crisis is the activities of large MNCs. These companies are the largest emitters of greenhouse gases (GHGs). The top ten polluting companies produce more than a billion tons of greenhouse gas annually. More open than most, Royal Dutch Shell reported in 2011 that the company had emitted 74 million tonnes of greenhouse gas into the atmosphere (Royal Dutch Shell, 2011d). In their 2013 sustainability report, greenhouse gas emissions totalled 73 million tons (Royal Dutch Shell, 2013). When we consider that this is the result of one company's operations, it is not difficult to consider the end result of over 77 000 companies and their affiliates polluting the environment.

Not only are MNCs the largest emitters of GHGs, anti-corporate activists charge that they are irresponsible emitters. They continue to pollute the environment even though they understand the consequences of their actions. Monsanto knew that its polychlorinated biphenyl (PCB) plant in Anniston, Alabama, was poisoning the local environment (and residents) for more than 40 years.[27] An internal memo showed that the company kept the problem a secret for many years (Beiles, 2000). After the US Environmental Protection Agency ordered them to clean up the site, the company was found to have interred millions of tonnes of PCB waste into the hillsides around its plant. As Barlett and Steele (2008) note, 'the old Monsanto plant remains one of the most polluted spots in the US'.[28]

Pollution is an industrial by-product of our modern lifestyle. As a consequence, we are all to blame to some degree. However, the issue becomes sinister when companies hide the fact that they have poisoned the environment and actively seek to prevent people from knowing the truth. One of the notorious examples of this approach was the formation of the Global Climate Coalition in 1989. Its members included some of the world's most significant polluters, including British Petroleum (now BP), DuPont, Exxon, Ford Motor Company, General Motors Corporation and Shell Oil USA. The purpose of the coalition was to mount a campaign to challenge the veracity of climate science and global warming, for purely commercial advantage.[29] At its height in the mid-1990s, the organisation spent more than US$1 million on consultants and US$100 000 a year lobbying politicians and developing public relations strategies to combat climate science.[30] However, the companies soon realised that membership in the coalition undermined their already fragile reputations and most left the organisation. In 2001, the coalition became defunct (Hoffman, 2001; Gewin, 2002).

According to anti-corporate activists, corporate irresponsibility extends to 'pollution havens' as well (Grether and Melo, 2003; Fullerton, 2006).[31] In order to escape the high cost of maintaining environmental standards at home, anti-corporate activists argue that MNCs sometimes move their operations to places that have low or non-existent environmental standards. The argument is that these MNCs move their operations to developing countries because host governments are more willing to tolerate environment degradation in order to gain much-needed investment. In this way, companies escape the need to reduce the polluting effects of their operations in their home country and the regulatory burden that goes with it.

Perhaps the issue that concerns anti-corporate activists the most is the recent trend among MNCs to paint themselves as environmentally friendly actors. Anti-corporate activists refer to this as 'greenwash'. This tactic is seen as little more than a shallow attempt to convince the public that buying their products is an environmentally sensible thing to do. To achieve this, companies use the language of sustainability and corporate social responsibility. But, according to anti-corporate activists, there is little tangible evidence to suggest that many of the world's largest polluters are actively working to reduce their emissions. Consequently, the much-needed change, according to activists, cannot occur while MNCs are privileged economic actors. As Hawken (2005: 3) argues, '[s]tanding in the way of change are corporations who want to continue worldwide deforestation and build coal-fired power plants …'.

They are Making the World Culturally Uniform

The impact of MNCs on the environment is easy to document. Oil spills, deforestation and polluted rivers all leave tell-tale signs. They also tend to receive extensive coverage in the media. However, determining whether, and to what extent, MNCs affect local cultures and traditions is a much more difficult undertaking: not least because cultures are 'lived'. As such, they are dynamic and adaptive and, over time, local, regional and international pressures influence them. No culture is now, or has ever been, immune from change. Furthermore, MNCs are only one force exerting pressure on various cultures.

Culture refers to the ways in which people make their lives meaningful (Tomlinson, 1999: 18). A culture is made up of a number of attributes. These include language, histories, stories and traditions, customary practices, ideals and norms of behaviour, ethics and law, religious practices, and symbols. While these attributes give meaning to people's lives, they also orient them along a continuum between their past and future. To some extent, culture determines where individuals locate themselves in the social and spiritual world. Accordingly, it performs a critical function in human development. It is also the glue that binds communities together.

But anti-corporate activists argue that MNCs undermine the cultural traditions of the countries in which they operate. First, they weaken cultural diversity because they are making the world more culturally uniform. This is leading to the creation of a new American-style global culture. Second, the cultural goods and services sold by these companies are often identified with the home country, regardless of where they are produced. Coca-Cola and Pepsi are uniquely American, just as Peugeot and Renault automobiles are French. Third, while corporate advertising campaigns are designed to sell products and services, they are inevitably advertisements for particular cultural values and practices. When Nike employed Michael Jordan to sell its shoes, American basketball increased in popularity around the world. Young males in Australia, the United Kingdom and elsewhere began to dress in NBA singlets, watch American basketball games, and aspired to be like Jordan. In other words, these campaigns changed young people's perceptions and preferences. Fourth, when backed by global marketing campaigns, Western cultural products are inherently seductive. Many young people, especially teenagers, see them as status symbols. Often, too, young people both in the global North and South see these products as liberating and a sign of affluence. Finally, the language of MNCs is traditionally English and, as Drohan and Freeman (2000: 429) note, 'the English juggernaut is often blamed for the death of minority languages'.

Barnet and Cavanagh (1996:74) argue that it is not just the interaction between MNCs and traditional cultures that is a problem, or even the products and services that they sell. Rather, it is the sheer volume of cultural goods flowing into local communities that undermines cultural diversity. According to them, MNCs, especially those in the entertainment industry, crowd out locally produced film, television and music. The giant media and entertainment MNCs have been able to use new digital technologies to heighten the profile of their products in host markets. Moreover, there are often more American cultural goods being consumed in non-American markets than local products. The presence of these MNCs acts as a medium through which American cultural values are being articulated and spread globally.

There is a range of data that potentially highlights just how embedded American culture is around the world. Starbucks has more than 16 000 stores worldwide; Coca-Cola products are advertised and sold in more than 200 countries. In 2009, McDonald's had more than 30 000 local restaurants in 118 countries. American banking giant Citibank has offices in over 100 countries and more than 200 million customers worldwide. Viacom, the world's largest entertaining company, has a media presence (motion picture, television mobile phone, and online platforms) in over 160 countries and territories. Viacom Media Networks have over 200 locally programmed and operated television channels across the globe, in regions such as Western and Eastern Europe, Russia, Africa and Latin America. In September 2012, the company's flagship music programme, MTV, was available to 600 million households (Viacom Inc., 2012). If you add the entertainment content of the other five major players in the entertainment space, it is easy to see why critics worry about the loss of cultural diversity.[32] Consequently, Barnet and Cavanagh (1996: 75) warn that local cultural practices and traditions are in danger of being lost.

The feeling that world culture will be degraded if diversity is lost is widely shared among artists, cultural conservatives and nationalists. Yet these concerns are overwhelmed by the sheer power of global popular culture, which threatens local cultural traditions and the traditional communities from which they spring.

The dominance of global popular culture gives rise to concerns about homogenisation and cultural imperialism. As American MNCs are the leading suppliers of these 'goods', it is their values that are being 'imposed' upon local communities, whether these communities want them or not. The American sociologist Herbert Schiller once described this as 'homogenized, North Atlantic cultural slop' (Tomlinson, 1999: 81).

SEATTLE AND AFTER: SHOWDOWN OR SLOWDOWN?

These four criticisms lie at the heart of the anti-corporate activist critique of MNCs. While they are not in themselves new criticisms, they have taken on a new sense of urgency for activists as a consequence of globalisation. This has been an important driver of MNC growth around the world. But, as these companies have become more powerful, opposition to them has grown. Concern about the behaviour of MNCs manifested itself most visibly at the anti-globalisation protests in Seattle on 30 November 1999.[33] Tens of thousands of protestors converged on the city to protest against the growing power of MNCs, globalisation and unfair trade arrangements between rich and poor countries.

Not since the Vietnam War has there been such a groundswell of opposition to a set of public policy issues. Indeed, the World Trade Organization (WTO) conference had to be cancelled.[34] The response from some of the attendees was predictable and dismissive. Michael Moore, the Head of the WTO at the time of the riots, called the protesters selfish protectionists unconcerned about the world's poor (cited in Klein, 2002a: 3). Other politicians incredulously asked how anyone could argue that globalisation was not beneficial to both rich and poor nations.

Seattle ushered in a new era of protest (Rikowski, 2001; Cockburn et al., 2000). What is interesting about this latest form of activism is that its character was very different to that of the 1960s protest movement. That movement was generational in character. For progressive young people living at that time, the institutions, policies and values of their leaders had failed them. The Cold War had brought them precipitously close to a nuclear holocaust and the US and Australian governments were sacrificing their young men and women in an unwinnable war in Vietnam. As Roszak (1970: 46–7) commented at the time:

[i]n an historical emergency of absolutely unprecedented proportions, we are that strange culture-bound animal whose biological drive for survival expresses itself generationally. It is the young, arriving with eyes that can see the obvious, who must remake the lethal culture of their elders and who must remake it in desperate haste.

Inspired largely, but not exclusively, by socialist values, these political activists sought to remake the world by attacking social and sexual conservatism, racial intolerance, the unequal treatment of women and minority groups, conformism, and the war mentality of Western policy makers.

A very different kind of protest movement emerged in Seattle, although the urgency was the same as earlier protest movements. It symbolised the beginning of a global movement opposed to the power of MNCs. Coming together under the umbrella of the Direct Action Network (DAN), the 50 000 or so protestors represented 'an emerging species of political organization based on networks, rather than institutions' (De Armond, 2000). Various participant groups mobilised using cell phones, police scanners and wireless laptops. Walkie-talkies continually fed information to protesters operating in and around the downtown area. Much of this information was also uploaded to the Internet, and became available to millions of people around the world, who sought to draw inspiration from the protests.

So diverse was this movement that Crossley (2002: 674) questioned whether it was appropriate to call it a movement at all. Instead, he suggested that it is better described as a 'protest field'. It was also a slightly more flamboyant and theatrical movement than the counter culture of the 1960s. Boyd (2000) describes the Seattle protests as a 'costume ball'. At the time, both *Newsweek* and *The Economist* highlighted this with pictures of sea turtles and people dressed as Santa Claus staring down riot police. Irreverent parodies of US presidents also added a sense of theatre and art to the movement. Indeed, it gave it a sense of spontaneity, vibrancy and optimism for the future.[35]

None of this apparent gaiety and diversity should gloss over the fact that Seattle was a very violent confrontation between police and protesters. The police used tear gas, concussion grenades, CN gas, pepper spray and rubber bullets in an attempt to quell the crowd. By most accounts the police were quite vicious, bludgeoning people whether they were protestors or not (Cockburn et al., 2000: 13–52). Even some legitimate WTO delegates were targeted by police and beaten.

Protestors were also violent in response to police brutality. The Black Bloc anarchists came armed with hammers and crowbars ready to vandalise shop fronts and damage property, especially those of MNCs like GAP. Moreover, the Seattle police claimed they were pelted with stones, glass bottles and Molotov cocktails.

In all, some 500 people were arrested. Retailers estimated that the riot caused about US$20 million in property damage and lost sales. Furthermore, it led to the resignation of the Chief of Police, and the Mayor of Seattle failed in his subsequent bid for re-election in 2001.

The Seattle protest movement, also known as N30, had an enormous impact on the protest movement as a whole. First, the protest represented a new beginning for anti-corporate activists. Second, it also drew attention to the WTO, a relatively unknown international institution. Indeed, the turmoil in Seattle became something of a curse for the WTO. Since N30 new agreements on trade and investment have been dogged by failure. The Doha round only agreed to a new agenda for discussion. This agenda subsequently broke down in Cancun, Mexico, amid further protests and a revolt from developing countries participating in the talks. Third, it emboldened the protest movement globally. The N30 protesters were successful in their protests in Seattle and continued their efforts at a number of follow-up protests at International Monetary Fund (IMF) and World Bank meetings, and at meetings of the World Economic Forum (WEF). Fourth, it was really the first anti-capitalist movement of modern times. As Rikowski (2001: 2) notes: 'it was *against capitalism* as a way of life'. Fifth, while it is true that the protests were broadly anti-capitalist, there were deep ideological divisions between the protesters. However, Cockburn et al. (2000: 65) seem to suggest that it was the street 'warriors' who won the Battle for Seattle, not the various labour unions and liberals in attendance. Put differently, the battle was won by the anti-corporate left. Finally, and perhaps most importantly of all, it demonstrated how new communications technologies could be used to connect people in multiple locations, not just around the Seattle area during the riots, but globally as well.

The euphoria of the 'victory' in Seattle is evident in a number of publications that followed the event. According to Nace (2005: 200), N30 was a 'blossoming' of opposition to corporate power. Danaher and Mark (2003: 18) describe the occasion as the 'rebirth of an American anti-corporate movement' and 'a coming-out party for a movement long in gestation'.

Perhaps the author who most embodies the sentiment of the protesters in Seattle is Naomi Klein. Klein has written for a range of newspapers including, *The Guardian*, the *New York Times* and Canada's *Globe and Mail*. She is also published in academic journals, such as the *Socialist*

Register (2002b). Klein is a committed radical and is staunchly anti-corporate and anti-capitalist. Her well-publicised book *No Logo* appeared a year or so after the Seattle riots. While the book is focused mainly on the impact of corporate branding on communities, especially in the US, it is also an articulation of many of the issues that activists were voicing at Seattle. As one reviewer of the book concluded, 'This is a book to galvanize the resistance that began at Seattle' (Mertes, 2000). Klein's subsequent book *Fences and Windows* is an interesting exploration of the values and goals of the new anti-corporate/anti-capitalist movement.

Over the last ten years, Naomi Klein has received numerous awards for her work, and is now largely a full-time political activist. In 2011, she attended the 'Occupy Wall Street' (OWS) rally and gave a speech to the protestors. In that speech, she referred to their protest as 'the most important thing in the world now'.

One of the things Klein shares with many other activists is a perception that a showdown between MNCs and anti-corporate activists is imminent.[36] If, by 'showdown', is meant a confrontation between opposing sides that leads to some ultimate resolution, it would appear that this has not yet materialised, and may never do so. Certainly there is a plethora of alternative radio stations and Internet sites in existence that are broadly anti-corporate, and there have been some examples of direct protest and resistance around the world. As we noted earlier in the chapter, the protests in Bolivia against the privatisation of water is a good example (Olivera and Lewis, 2004; Polet, 2007). In addition, the World Social Forum (WSF) provides an important space for dialogue between various activist groups. So important is this forum that Chomsky (2004: 236) once described it as a 'second superpower' and suggested that it showed considerable promise in bringing about positive change. There are also many academic studies which target aspects of MNC behaviour, as well as celebrating the virtues of political resistance (Willis and Hardcastle, 2004; Amoore, 2005). But there does not appear to be any visible momentum at present, especially if we consider the 1999 Seattle protests as the high water mark of the latest wave of anti-corporate activism. This does not mean that the anti-corporate movement is a spent force, only that the early optimism of Klein and others appears to have dissipated over the past few years, rhetoric to the contrary. OWS is hardly a movement with any real capacity to effect broad social or economic change, especially at the global level.

There are a number of reasons why the change they desire so much has not materialised. The coordinated attacks on the World Trade Center on 11 September 2001 changed the global political landscape and the priorities of national governments everywhere. A discourse about the evils of globalisation and MNCs gave way to one dominated by the war on terror, personal and national security, and why the tragedy happened to the US.

Put differently, the anti-corporate activist agenda was supplanted by a different set of political issues and problems. First, the American Left were quick to blame the United States for the attacks. Sontag (2001) noted in *The New Yorker*, '[w]here is the acknowledgement that this was not a "cowardly" attack on "civilization" or "liberty" or "humanity" or the "free world" but an attack on the world's self-proclaimed superpower, undertaken as a consequence of specific American alliances and actions'. Similarly, in a public lecture at the Massachusetts Institute of Technology (MIT) a few weeks after the attacks, Chomsky (2001: 35) delivered a lecture titled 'The new war against terror'. He argued that America had it coming because it had been practising terror on a global scale for more than 100 years. He stated that we 'can think of the United States as an innocent victim only if we adopt the convenient path of ignoring the record of its actions and those of its allies ...'.

Chalmers Johnson (2004) refers to this viewpoint as 'blowback'. According to him, the CIA first used the term in a briefing document in the 1950s, referring to the consequences that followed from certain courses of action. In 1953, the CIA helped to overthrow the Mossadegh Government in Iran and return the Shah to power.[37] This, in turn, led to a quarter of a century of tyranny and oppression. The Shah was once again removed from power by Ayatollah Khomeini and other religious clerics. This, in turn, led to the Tehran hostage crisis (Buchan, 2013). The theory holds that September 11 was the unintended consequences of decades of American imperialism. It symbolised the collective anger of peoples and states around the world that had suffered, and are still suffering, at the hands of successive US governments.

At a time of national tragedy, however, such arguments seemed to many to be callous and unpatriotic and, once again, showed the political mainstream why left-wing activists had little to contribute to serious public and foreign policy debate (Flynn, 2004). As Kazin (2002: 42) pointed out at the time, '[i]t's difficult to think of any radical or reformer who repudiated the national belief system and still had a major impact on U.S. politics and policy'. As a result, activism lost some of its credibility during this period. This weakened the anti-corporate movement significantly.

The wars in Iraq and Afghanistan further muddied the waters for activists. Debate raged about whether or not Saddam Hussein had weapons of mass destruction, rather than intense scrutiny about whether Halliburton and other large MNCs were entitled to lucrative contracts to support US operations in Iraq and in Afghanistan.[38] Perhaps the most obvious point to make is that despite numerous protests against the war, mass opposition to it soon dissipated after the fighting had started. Despite the failure to find weapons of mass destruction, the growing body count, numerous congressional and senate inquiries, and ongoing carnage from suicide bombers, George Bush Jr, Tony Blair and Australia's Prime Minister John Howard were all returned to power in subsequent elections. Indeed, Bush and Howard increased their majority in government.[39] That President Aznar of Spain lost the 2004 election had more to do with the timing of the bomb blasts in Madrid. Had those blasts not occurred, most electioneers in Spain predicted that Aznar would have been returned to power as well (Luttwak, 2004).

Finally, the Global Financial Crisis (GFC), the state of the American economy, unemployment, Hurricane Katrina, and the BP oil spill in the Gulf of Mexico tended to overshadow issues relating to globalisation and MNCs. It is not that these issues went away exactly, as much as changes in the global political landscape impacted on the anti-corporate message. Only with the OWS did some fire return to anti-corporate activism.

On a more practical note, it is difficult to see how a global 'showdown' could emerge out of a movement that is, by and large, anarchic and decentralised. Cohesion is important for coordination. Indeed, this is a lesson that Lenin learned from the failure of nineteenth-century anarchism to bring about a revolution in Europe. The Vanguard Party was Lenin's solution to the shortcomings of decentralised protest. This suggests, then, that there is a high degree of wishful thinking in the writings of those who have posited a possible confrontation between anti-corporate activists and MNCs that would lead to a restraining of their power, or other similar outcome.

Two years after Seattle, and in the wake of the collapse of Enron, some journalists were beginning to question whether the enthusiasm for protest by these activists had dissipated. Writing in *The American Prospect*, Penniman (2002) asked:

> [w]hy hasn't the moment been seized? It's been almost a year since Enron evaporated and two years since the 'new economy' lost its giddiness. But where's the grass-roots ground swell? What happened to all of those daring anticorporate protestors who paralysed Seattle during the World Trade Organization meeting?

Two years later, *The Economist* (2004a) also reported that the movement was faltering because of a range of organisational and ideological problems, including apathy amongst the rank and file, a breakdown between various factions, and a lack of attendance at meetings. Somewhat cheekily and cynically, the well-known magazine argued that:

> Given that the anti-globalization movement has lent ideas to capitalism – at the mushier end of corporate social responsibility, for instance, where fear and conscience meet to try to placate the mob – capitalism should surely return the favour in anti-globalization's dark days. There are plenty of modern management techniques which the movement could employ to reinvigorate itself. Has it, for instance, tried benchmarking itself against comparable movements? If street protest is too arduous for the membership, should it not think of outsourcing its more strenuous activities to the immigrants who already do most of Britain's tougher jobs. Taking that argument further, if domestic apathy is the problem, perhaps the answer is offshoring. A Mayday protest organized in, say, Libya or North Korea would really make a splash.

It is unclear whether the hype surrounding the rise of the anti-corporate movement was ever going to deliver the kind of economic reforms that these activists desired. Walker (2005: 699) once described anti-corporate activists as 'mosquitoes on the evening breeze, irritants to those who claim maturity and legitimacy at the centers of political life'. If such a movement can only ever be an 'irritant' to those in power, it is difficult to see how these activists can fulfil their long-term aspirations to remake the global economy and reign in the power of MNCs.

It is also a fact that many of the larger organised protests groups have been steadily losing members, rather than gaining them. Greenpeace membership has fallen from a high point of nearly 5 million members to approximately 2.8 million. Moreover, the number of protesters turning up to WTO and WEF meetings appears to be dwindling as well. Rather than an increase in opposition to MNCs, the opposite appears to be the case. The mass protest movement which was born in Seattle may have all but run its course.

The final point to make with respect to the anti-corporate movement losing momentum in the aftermath of September 11 is that their entrenched dislike of MNCs has meant they have not been able to see what is taking place around them. Zadek (2001: 1–2) observes that many of the '[a]ctivists leading the assault on corporate power and influence have in the main remained entrenched in their negative critique'. Anti-corporate activists paint a picture that is too black and white. While there are companies who greenwash their image, there are as many who are genuine about balancing social and environmental imperatives with profit maximisation. We will examine the efforts of Interface Inc. in this regard in Chapter 6. Their efforts to become a sustainable enterprise have been celebrated as a model for the future of capitalism.[40] Thus, it is not the case that MNCs cannot get beyond greenwash and marketing. On the contrary, it is the success of the early anti-corporate movement in shaping current MNC behaviour that has brought about an ideational shift in business thinking. What began as a campaign against MNCs by anti-corporate activists demanding change has increasingly come to frame and instantiate new norms of corporate conduct.

Largely in response to the anti-corporate activist agenda, the literature on corporate social responsibility and the future of business has grown dramatically since the Seattle riots. Zadek (2001: 13) argues that '[c]orporations can be civil', while Parker (2002: 30) speaks about the possibility of an 'open corporation' that is strongly committed to corporate social responsibility. Hopkins (2003: xii) predicts that soon 'it will not be possible to conduct business without being socially responsible'. Finally, Vogel (2005: 162) argues that there is now a 'market for virtue'. While this is not definitive evidence, it is clear that a growing number of writers are pointing to the emergence of a different kind of MNC. While anti-corporate activists continue to be mired in a negative critique, the movement is likely to continue to lose momentum. Thus, the much anticipated 'showdown' appears to have turned into a 'slowdown'. The anti-corporate movement has been extremely successful in effecting change in the behaviour of MNCs. This is not simply because of their capacity for protest, but because they have turned corporate reputation into a political issue, subsequently exposing the Achilles heel of all modern MNCs. However, they now find themselves in a bind. On the one hand, they have been successful in achieving a significant degree of ideational change in MNC behaviour through the strategic use of political power yet, on the other hand, they cannot accept their success in modifying that behaviour (Spar and La Mure, 2003).

None of this is to suggest for a moment that activists do not have other avenues to attack MNCs. This includes an explosion in the number of websites devoted to anti-corporate themes. Some examples of these include the *Multinational Monitor, Mines and Communities* and *Corporate Crime Reporter*. Other sites offer more targeted critiques. These include sites that are devoted to attacking specific MNCs like Nike and Nestlé, as well as those targeting specific social and political issues.[41] Moreover, *The New Internationalist* continues to provide a well-established voice in magazine form, and has been doing so since the early 1970s. So while organised protest appears to have dissipated, the activists' agenda continues to be articulated with gusto. MNCs would be well advised not to backslide on their evolving social and environmental credentials as a consequence.

INTERNATIONAL INSTITUTIONS AND MNCS

Anti-corporate activists are not the only force in international relations (IR) exerting pressure on MNCs. International institutions such as the UN, the Organisation for Economic Co-operation and Development (OECD), and other agencies are having an influence in this regard as well. Through a range of institutional frameworks and partnerships, these organisations are attempting to improve the contribution of MNCs to society and to development.

One of the first initiatives of this kind occurred in 1973. In the middle of 1972, the UN Economic and Social Council asked the Secretary-General (SG) to examine the role of MNCs in the development process, as well as assess their impact on IR. The SG appointed an Eminent Persons Group to consider the matter. A report titled *Multinational Corporations in World Development* (United Nations, 1973) was provided to the group to facilitate the work. The group recommended the establishment of a special commission on MNCs. The UN Centre on Transnational Corporations (UNCTC) began work in 1974, guided by three broad objectives:

1. To further the understanding of the political, economic, social and legal effects of TNC activity, specially in developing countries [sic];
2. To secure international arrangements that promote the positive contributions of TNCs national development goals and world economic growth while controlling [and] eliminating their negative effects; and
3. To strengthen the negotiating capacity of host countries, in particular developing countries, in their dealings with TNCs.

The UNCTC lasted for almost two decades and was eventually absorbed into a newer commission, more broadly devoted to international investment. However, the underlying rationale remained the same for the successor organisation; that is, to promote investment in the developing world, while reducing the negative impacts associated with MNC activity.

The most recent attempt to engage MNCs is the United Nations Global Compact (UNGC). The concept of the Compact originated within the office of the former UN Secretary-General Kofi Annan (1999). In a speech to the WEF, Annan argued that the global economy remained vulnerable to a range of threats and suggested that MNCs could contribute to reducing threats that might emerge in the future.

In July 2000, the UNGC was launched in New York. Present at the launch were representatives from some of the world's largest MNCs, NGOs and members of the trade union movement. The UNGC is both an acknowledgement of the contribution that MNCs have made to global economic growth, but that it needs to focus more explicitly on human rights, labour issues, the environment and corruption.

The UNGC has two main objectives. The first is to embed its core principles in MNC thinking globally. The second is to get MNCs to support the broader UN agenda, particularly the Millennium Development Goals (MDGs) and now, the newly developed Sustainable Development Goals (SDGs). At the heart of the Compact are ten core principles covering four areas of importance. These are:

Human Rights

1. Businesses should support and respect the protection of internationally proclaimed human rights;
2. make sure that they are not complicit in human rights abuses.

Labour

3. Businesses should uphold the freedom of association and the effective recognition of the right to collective bargaining;
4. the elimination of all forms of forced and compulsory labour;
5. the effective abolition of child labour;
6. the elimination of discrimination in respect to employment and occupation.

Environment

7. Businesses should support a precautionary approach to environmental challenges;
8. undertake initiatives to promote greater environmental responsibility;
9. encourage the development and diffusion of environmentally friendly technologies.

Anti-corruption

10. Businesses should work against corruption in all its forms, including extortion and bribery.

The UNGC is not a regulatory body, and has no power to compel MNCs to abide by these principles. Adherence to the principles is on a voluntary basis only. According to Ruggie (2002: 23) the UNGC is best viewed as a 'social learning network'. It is a site for various groups to engage with each other and work together to achieve mutually beneficial goals. It does this in three ways: through international sharing and learning, policy dialogues, and partnership projects. In March 2004, 1366 formal corporate participants were involved in the activities of the Compact. Today, there are around 10 000 corporate participants. In a review of its performance in 2004, McKinsey & Company (2004: 2) concluded that '[o]ur impact assessment has found that the Global Compact has had noticeable, incremental impact on companies, the UN, governments and other civil society actors and has built a strong base for future results'. In the 2011 annual review, the UNGC had added a further 1861 new companies to the initiative. This seems to suggest that it is a positive vehicle for the promotion of change in corporate behaviour (United Nations Global Compact, 2011).

The OECD has also moved in this direction. The organisation has developed its own set of principles, contained in the OECD Guidelines for Multinational Enterprises (2000: 9). These guidelines take the form of recommendations from governments to MNCs in order to bring harmony between corporate activities and government policy, to strengthen relations between MNCs and the societies in which they operate, to improve the foreign investment climate, and to contribute to sustainable development.

Inevitably these, and other similar institutional initiatives, appear to critics as a palliative, rather than a concerted effort to curb the behaviour of MNCs. Critics have accused these initiatives of providing a basis for MNCs to 'blue wash' their dishonest activities (Oldenziel, 2005: 12). But, most importantly, the key problem that anti-corporate activists have with these approaches is that they lack credible accountability and enforcement mechanisms. Zadek (2001: 84–9) summarizes the criticism in the following way. First, companies can gain reputational value in being associated with these institutions, but do not actually have to change their behaviour. Second, companies are able to avoid being more heavily regulated by national governments by associating with the UN. Third, the legitimacy of globalisation remains intact. In the final analysis, it is legislation and regulation anti-corporate activists want, not partnerships and multi-stakeholder dialogues.

Ruggie argues that voluntary approaches by themselves will not satisfy everyone or provide an adequate solution to global governance issues. But he argues that 'these company-based initiatives are significant not only for what they achieve directly, but because they are also triggering broader second-order consequences' (Ruggie, 2002: 25). Most importantly, they demonstrate that a 'global public sector' (Ruggie, 2002: 26) is emerging. He defines this as an:

institutionalized arena of discourse, contestation, and action organized around the production of global public goods. It is constituted by interactions among non-state actors as well as states ... The effect of the new global public domain is not to replace states, but to embed systems of governance in broader global frameworks of social capacity and agency that did not previously exist (Ruggie, 2004: 519).

Ruggie offers a few examples of this but the main point he is making is that the relationship between states, non-state actors and MNCs is changing, and new forms of governance are emerging. Arguments about the inherent weaknesses in international partnerships and voluntary codes miss this important point. They also fail to take account of the importance of the corporate reputation to MNCs today. How activists have brought corporate reputation into the political debate about the behaviour of MNCs is the topic I turn to now.

THE 'POLITICISATION' OF THE CORPORATE REPUTATION

A number of business advocates have clearly understood the link between anti-corporate activism and corporate reputation, with Peters (1999) being one of the first. Others have also noted the connection. Albrecht (1996: 18–19) warns that '[t]he activists who protest at your doorstep will have a very vocal agenda – publicity for their cause, the need to express their anger over what they feel is corporate greed or apathy, and the desire to create change through the infliction of real pain or other media-generated discomfort'. Larkin (2003: 18) argues that activism 'is an established feature of modern day society and must be factored into reputation risk planning'. Similarly, Alsop (2004: 45) bluntly notes that '[i]gnoring activists can be dangerous'.

Over the years, activists have used a number of methods to undermine MNC credibility and their activities. Perhaps the worst example of this is tree-spiking. Advocated by Earth First, it involves activists deliberately inserting metal spikes into trees to prevent them from being harvested. Attempts to harvest spiked trees with chainsaws had the potential to seriously injury or even kill forest workers.

People for the Ethical Treatment of Animals (PETA) is also known to advocate violence against MNCs who test their products on animals. PETA has been responsible for destroying animal testing laboratories and liberating caged animals. In the US, where they are headquartered, PETA has been accused of being a domestic terrorist organisation. Their signature mode of protest has included naked men and women advertising their cause. In this, they have been heavily supported by celebrities such as Alicia Silverstone, Charlize Theron and Pamela Anderson.[42]

King (2000: 2) argues that the purpose of these activities is to humiliate MNCs in order to undermine their reputations.[43] As noted earlier, this is based on shaming MNCs or by influencing consumer and investor behaviour. This strategy has led to a 'politicisation' of the corporate reputation.[44] While not the most eloquent of terms, the notion that corporate reputations have become 'politicised' provides an important insight into the shift in the bargaining relationship between anti-corporate activists and MNCs. Further, as King (2000: 2) notes:

> the contest over corporate reputation includes, but goes beyond issues surrounding the implementation of technology and workplace reforms to incorporate business ethics, environmental sustainability, community involvement, corporate governance and community development. It is a contest that has stimulated the rephrasing of questions about the responsibilities of business in society: What are corporations for? What is the extent of their fiscal, social and environmental responsibilities? To whom are corporations accountable?

King's argument is that, as corporate reputations have become a more significant part of the success of MNCs, this has exposed them to the political power of anti-corporate activists. Put differently, the increasing importance of the corporate reputation to MNCs has weakened their bargaining position and made them more vulnerable to activist pressure. It means that reputational capital is put at risk whenever an MNC finds itself in the cross-hairs of anti-corporate activists' gun sights.[45]

How has this occurred? One way of thinking about this issue is through the social amplification of risk framework (SARF). It offers an interesting account of this process.[46] The SARF concept seeks to account for the way risks are communicated across societies and institutions. At its heart is the idea of social amplification. When risks are communicated through any medium, such as face to face, within the workplace, or through the media, SARF suggests that two things occur. First, these risks tend to be amplified as they are transmitted. Second, the potential exists for ripple effects to occur. These may have secondary and tertiary impacts that grow beyond an original risk event and 'interact with a wide range of psychological, social, institutional, or cultural processes in ways that intensify perceptions of risk and its manageability' (Kasperson et al., 2003: 13). The strength of SARF is its ability to describe how risk signals, in the form of images, stories, signs and symbols, are received and transmitted to a range of social agents. These signals pass through so-called 'amplification stations' (Kasperson et al., 2003: 15). They filter and interpret the information, which then leads to particular responses from participants in the social system. Amplification stations include an array of individuals and groups within society, including activists, government agencies, communities and politicians. However, in SARF, the media is the primary amplifier.

In essence, anti-corporate activists have been adept at communicating and amplifying risks. They have been able to gain maximum exposure for their causes in various media by highlighting the risks that MNCs pose to human well-being. The media, then, is a primary amplifier of the real or perceived risks. The ripple effects of amplification travel across borders and around the world. The Seattle riots are an excellent example of this phenomenon.

There are numerous other examples that highlight this phenomenon. Many people fear being attacked/eaten by a large shark. Yet the reality is that they are more likely to get badly injured or killed in their home than attacked and killed by a shark. When a shark attack occurs, it generally makes headline news. This tends to heighten our awareness of the danger of shark attacks, well out of proportion to the real danger these creatures pose to humans.

Fear is a crucial ingredient in the amplification process. Anti-corporate activists are very skilled in the use of rhetorical language to heighten community fears about MNCs. I have referred to this elsewhere as the 'rhetoric of moral outrage' (O'Callaghan, 2007b: 197). The purpose of such rhetoric is not objectivity or truth, but to paint a dire picture of the state of the world, a picture so bleak that it will shock individuals and push them to mobilise against MNCs. Chomsky is one of the best exponents of this strategy, although it is a common style of argumentation of those at the extreme ends of the political spectrum.

Whatever the academic merit of this approach to argumentation, it is difficult for MNCs to counter. The Achilles heel of most corporate leaders is that they are generally politically naive. A comment from Monsanto's Director of Corporate Communications illustrates the point: 'Monsanto should not have to vouchsafe the safety of biotech food. Our interest is in selling as much of it as possible. Assuring the public safety is the Fed's job' (Starr, 2000: 9). Given the community's concern, real or imagined, about the possible dangers of genetically modified (GM) foods, such a rash statement does nothing to enhance Monsanto's reputation as a responsible company, or improve public perception of GM foods. Indeed, it is this sort of comment that activists seize upon to show that MNCs are uncaring and that they should not be trusted. Astoundingly, this person is a communications 'expert'.

What this suggests is that many corporate managers are at their weakest where anti-corporate activists are at their strongest. The latter are by nature political animals. They are socially, politically and culturally aware, and have no trouble outflanking unreflective corporate managers. When this political astuteness is coupled with a capacity to amplify risks and heighten community fears, it is a force to be reckoned with.

CONCLUSION: TOWARD CORPORATE SELF-REGULATION

Anti-corporate activists' pressure has led to MNCs seeking to improve their performance on social and environmental issues, but it is important not to lose sight of the fact that MNCs have shown a willingness to adjust to this new reality. The various means by which MNCs are expressing this commitment should not be interpreted as an attempt by these companies to appease public opinion while protecting their profits. Rather, the shift in their behaviour represents a genuine ideational shift in the thinking of corporate managers. This shift is pushing them towards corporate self-regulation. It is a long journey, but one which many MNCs are embarking on. Some are further along the road than others. Some have just begun the journey. Still others do not fully appreciate what is at stake. Over the next decade or so, no MNC will be able to do business without taking responsibility for their social and environmental footprint, or adding significant value to the communities in which they operate.

NOTES

1. For an earlier version of this argument see O'Callaghan (2007b).
2. Erin Brockovich is, perhaps, the most notable example. See Brueckner and Dyann (2010); Perlman (2004).
3. Dangl (2007) argues that the popular protests in Bolivia began with a confrontation between local miners over access to mine leases and then spread to a violent confrontation regarding access to water in Cochabamba. As he (2007: 8) notes, '[t]he residents of Cochabamba rose up when the multinational Bechtel Corporation bought their public and communal water systems. In a classic example of the failure of the privatization of a basic resource, the company's rate hikes and exclusive water rights sparked a revolt that continues to rock the country's social and political landscape'. Also see Barlow and Clarke (2002: 154–80).
4. These include ethical codes of conduct, targeted philanthropy, citizenship programmes, employee development and equity programmes, and new social and environmental reporting initiatives.
5. Hereafter referred to as 'Shell'.
6. A transaction cost economics perspective sees the impact of the pressure exerted by activists on MNCs in a slightly different way. It is not a concern with reputation, but the

cost of doing business. Using their example of a pharmaceutical company selling drugs into developing countries, Vachani et al. (2009: 448) argue that activism can 'result in high transaction costs for the MNE as it is forced into a public relations campaign to address accusations of attempting to exploit developing-country customers, as well as incur legal and lobbying costs of dissuading the local government from sanctioning local manufacture of generic drugs. These escalating transaction costs can change the balance of costs and benefits of the pricing policy, forcing the MNE to change strategy and seek new governance mechanisms to implement a differential pricing strategy'. On this view, the change in behaviour is driven by transaction costs, rather than concerns with corporate reputation.

7. The term 'business advocate' is used here to refer to authors who seek to advocate on behalf of business interests. This may be in matters of corporate strategy and governance, advice on how to meet particular challenges, or simply to show how business can perform better. In the case of Peters, the main aim of his book is to demonstrate to MNCs how they can protect their reputation from anti-corporate activists.

8. These authors follow in the footsteps of, among others, Barnett and Cavanagh (1976; 1995) and Falk (1999).

9. They are also referred to as multinational enterprises (MNEs), transnational corporations (TNCs), and firms.

10. Many anti-corporate activists are also staunch anti-Americans. I leave that controversial issue aside here, as I am interested in anti-corporate activist views about MNCs, not the foreign policies of successive US governments. The most comprehensive treatment of anti-Americanism is O'Connor (2007).

11. The obsolescing bargain (OB) is an interesting theoretical concept. Developed by Vernon (1971), the concept highlights the dynamic bargaining relationship between MNCs and host governments, within a particular investment cycle. A developing government needs investment. It offers a contract to an MNC to build a new utility. This might be to construct a new power station, a sanitation plant, or a transportation network. Initially, the host country is a beggar. It needs investment and so is willing to offer the winning MNC lucrative conditions to invest. These may include tax holidays, low tax rates and other concessions. After the investment is established and has become profitable for the MNC, the host government wants a greater share of the profits from the investment. Gradually, the government changes the regulations governing the investment. Over time, the original bargain obsolesces. The project loses its value and becomes unprofitable. The result is that the MNC may leave the project. On the various aspects of this idea see Spagnoletti and O'Callaghan (2011); Grosse (2005a).

12. This issue is treated in more detail in Chapter 4, where I examine Shell's rationale for not supporting the release of the Ogoni Nine.

13. See Grosse (2005b); Eden and Appel Molot (2002); Fagre and Wells, Jr (1982).

14. According to Sell (1999: 172), the impetus for the Trade Related Aspects of Intellectual Property Rights (TRIPS) accords came from the CEOs of 12 large American MNCs. 'In effect, twelve corporations made public law for the world'.

15. One of the best discussions of this period is Moran (1974). See also Harmer (2011).

16. A similar story can be told of the United Fruit Company's role in supporting a coup in Guatemala in the 1950s. The long-term consequence of this coup also led to many years of repression and hardship for the Guatemalan people. See Schlesinger and Kinzer (2005).

17. This is also the central theme of Hartmann's (2007) book on the demise of the middle class in America.

18. These include the exploitation of workers, financial support for militia groups that torture and kill innocent people, inadequate attention to the welfare and safety of employees, forced removal of locals from traditional lands, and collusion with unscrupulous host governments.

19. See the website 'Killer Coke' (n.d.).

20. *Doe v. Unocal.* See also Spar and La Mure (2003); Dale (2011). Human Rights Watch (2012) has recently stated that Burma's military are as violent as ever and the opening up of the country in the last two years has done little to improve the country's human rights record.
21. These include PepsiCo and French oil company Total S.A.
22. See the website 'Boycott Nike', accessed 8 August 2015 at http://boycott-nike.8m.com/. See also Sage (1999).
23. For critiques of MNCs' labour record see Armbruster-Sandoval (2005); Locke et al. (2009); Williams et al. (2014).
24. Mining companies have improved their behaviour in host countries. See the Mining, Minerals and Sustainable Development (MMSD) project, located within the International Institute for Environment and Development (IIED). A range of position papers have been developed within the institute to help mining companies navigate their host country relations and their environmental and social obligations. The International Council on Mining and Metals (ICMM) has a similar function.
25. This has been a particular problem for the automotive industry. See also Paterson (2000); Kolk and Levy (2004); Paterson and Dalby (2006); Paterson (2007); Mikler (2009); Orsatto and Clegg (1999: 264).
26. World Health Organization 'Air quality and health' (n.d.). A large percentage of these deaths occur in the family home due to smoke inhalation from biomass and kerosene cooking fires. See Spagnoletti and O'Callaghan (2013).
27. Polychlorinated biphenyl is an industrial coolant.
28. Monsanto was one of the first companies to openly challenge the findings of Rachel Carson's *Silent Spring*. The company tried unsuccessfully to have the book banned (Carson, 2002; Stauber and Rampton, 1995: 123–42).
29. The release of a number of reports by the UN's Intergovernmental Panel on Climate Change (2007) (IPCC) triggered the formation of the coalition.
30. The vast majority of scientists think that the climate science modelling is accurate. For a defence of climate science see Flannery (2009). On climate scepticism see Paltridge (2010); Kehr (2011); Robinson (2013). Also researchers from the Lavoisier Group refute the science of human-induced climate change, and criticise the policy responses proposed by the Rudd and Gillard Governments in Australia. See Evans et al. (2009).
31. The so-called 'pollution haven' hypothesis has been a hotly debated topic among environmentalists over the last two decades. However, most commentators now appear to agree that the hypothesis is not proven. Mani and Wheeler (1997) argue that an examination of data over a 30-year period appears to show that pollution havens are as transient as low-wage havens. Smarzynska and Wei (2001) reach a similar conclusion.
32. These are The News Corporation, The Walt Disney Company, Time Warner, Sony Corporation of America, and NBC Universal.
33. Often called N30 by activist groups.
34. The organisation was formally known as the General Agreement on Tariffs and Trade (GATT).
35. In Seattle, there were intellectuals, socialists, anarchists, environmentalists, human rights activists, land reform groups, women's groups, gay and lesbian networks, farmers, religious groups, animal rights activists and politically engaged musicians.
36. This theme is most thoroughly discussed by Barlow and Clarke (2001). The title of the book is *Global Showdown: How the New Activists Are Fighting Global Corporate Rule*.
37. On the rise and fall of the Shah, see Saikal (2009).
38. On the history of Halliburton, including its activities in Iraq, see Briody (2004).
39. These were not just three members of the so-called 'Coalition of the Willing'. Other members included Afghanistan, Albania, Azerbaijan, Bulgaria, Colombia, the Czech Republic, Denmark, El Salvador, Eritrea, Estonia, Ethiopia, Georgia, Hungary, Italy, Japan, South Korea, Latvia, Lithuania, Macedonia, the Netherlands, Nicaragua, the Philippines, Poland, Romania, Slovakia, Spain, Turkey and Uzbekistan. Two points are worth making about the list. First, the number of official participants in the coalition had changed

considerably by 2006, as some governments bowed to domestic pressure to exit the conflict. This was particularly the case with Spain. Second, while Kuwait, Bahrain and Qatar were used by the United States to prepare for the conflict, none were officially listed by the State Department as being members. See Shifferes (2003).

40. Holliday et al. (2002) and Arena (2004) offer some other examples of companies moving in this direction. Also see Mirvis et al. (2010); Seeger and Ulmer (2001).

41. These range from informing the media and the public about the activities of MNCs, handing out leaflets in public places, picketing corporate headquarters, publishing detailed anti-corporate reports, and publishing embarrassing photographs of environmental damage.

42. See Huffington Post (2011) slideshow.

43. Sasser et al. (2006: 4–5) refer to this political strategy as 'direct targeting'. As they note: '[d]irect targeting enables NGOs to exert maximum pressure on firms to join the NGO-preferred program'.

44. The concept of 'politicisation' is a term familiar to political theorists. It generally means two things. First, it refers to a revealing of the power relations inherent in a particular social construct. In this sense, feminists have 'politicized' gender. See Brown (2004: 116). A second usage of the term is when a particular issue moves from being a non-political issue to become a political one. Scruton (2007: 534) uses the example of Frankfurt School theorist Walter Benjamin, who advocated the politicisation of art in order to promote revolution in Europe. It is in this latter sense that the term is used here. It suggests that at one time corporate reputation was not seen as a political issue. The skill of anti-corporate activists is being able to turn it into one.

45. Reputation capital has been defined by Fombrun (1996: 11) as 'a form of intangible wealth that is closely related to what accountants call "goodwill" and marketers term "brand equity"'.

46. An alternative explanation for the success of NGOs can be found in 'agenda setting theory'. See Ragas (2013).

2. Disciplining MNCs: corporate reputation as a driver of ideational change

A strong reputation is a prized commodity. It affords the bearer with advantages not readily available to others. Think of the financial value famous athletes are able to bring to a brand or product. Retired politicians with an unblemished record in government are often offered ambassadorial posts, or positions in international organisations, such as the UN. Judges are sometimes chosen to head parliamentary inquiries into matters of public concern because they are trusted to act honourably and in the interest of the whole community. The essence of a strong reputation is how a person is regarded by others. It is therefore exogenously derived. One can only earn a reputation in the context of a community. Robinson Crusoe, perhaps the most celebrated castaway of all times, lacked a reputation until he saved 'Friday' from certain death at the hands of his enemies. The ensuing relationship between master and servant restored something that Crusoe had lost when he became shipwrecked (Griffin, 2002: 8–9).

The importance of a strong reputation to individuals, then, is nothing new. It is something that human beings have sought after for hundreds, perhaps thousands of years. Some have it. Some lose it. Some spend their entire lives striving for it. Reputation is one of those values that distinguish individuals from a social group. It means that they are held in high esteem. It is a relational quality and a quality that rests on trust and admiration.

Like individual reputations, corporate reputations are also derived from the community. Stakeholders decide whether a company has a strong reputation or not.[1] Equally, they decide who has a bad reputation. Stakeholders can be individuals or groups, including shareholders, customers, employees, sub-contractors, regulators and various communities. How a company manages its stakeholder relations has a significant impact on its reputation (Freeman et al., 2007). As one public relations firm expresses it, 'reputation is in the eye of the stakeholder' (cited in King, 2000: 3).

Fombrun (1996: 37) defines corporate reputation as: 'the overall estimation in which a company is held by its constituents. A corporate reputation represents the "net" affective or emotional reaction – good or bad, weak or strong – of customers, investors, employees, and the general public to the company's name'.[2] This 'emotional reaction' is derived from the goods and services the company provides, as well as the values and principles it espouses. A company that advocates values that its stakeholders find offensive will never develop a strong corporate reputation. The same applies to a company that uses deceptive tactics in an attempt to make it more attractive to stakeholders.

There has been an increase in interest in the study of corporate reputation over the last decade or so. As a result of this increasing interest, a number of dedicated reputation research companies have emerged. These include the Reputation Institute in the US, Ipsos MORI in the UK and Reputex in Australia. In addition, the peer-reviewed journal *Corporate Reputation Review* now serves as a channel for new academic research in the field.

Yet this upswing of interest has not led to greater clarity around the concept of corporate reputation. Some writers argue that corporate reputation is another way of describing the corporate image. Markwick and Fill (1997: 398) suggest that '[t]he term "reputation" is often used synonymously with image and this can lead to confusion'. Others see corporate reputation as the sum total of corporate image and corporate identity. Still others view it through the lens of corporate communication (Griffin, 2002: 10–11; Doorley and Garcia, 2007). These variations have led to a degree of frustration among some scholars and practitioners. Gotsi and Wilson (2001: 24) lament the fact that 'there is no unambiguous, generally accepted definition for the term corporate reputation'. Moreover, Wartick (2002: 371) notes that 'many deficiencies in definition and data can be attributed to the fact that theory development around corporate reputation has been insufficient'. The need for a common definition of corporate reputation is also echoed by Barnett et al. (2006: 28). They argue that '[t]here is an urgent need to create a unifying framework'.

Attempts to find definitional consensus are likely to prove elusive, given the interpretive nature of the social sciences.[3] Despite this apparent (and contested) weakness in the field, it is broadly accepted that corporate reputation is an amalgam of three broad concepts: corporate image, corporate identity and corporate behaviour. This is how corporate reputation is understood in this book.

IMAGE, IDENTITY AND BEHAVIOUR AS ATTRIBUTES OF A STRONG CORPORATE REPUTATION

The study of corporate reputation has been shaped by three twentieth-century developments. The first is the liberal economic trading system, which emerged out of the ashes of World War II. The second is the spread of MNCs around the world in the 1960s. The third is the revolution in information and communications technology associated with globalisation.

As the world recovered from war, a new economic system based upon the principles of free trade and open access to national markets paved the way for the spread of multinational MNCs (primarily US multinationals) around the globe.[4] These companies offered unique products and services to the public. However, competition was fierce. The automobile industry in the United States during the 1950s and 1960s is a good example. Ford, Chevrolet and GM fought a pitched battle to win over the hearts and minds of potential purchasers.[5] These, and other companies, quickly realised that they were not only making and selling a product, but also promoting an image, a brand and a lifestyle. It was in this post-war environment that researchers began initially to look at how companies presented themselves to their customers. They focused their attention on the corporate image.

Corporate image refers to those visual aspects of a company that make it noticeable to stakeholders. These include its symbols, logos, slogans, brand design and other ways of engaging potential consumers. The visual arts, particularly graphic design, played an important part in the early development of the corporate image.[6] As Balmer (1998: 966) notes, 'Graphic design exerted a powerful influence on corporate image with corporate image being interpreted as how an organization communicates an image through a name and/or icon'.

The second aspect of corporate reputation is corporate identity.[7] This refers to the way that a company views itself, that is, its philosophy, values, products and services, and how it communicates these to stake-holders (Davies et al., 2001: 114). According to Balmer, the shift of emphasis from corporate image to corporate identity began in the 1970s. This is an important period in the evolution of corporate reputation because it demonstrated that MNCs were beginning to see themselves as more than just an amalgam of logos, symbols and slogans. They were forging distinct identities. While still employing the language of corporate image, Kennedy (1977: 123) noted the positive role of employees in nurturing a company's image. According to her, '[r]ealizing that every employee is a potential salesman for the firm, and that the firm is selling much more than its conventional product range, brings the employee into the centre of image formation'. Kennedy's point is that it deepens the concept of corporate image. She is one of the first authors to look beyond the marketing and graphical representation of a company's activities and to suggest that their identity is an important part of their outward appeal. This might also be referred to an identity formation. Similarly, and with even greater clarity, Olins (2003: 64) explicitly moves beyond corporate image in his work. As he notes:

> This is why corporate identity cannot be confined to graphics. If a company puts fresh bright signs on a squalid and decaying edifice, it indicates not only that it has the wrong priorities, but also that it is not sensitive to the spirit of the age in which we live ... Corporate identity must take into account not just the package but the product that goes inside it and the service that backs it up, not just a sign but a building on which it is placed. Not just uniforms but the way in which people who work for the company think about themselves in relation to it.

The third, and arguably most important aspect of corporate reputation, is the way that MNCs conduct themselves in their commercial activities. Larkin (2003: 1) argues that '[r]eputation in a corporate context is based on perceptions of the characteristics, performance and behaviour of a company'. Barnett et al. (2006: 34) define corporate reputation as '[o]bservers' collective judgment of a corporation based on assessments of the financial, social, and environmental impacts attributed to the corporation over time'.[8] Doorley and Garcia (2007: 4) put the point even more succinctly: 'Reputation = Sum of Images = (Performance and Behaviour) + Communication'. In other words, a strong reputation hinges on how well a company is able to convey to its stakeholders that it is a good corporate citizen.[9] Indeed, where corporate behaviour is concerned, actions speak louder than words.[10]

It is important not to confuse or conflate image, identity and behaviour because we are dealing with discrete concepts (Jackson, 2004: 41). Each has a different set of assumptions, practices and mechanisms that contribute to a strong corporate reputation. Corporate image has nothing to do with the way in which a company behaves. It is purely a way to attract customers and clients by instilling in them an emotional attachment to a particular product or service. One of the difficulties with the concept of corporate image is its shallowness. Often its value is fleeting, and lasts only as long as the marketing budget exists. Moreover, where there appears to be a longer-term benefit for a company through its use of powerful imagery, anti-corporate activists question whether such imagery

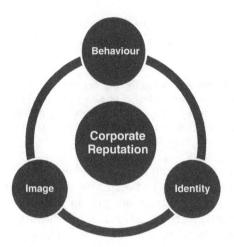

Figure 2.1   Elements of corporate reputation

is disingenuous. BP is one of the world's heaviest polluters, yet its green and yellow logo appears to suggest that the company is environmentally benign. The golden arches of McDonald's may well signify quick meals of consistent quality, but to some it symbolises obesity, heart disease and diabetes. Morgan Spurlock's documentary *Super Size Me* is a timely reminder that corporate imagery is a double-edged sword. It can be beneficial to a company, but it can also lead a company into contradiction and ridicule. It is for this reason that Grunig (in Balmer and Greyser, 2003: 209) dislikes the concept of corporate image because it focuses solely on symbolic relationships, rather than behavioural ones. It lacks the capacity to guide MNCs ethically.

It is no longer possible for MNCs to think about corporate reputation as something which can be enhanced solely through the use of traditional marketing and public relations practices, or through introspection about their identity. While these are obviously important to a company in order to influence stakeholders and be distinctive in the marketplace, it is their behaviour which is now the most important ingredient for building a strong corporate reputation.

THE IMPORTANCE OF AUTHENTICITY

Fombrun and Van Riel have used the term 'authenticity' to highlight the importance of corporate behaviour in building a strong corporate reputation.[11] Authentic companies are 'real, genuine, accurate, reliable, and trustworthy' (Fombrun and Van Riel, 2004: 163). In their view, the behaviour of the company in its commercial and public activities is what counts:

> being authentic means narrowing the gap between claims and deeds, between who you are, what you say, and what you do ... Unfortunately, consumers are well aware of it, and to them, good intentions aren't enough – companies should be judged on their actions and behaviours. (Fombrun and Van Riel, 2004: 165)

It is unclear why it is unfortunate that consumers are better educated about the gap between claims and deeds, but it is true that consumers are now aware that good intentions are not an adequate defence against corporate impropriety. If the old adage that 'the customer is always right' continues to have currency, then there is nothing unfortunate about MNCs being judged by their performance, rather than their marketing skills. This is why Fombrun and Van Riel (2004: 145–52) believe it is crucial for companies seeking to build a strong corporate reputation to develop authentic corporate stories about themselves.

Godin (2005) makes a similar point. He argues that we live in a world where public trust of MNCs is low and, as such, the best marketing strategy for MNCs is to tell the truth. Or, as he puts it, to tell an authentic story.[12] Godin examines Nestlé's sale of powdered milk formula to breastfeeding mothers in the developing world. He argues that Nestlé's problem was that they told an inauthentic story about the worth of the formula.[13]

During the 1970s, Nestlé marketed this product to women as a substitute for breastfeeding. However, living conditions in the developing world made the use of the formula particularly dangerous to the health of infants.[14] First, the formula needed to be mixed with water. With much of the water contaminated, it exposed infants to an increased risk of disease. Second, formula is no substitute for breast milk, which provides infants with a natural immunity, something especially important in countries with a high disease burden. Third, while breast milk is free, artificial formula is an added expense to poor families.

The United Nations International Children's Emergency Fund (UNICEF) has suggested that as many as one million children may have died from drinking the formula (Godin, 2005: 99). Of course, there is no way to test the truth of this allegation, but it does highlight the magnitude of the problem for Nestlé. The crisis, and the bad publicity that followed, had a significant impact on the company's reputation, with critics boycotting Nestlé's products for years afterwards. Godin's (2005: 100) argument is that Nestlé told mothers that the company's formula was better than breastfeeding.

They could have just as easily told a truthful and authentic story which marketed their product to those mothers who had difficulty in breast-feeding their infants or who had Acquired Immune Deficiency Syndrome (AIDS). In this case, the story would have been true. Nestlé may not have sold quite as much product, but its reputation would have remained intact, and it would have built a long-term business line in the developing world. As Godin (2005: 100) concludes, '[j]ust because people might believe your story doesn't give you a right to tell it!' Conveying authentic stories to consumers, for Godin, is essential to good corporate conduct and the key to building a strong reputation. For him, the Nestlé example demonstrates the costs to companies that forget this important message.[15]

Wicki and Van der Kaaij (2007) use a case study of Chiquita to demonstrate the gap between word and deed.[16] For many years, the company had a poor reputation both in the US and in Latin America. By the early 1990s, the company was faltering; a bad reputation and poor economic performance saw the share price fall dramatically and, at one stage, the company filed for Chapter 11 in the US courts.[17] In addition, the company had been receiving bad media coverage, with one news-paper painting it as 'a rapacious exploitative company with no con-science' (Werre, 2003: 251). Like most companies that find themselves in a vulnerable commercial position, Chiquita understood that it had to change. By developing a relationship with the Rainforest Alliance, and by employing a corporate social responsibility (CSR) approach to business, the company worked to reinvent itself as an ethical and socially respons-ible company.[18] It is interesting that the company's new approach was developed without the usual marketing campaigns that generally surround such reinventions. However, after 12 years of quietly developing a new ethical approach to its business, the company decided to launch a very high-profile campaign in Europe, intended to show Europeans that they were leaders in CSR and were an ethical company. Instead, the company provoked a strong negative reaction from NGOs suspicious of the company's claims.

What this case highlights is that it does not matter what the company thinks of itself, but rather, how the community (stakeholders) view them. The 'gap', then, is the difference between actual reputation and what the company believes its reputation to be.

> The distance between the projected external CSR identity of a company as perceived in the marketplace is the so called 'authenticity gap'. This is not the gap between what is true or false. It is the gap between the CSR image that

companies are pursuing as a brand and the actual identity of that brand as a corporate citizen (Wicki and Van der Kaaij, 2007: 317).

THE ROLE OF CSR IN BUILDING A STRONG CORPORATE REPUTATION

What does behaving well mean in the context of building a strong corporate reputation? Like Chiquita, for most companies, it means adhering to principles of CSR.[19] CSR is essentially the voluntary integration of social and environmental factors into a company's business plan. It covers a range of issues, including labour rights, environmental sustainability, the protection of human rights, respect for local communities, and fair play in their commercial activities (Larkin, 2003: 18; Makower, 1994). As one CEO noted, 'any multinational needs to be more transparent, open and fair. Over the next ten years CSR is the major issue for multinationals. They (we) have huge impacts on the world and we have to step up to it' (cited in Freeman et al., 2007: 98).

The number of companies now embracing a CSR agenda has grown significantly in the last decade. For example, almost 70 per cent of United Nations Global Compact UK Network member companies are actively promoting the UN's MDGs as part of their CSR commitments (Department for Business Innovation and Skills, 2010: 7). The promotion of these goals is especially prevalent in industries that traditionally have a poor social and environmental record. The extractive industry has employed CSR as a way of avoiding confrontations with host governments, traditional landowners and anti-corporate activists. Barrick Gold's website provides a good example of a company that integrates CSR into its business activities. As the company notes in its CSR Charter:

> We endorse the definition of Corporate Social Responsibility as proposed by the World Bank: Corporate Social Responsibility is the commitment of business to contribute to sustainable economic development – working with employees, their families, the local community and society at large to improve the quality of life, in ways that are both good for business and good for development.

Similarly, Goldcorp notes that '[c]orporate responsibility is at the core of all our business decisions, and our way forward will always be shaped by a balance of social, economic and environmental considerations'.[20]

CSR is a diverse idea. A recent analysis of the concept determined that there are at least 37 separate definitions of the idea (Dahlsrud, 2006). However, according to Dahlsrud, these are reducible to five broad dimensions. These include (a) an environmental dimension; (b) a social dimension; (c) an economic dimension; (d) a stakeholder dimension; and (e) a voluntariness dimension. As with the concept of corporate reputation, the study concluded that it was not possible to develop an objective definition of the concept. CSR is a social construction. In other words, the various definitions are context dependent. Despite these variations, the five dimensions highlight the broad categories and ideas which are at play in the CSR discourse. For example, one version of CSR integrates financial, social and environmental data as part of a company's annual reporting. This is referred to as 'triple bottom line' reporting. Wilson and Lombardi (2001: 69) call this 'a new definition of corporate social responsibility'. Other approaches focus more on sustainability. Still others prefer to employ voluntary codes such as the ISO 14 000 family of Environmental Management Systems standards.[21] Whatever the focus, the context is generally a sector-specific one ('context dependent' in Dahlsrud's language).

Yet the concept of CSR is not without its critics. Henderson (2001a; 2001b; 2009), a former chief economist of the OECD, argues that business acceptance of CSR is a form of 'appeasement' to the demands of anti-corporate activists (Henderson, 2009: 13). While acknowledging the pervasiveness of the concept, he argues that it pushes up costs, impairs corporate performance, lessens competition and 'will make the world poorer and more over-regulated'. Griffin (2008: 24) asserts that CSR is 'implemented very inconsistently', is 'unwieldy', and 'ill thought through' in most organisations. Moreover, he suggests CSR is often interpreted as if it is embraced by MNCs to correct their corporate 'irresponsibility'. For Griffin, the assumption hidden within CSR is that it is a corrective or reactive response to external pressures. Consequently, he prefers the notion of corporate citizenship because it conveys a more positive meaning.[22] As he notes (Griffin, 2008: 154), 'The language of "corporate citizenship" is much more helpful. It is far more positive and describes more accurately the desired positioning of companies in wider society. Good companies should behave like good citizens'. What should not be overlooked here is that while Griffin's criticism may be valid, CSR is having a positive impact on corporate behaviour, regardless of its inefficiencies and the negative perception some have of the idea.

It is creating internationally accepted standards of behaviour in human rights and labour rights and the environment. Ruggie's point in Chapter 1 is reiterated by Spar. As she (1998: 12) notes, 'U.S. multinationals could be – indeed, may already be – a powerful instrument in the pursuit of human rights'. There are also other high-profile examples where companies have decided not to undertake investments because of the controversial nature of doing so. The exodus of a number of companies from Myanmar in the early 1990s is a good example of this. There is also evidence that CSR initiatives have made a clear difference in particular issue areas. A number of companies have stopped selling timber products that have been logged from old growth forests in developing countries (Vogel, 2005: 114–17). Finally, while it may be true that some companies use CSR as a means of avoiding their social obligations, it is not true in all cases. Critics of CSR often ignore the fact that many local communities are actively seeking meaningful partnerships with resource companies. The principles of CSR often provide a framework for negotiation and engagement with traditional landowners. Polaris Materials, a US-based construction aggregates company, has a strong partnership with the Namgis people of Vancouver Island (Bowes-Lyon et al., 2009).[23] The partnership provides training and jobs for the Namgis people and generates income that facilitates local development. CSR has been a critical factor in fostering the relationship between the two parties. CSR, then, has helped MNCs to think more deeply about who they are, what they do, how they interact with their stakeholders, and the value they place on their reputations (Plate et al., 2009).

THE VALUE OF A STRONG CORPORATE REPUTATION

What is the value of a strong corporate reputation? How do you measure it? These are not simple questions to answer because a strong corporate reputation is an intangible asset. It cannot be seen or felt, nor can it be traded, like property or stock. Yet there is no doubt that it is an invaluable asset to all companies, large and small.

The most common way to test the quality of a company's reputation is through stakeholder surveys.[24] They generally ask respondents to rate companies according to a range of criteria, such as quality of products or brands, financial performance, philosophy, behaviour and so on. These are then weighted by respondent attributes such as age, gender, income and educational background, to provide a quantitative assessment of where a company stands in relation to its competitors. Many popular periodicals and newspapers publish annual rankings of the top 100 companies, according to these methods, with *Fortune* being the most well-known. Such surveys can also be narrower in focus in order to test a particular issue or attribute of a company. The Australian corporate intelligence company, Reputex, publishes a ranking of Australia's best 'low carbon' companies (Reputex, 2008).

One of the more sophisticated attempts to measure corporate reputation is the so-called Reputation Quotient (RQ).[25] This is a survey-based attempt to determine which companies have the strongest corporate reputations. According to its proponents, the 'resulting instrument ... has emerged as a valid, reliable and robust tool for measuring corporate reputation' (Gardberg and Fombrun, 2002: 306).

Just how these surveys demonstrate the value of a strong corporate reputation is not at all clear. As Larkin (2003: 5) rightly points out, there is often a lack of precision in the criteria for assessment. What these surveys can determine is how popular a company is, and where it sits on a league table, compared to other similar companies. It does not actually tell us much about the real or potential value of individual reputations.

There are a number of reasons why a company might rank higher or lower than a competitor and these may have little, if anything, to do with its reputation in the marketplace. A successful advertising campaign in the weeks prior to the distribution of the survey may well sway the results significantly. In addition, survey questions change annually, and respondents often lack the knowledge to rate companies accurately. The surveys are also generally applied only to publicly listed companies and often ignore small and medium enterprises (SMEs). At best, these surveys are a subjective, opinion-based measure of the value of a corporate reputation. They tell us little about the real value and benefits of a reputation to a company strategically and operationally.

It would, however, be a mistake to dismiss them as a means of measuring corporate reputation. If they do not have any other effect than to focus attention more closely on corporate reputation, they serve a useful purpose for both MNCs and society. The important point is that the value of a strong corporate reputation lies in the benefits it brings to the company, not where it sits on an annual league table.

It is now almost universally accepted that a strong corporate reputation adds considerable value to a company. Gibson et al. (2006: 15) argue that it is the 'single most valued organizational asset'. Gaines-Ross (2008: 7) suggests that 'there are very real, tangible, "hard" payoffs to maintaining a good reputation'. Consequently, the value of a strong corporate reputation lies in how it contributes to a company's capacity to perform and meet particular market outcomes over time.[26] These market outcomes should not simply be confined to profit maximisation. While this is a crucially important part of MNC success, the real issue is how this profit is generated. A strong corporate reputation comes to companies which generate low (or no) negative externalities.

There are a number of benefits which may flow to companies who have developed strong corporate reputations. These include, among other things, a higher market profile, lower cost of finance, better product placement, opportunities to partner with other companies, and the building of trust with stakeholders (Dowling, 2002: 12–13; Jackson, 2004: 51). There are a number of points worth making here. First, the benefits of a strong corporate reputation are potentially broad. We are not simply talking about a narrow range of financial benefits here. Almost all aspects of a company's operations can derive some noticeable benefit from a strong corporate reputation, including in areas such as human resources, strategic management and customer satisfaction.

Second, a strong corporate reputation can help promote valuable relationships with stakeholders. It helps MNCs to understand their interests and contributes to the building of trust. As Fombrun et al. (2000a: 90) argue: 'corporate citizenship creates reputational value and so provides a platform from which other opportunities may spring'. A company that gains a deep appreciation for the culture, language and interests of society and its various stakeholders, is likely to have fruitful engagement and dialogue with them. Peters (1999: 17) nicely sums this up: 'reputation has an etiquette that translates into how a company behaves with regard to certain common principles that build integrity and trust with stakeholders'.

Third, a strong corporate reputation adds financial value. In some respects, the idea that corporate reputation is an intangible asset is an unfortunate one. It implies that these are second-order assets which do not need to appear in annual reports. Doorley and Garcia (2007: 8) are correct to argue that this is the wrong way to think about corporate reputation. In their view, this form of capital has 'real tangible value (dollars, for example) that can be measured'. Gaines-Ross (2008: 12) argues that as much as 70 per cent of a company's market capitalisation today could come from its intangible assets. Nakamura thinks that intangible assets are worth in the order of US$1 trillion a year to the US economy and argues that there is a strong correlation between the rise in the value of intangible assets and rising stock market values (cited in Hand and Lev, 2003: 29).

Fourth, a strong corporate reputation has immense strategic value. Imagine a situation where a company is seeking a licence to operate a mine in a particular country. If that company has built a strong reputation with respect to the treatment of local communities in other jurisdictions, governments may be more willing to grant the company an operating licence. A strong corporate reputation, then, provides opportunities and benefits that may not available to weaker performing MNCs. In Fombrun and Van Riel's (2004: 5) words, it creates 'differentiation and competitive advantage'.

Finally, a strong corporate reputation protects a company during a crisis.[27] Morley (2002: 5) calls it a 'crisis shield' during a time of adversity, and notes that '[w]hen a company with a strong reputation is confronted by a crisis or a serious problem, it gets the benefit of the doubt'. It is generally agreed that Johnson and Johnson survived the Tylenol tampering crisis in the US because the company had built up a strong corporate reputation among its consumers over many decades.[28] When a similar problem occurred in Australia with Herron's paracetamol tablets, the Australian media were particularly supportive of the way the company dealt with the crisis. In a slightly different case, when some of Cadbury's chocolate lines tested positive for salmonella, the company averted severe reputational damage by pleading guilty to health and safety violations. This meant it did not have to endure a long court battle and media attention. This limited the damage to its reputation.

Crises are also very costly to rectify. The Cadbury crisis cost the company £37 million pounds (Carroll, 2009: 72). Larkin (2003: 6) thinks that the case for maintaining a strong corporate reputation can easily be made if one considers the potentially significant costs involved in managing a corporate crisis.[29] Larkin (2003: 6) demonstrates the costs of a crisis. For example, the Exxon Valdez oil spill cost the company around US$16 billion. Some estimate that the BP disaster in the Gulf of Mexico could ultimately cost the company US$80 billion.

Not only are crises themselves extremely costly, but the potential supplementary effects, such as litigation, loss of stock value, clean-up costs and compensation, further add to the damage bill. Having a strong corporate reputation may prevent many of these problems from occurring in the first place. In reality, it is difficult to determine accurately the total financial and non-financial costs that might arise from a reputational crisis. Even if Arthur Andersen's reputation had survived the Enron debacle, how much would the scandal have cost the company over a 10-, 20- or 50-year period? How can one put a figure on the loss of morale among employees, the loss of earnings, and the loss of clients who would never again trust Arthur Andersen with their accounts? We do not know enough about reputation risk to put a figure on this. Undoubtedly, though, the losses are likely to be substantial.

All of these points lead to the conclusion that the overriding value of a strong corporate reputation is that it builds resilience in companies. Resilience is the ability of an individual or group to cope with a crisis successfully, despite substantial adversity. The term is often used in psychiatry, where it refers to the ability of children and adolescents to handle traumatic events, such as sexual abuse or the loss of a parent. More recently, the term has been used in terrorism studies, where researchers attempt to measure the capacity of modern, complex cities to recover from a catastrophic terrorist attack. The commonality in these two areas of study is the role of protective factors. In the case of the death of a parent, a person's social positioning, support network and temperament may assist them in dealing with the grief. In the case of terrorism, the protective factors that allow a city to recover from a terrorist attack include the preparedness of emergency services personnel, the availability of hospital beds and trained medical professionals, and the existence of high-quality back-up systems for power generation and the provision of potable water.

While a strong corporate reputation builds value, it is a fragile value which can easily be destroyed. In the next section of this chapter, I argue that reputation risk is the pre-eminent threat facing MNCs today. There are at least three reasons for this. Managing reputation risk is not well understood by risk managers and senior executives. Second, while there are innumerable practitioner resources available on the subject of reputation risk management, it is evident that the risk mitigation techniques have not established themselves within most organisations to the extent that managers can have confidence in their protective capacity. Finally, a reputational crisis can occur from a relatively minor source, but may result in severe and unintended reputational consequences.

CORPORATE REPUTATIONS AT RISK

When Enron, America's largest energy trader, filed for bankruptcy in 2001, it earned the dubious distinction of becoming the largest corporate collapse in the country's history. What made this collapse distinctive, however, was not so much the enormous debt that it left behind, but that it simultaneously destroyed the reputation of one of the world's top five accounting firms. Initially, Arthur Andersen sought to place the blame for Enron's predicament squarely at the feet of the company's Board of Directors, a tactic that was met with a certain degree of criticism from financial analysts and media commentators. However, allegations that staff at Arthur Andersen had destroyed important documents relating to Enron's business dealings only compounded their troubles. Not surprisingly, the company lost its major accounts and eventually filed for bankruptcy. At the time, Al Bows, a retired senior partner of Arthur Andersen, commented that 'we worked so hard to get all these clients, and it just breaks my heart they're gone' (cited in Dugan, 2002: A1).

According to one report, the directors of Arthur Andersen considered cutting ties with Enron the previous year, but determined that the lucrative earnings from the affiliation outweighed the risks of continuing the relationship. This amounted to about US$52 million dollars annually. This decision proved to be Arthur Andersen's undoing, and a few months after Enron collapsed, the company had all but disappeared.

Arthur Andersen is not the only company to meet its demise following a reputational crisis. In the early 1970s, A.H. Robins, a popular and respected pharmaceutical company, marketed a new contraceptive device known as the Dalkon Shield (Sobol, 1993; Hawkins, 1997).[30] Within a short period of time, the product became the biggest selling contraceptive device of its kind on the market. Despite its early success, evidence began to emerge that the product could cause serious infection in the women who used it. It took three years, and the death of two women, before the product was finally withdrawn from sale in the US. By 1975, 15 women in the US had died, and a class action suit was launched against the company (Schwartz and Gibb, 1999: 56).

The actions of A.H. Robins were disturbing to say the least. First, even before the Dalkon Shield went on sale, there was scientific evidence from early trials to suggest that it was not safe to use. It appears that this evidence was ignored by the company. Second, even after the product was recalled in the US, the firm continued to sell it to women in the developing world. Third, although the product was recalled in 1975, and despite mounting evidence of the danger it posed to women's health, it took the firm another five years to recommend that doctors remove the Dalkon Shield from those women still using it. In addition, A.H. Robins' senior management dealt with the crisis in a less than sensitive manner, claiming in court that the central source of the infection was the promiscuous sexual behaviour of the victims. By the mid-1980s, the crisis had cost the company US$2.45 billion and A.H. Robins' stock price had dropped by 50 per cent. In August 1985, the company filed for bankruptcy and was eventually sold to American Home Products.[31] In a rather perverted twist, the new owners of the Dalkon Shield continued to fight the law suits for many years after the acquisition.

A.H. Robins' decision not to recall the product was clearly made for financial reasons. A Minnesota judge hearing the case remarked to defence lawyers during the trial: '[p]lease, in the name of humanity, lift your eyes above the bottom line' (Schwartz and Gibb, 1999: 57). More than 300 000 law suits were filed against the company, making it the largest class action against any MNC in US history.

The cases of Arthur Andersen and A.H. Robins illustrate just how damaging a reputational crisis can be to a company. A crisis can emerge from a wholly unexpected source, and without warning. One of the interesting features of Royal Dutch Shell's confrontation with Green-peace over the proposed at sea dumping of the Brent Spar oil storage facility was the company's genuine sense of incredulity at what had occurred. In the space of a week they were seen as environmental vandals, and their reputation was in tatters. This is a good example of how fragile corporate reputations are. Despite a company's best efforts to 'do the right thing', a single miscalculation can seriously weaken its reputation overnight. As Buffett (1995) expresses it: 'it takes twenty years to build a reputation and five minutes to ruin it'.

Reputation risk is defined as that class of risks which occur when MNCs fail to adhere to community standards. It is a consequence of a breakdown in public trust and usually involves a change in the public's perception of the worth of a company. It can lead to a reduction in key corporate values.[32] Reputation risk also threatens a company's credibility among its various stakeholders.

It is possible to identify three key sources of reputation risk. The first are social and political in nature. The second are commercial in nature. The third occurs when senior executives display poor judgement and have poor communication skills in the face of a crisis.

Table 2.1 offers a list of some of the issues that can trigger a reputation crisis event. Undoubtedly, there are many other sources, but this list illustrates how easily a reputational crisis event can occur. Social, political and commercial reputation risks are fairly self-explanatory. The third class of reputation risk requires some explanation, as it is the most unpredictable class of reputation risk to guard against.

In 1991, a well-known British jeweller, Gerald Ratner, commented at a function that some of his product lines were of a very poor quality. He labelled a decanter and glass set as 'total crap'. Later in the speech, he suggested that the gold earrings his company sold were cheaper than a prawn sandwich from Marks and Spencer, and probably would not last as long.

After the comments were broadcast in the media, a reputational disaster followed that wiped £500 million off the value of the company. Some years later, the BBC (BBC News, 2002) suggested that this was one of the most famous gaffes in corporate history. They referred to it as an example of 'foot in mouth disease'. The phrase 'doing a Ratner' has also become shorthand for CEO verbal indiscretions.

More recently, BP's former CEO, Tony Hayward, brought about public disapproval of the company for insensitive comments concerning the disaster in the Gulf of Mexico (Lubin, 2010). He suggested that the environmental impact of the spill was 'very, very modest'. Later, he told the media, 'he would like his life back'. These sorts of comments display

Table 2.1   Key sources of reputation risk

Social and political	Commercial	Public errors of judgement and a failure to communicate
• Environmental problems • Exploitation of labour • Indifference to health and safety of workers • Cultural and ethnic insensitivities • Gender issues • Complicity in human rights violations • Lack of concern for the views of local communities • Indifference to human suffering • Corruption and bribery • Inadequate response to a crisis • Failure to uphold human rights	• Product failure/recall • Poor advice and service • Fraudulent activities • Poor governance and decision-making • Intervention by regulatory authorities • Fines/penalties • Litigation by stakeholders and regulators • Unethical behaviour towards competitors • Infighting among board members • Information and security leaks • Anti-trust issues and unfair use of market power	• Verbal gaffes • Acting in an insensitive manner during a crisis • Public arrogance • Failing to acknowledge the extent of a crisis or downplaying the seriousness of a crisis • Failure to communicate effectively with stakeholders • Poor public behaviour

an acute lack of judgement during one of the world's worst environmental disasters. It devastated the marine environment and affected the lives of tens of thousands of people living along the coastline.[33]

Unfortunately, this 'foot in mouth disease' is more common than we might think. In the last two years, a number of other examples have surfaced. In an interview, the founder of Lululemon suggested that his yoga pants were not suitable for all women because some women's thighs rubbed together. Guido Barilla, a family member of the famous Barilla pasta brand, stated in an interview that his company was pro-family. They did not do advertisements with gay people because the classic family was sacred to them. Finally, the CEO of AngelHack, Greg Gopman, posted the following on Facebook upon his return to the US:

> Just got back to SF. I've travelled around the world and I gotta say there is nothing more grotesque than walking down market st in San Francisco. Why the heart of our city has to be overrun by crazy, homeless, drug dealers, dropouts, and trash I have no clue. Each time I pass it my love affair with SF dies a little [sic].

The backlash on Facebook and Twitter was fierce. Despite an apology, Gopman resigned from the company and his Facebook page was deleted.

Companies are readily able to recover financially from market fluctuations, research and development failures, bad investment decisions, or other commercial problems. However, reputation risks infect the entire organisation, not just a single part of it. Reputation risk can also have transnational consequences in an era of globalisation. BHP's environmental disaster at their Ok Tedi mine in Papua New Guinea was played out in Victoria's Supreme Court in Australia. Freeport McMoRan's involvement in conflicts with local communities at its Grasberg mine in West Papua led to litigation and protests in Austin, Texas. Moreover, reputation risks have the potential to contaminate an entire industry. As Larry Parnell, former Director of Global Public Relations at Ernst & Young, noted in relation to the Enron–Arthur Andersen collapse, '[i]t has obviously called into question the entire industry's credibility and reliability' (PR News, 2002). Barnett and Hoffman (2008) refer to this as 'reputational interdependence'. Interdependence not only means that all companies in an industry sector are reliant on the behaviour of each other. It also means that they are mutually vulnerable. A reputational crisis can taint an entire industry sector. Goins and Gruca (2008) use the term 'contagion effect' to highlight the problem. One of the interesting side-effects of Arthur Andersen's role in the demise of Enron is that it led to a scramble by other auditing companies to ensure that they were acting with impartiality and honesty. Similarly, the Bhopal disaster produced a kind of reputational 'contagion' that spread through the entire chemical sector.

Referring to the spate of corporate collapses around the time of Enron, Alsop (2004: x) observed that:

> [l]ong before the scandals broke, I had a sense that companies were beginning to understand how important – but neglected – their reputations were. Whenever I wrote an article for the *Wall Street Journal*, I received calls and emails from managers hungry to know more about the subject. They asked me questions about how to get their arms around the concept. They didn't understand how to define reputation, how to measure it, or more important, how to manage it.

This view has remained practically unchanged over the last decade or so. A 2005 survey of 269 senior executives noted that more than 50 per cent believed the greatest risk they faced was managing their reputations (Economist Intelligence Unit, 2005: 19), while a 2009 McKinsey survey of senior executives around the world overwhelmingly pointed to the importance of corporate reputations for their businesses (Bonini et al.,

2009). The survey also highlighted their concerns over the loss of public trust in companies in the wake of the GFC.

CORPORATE REPUTATION AS A DRIVER OF IDEATIONAL CHANGE IN MNC BEHAVIOUR

The term 'ideational change' is a familiar one to comparative political economists, and to those scholars with an interest in how institutions change over time. Finnemore and Sikkink (2001: 405) refer to this literature, broadly, as the 'ideas literature'. An interesting feature of this large body of work is that it rejects the idea that institutional change occurs through the exercise of power, whether it be through the exercise of political power, military power or economic power. Instead, new thinking and new norms come about through 'dramatic policy shocks, failures, or crises' (Finnemore and Sikkink, 2001: 406). One particularly good example of this is Culpepper's (2005) study of institutional change in the financial systems of France, Germany and Italy since 1990. He argues that the key to making sense of institutional change at the time is to understand the role of 'triggering events'. As he notes:

> The sufficient condition for institutional change in such an institution is thus one of changed ideas, with change occurring via a causal mechanism I call *joint belief shift* – the process by which actors use triggering events to coordinate their future expectations around the new rules of the game, that is, around new institutions. The mechanism of joint belief shift is both ideational and rationalist, and it builds on the pioneering work of North and Aoki to identify the cognitive mechanisms that lie behind institutional change. (2005: 176)

While Culpepper's research focuses on large financial institutions in Europe, it is equally useful for accounting for what is happening to MNCs at present. The politicisation of the corporate reputation, as discussed in Chapter 1, has triggered a 'joint belief shift' in MNC behaviour, and this is instantiating a new set of norms and beliefs about the relationship between MNCs and society, and about how MNCs should operate within this changed context.

I use the term 'ideational change' to highlight the fact that, at play, are ideas about the role of MNCs as economic, social and political actors. This is occurring not only exogenously, as we have seen thus far, but also endogenously. Within organisations ideational change is being driven by such concerns as staff morale, the role of corporate social responsibility officers within a company, and how a company wants to represent itself to its external audience. The ideational change that I am suggesting is taking place is one where there is greater recognition by MNCs that their future expectations for profit, growth and a strong reputation now rely on a different way of understanding their interests.

It is not for purely ethical reasons that the change is taking place. Rather, MNCs understand how their business can benefit from a strong corporate reputation, and the potential costs of not sustaining one. Along the way, ethical behaviour is becoming instantiated in corporate structures and processes and, consequently, a new way of thinking about MNC interactions with society is emerging. Put differently, the action and behaviour of companies is being constrained by the need to protect their reputations in order to avoid the risk of substantial loss. This awareness is having a 'disciplining' effect on them, pushing MNCs in the direction of self-regulation (O'Callaghan, 2007b). This is the rationalist aspect of change that Culpepper refers to above.

Foucault uses the term 'governmentality' to refer to three related historical practices. First, the institutions, practices and strategies that allow power to be exerted over a population. Second, it refers to a tendency which led towards the pre-eminence of government in modern society, and the formation of various apparatus of government. Third, it refers to the transformation from the state of justice in the Middle Ages to the administrative state of the eighteenth century. At its broadest, Foucault thought of governmentality as the 'art' of government. But he did not confine the meaning simply to the activities of elected officials. He also used the term to refer to the array of practices and techniques that governments use to control a population. These are the social practices, ideas, rules and norms we find ourselves following every day. More subtly, governmentality exposes the techniques by which individuals and groups are governed by sovereign states. Foucault's death meant that he did not fully develop his thinking on the subject. However, numerous scholars have used the term to interrogate critically the idea of the neoliberal state (Larner, 2000; Lemke, 2000).

The key feature of the neoliberal state is that it 'involves both direct and indirect forms of governance. These encourage both institutions and individuals to conform to the norms of the market' (Larner, 2000: 11). Predating the neoliberal state model, governments used a welfare state model of governance (Castles et al., 2012; Pierson, 2013). They 'cared' for the population through social measures, such as unemployment benefits and subsidised education. In the neoliberal model, governments use direct forms of control with the help of state apparatus, but place greater emphasis on indirect forms of control.[34] These centre on a range of moral duties, such as the demand that individuals become responsible for themselves and for the quality of their society. As Lemke (2000: 12) argues, the strategy of rendering individual subjects 'responsible' (and also collectives, such as families and associations) entails shifting the responsibility for social risks such as illness, unemployment and poverty into the domain for which the individual is responsible and transforming it into a problem of 'self-care'.

Lupton (1999: 88–9) explores this idea with reference to a woman's pregnancy and how experts advise an expectant mother that she has a duty to regulate her activities in the interests of her child.[35] Lupton argues that '[a] crucial aspect of governmentality as it is expressed in neoliberal states is that the regulation and disciplining of citizens is directed at autonomous, self-regulated individuals. Citizens are positioned in governmental discourses as active rather than passive subjects of governance' (Lupton, 1999: 88). As active subjects of governance, individuals and institutions are exhorted to conform to the norms of the market, as well as those of society.

In the context of neoliberalism, the discourse of governmentality has both a critical function and an explanatory one. As a critical discourse, it is used to show that neoliberalism offers a very flawed, perhaps even insidious, approach to government and governance. As an explanatory discourse, in the context of understanding MNCs and why they are moving towards self-regulation, it has a great deal of explanatory power. Discussions about CSR, codes of conduct and other such regulatory devices for managing corporate behaviour are simply the indirect mechanisms by which governments, international institutions and non-state actors have adopted to govern MNCs. Rather than a critique of neoliberalism, then, governmentality can be interpreted as an interesting theoretical deliberation about the growing trend towards corporate self-regulation. The crucial point is that the norms of the neoliberal state have been an important contributing factor in the ideational shift in business thinking. 'Explanation' here should not necessarily be read as a vindication of neoliberalism. It is also only one part of a more complex process. Arguably, governmentality can be observed in multiple ways, as various actors seek to gain influence over each other. Host governments in the developing world, indigenous communities and international institutions have certain expectations of MNCs and seek to influence their behaviour. Moreover, it would be an interesting exercise to consider the contribution of anti-corporate activists to the process of the normalisation of corporate behaviour. It may even be the case that, ironically, anti-corporate activists themselves are agents of the neoliberal state. By putting pressure on MNCs and their corporate reputations, they have played an important role in moderating that behaviour.

There are a number of other factors that are driving change in MNC behaviour that follow on from this. First, public sentiment towards MNCs has altered in recent years. This has forced them to take social and environmental issues more seriously. Second, a convincing business case can now be made for taking self-regulation seriously. Third, MNCs are operating in multiple jurisdictions. This is creating reputational issues for them globally, not just in their home country.

Public Sentiment Matters

The Millennium Poll on Corporate Social Responsibility surveyed more than 25 000 people from 23 countries (International Business Leaders Forum, 2011). The poll highlighted seven interesting features regarding public perceptions of MNCs and CSR. First, a majority of citizens from 13 of the 23 countries surveyed believed that their country should pay more attention to social and environmental issues than to economic ones. Second, in developing impressions of companies, people tend to focus more on corporate citizenship than on branding or financial factors. Third, 66 per cent of those polled wanted MNCs to go beyond the historical idea of companies as profit maximisers and embrace broader societal goals. Fourth, contributing to charities and community projects was not enough to count as effective CSR. Fifth, half of the people surveyed indicated that they pay attention to the behaviour of MNCs. Sixth, 20 per cent reported that they had rewarded or punished companies in a 12-month period for their behaviour, either by switching brands or by no longer buying the product. Finally, the survey concluded that over the next ten or 15 years, public pressure will force MNCs to play a more useful role in the societies in which they operate. This is a significant shift in public sentiment compared to views of MNCs two decades ago.

MNCs have undergone a number of transformations in the past century and will continue to do so into the future. At the beginning of the twentieth century, mass production was born, bringing with it Fordist modes of production that allowed companies to produce more products and, at a quicker rate, for local and overseas markets (Harvey, 1992: ch. 8). After World War II, MNCs slowly began to change, not only in a managerial sense, but also in a technological sense, as they sought to sell more of their products overseas. More recently, globalisation has cata-lysed a revolution in the way MNCs think about the conduct and the management of their businesses. The point is that, just like most organisations, MNCs are evolutionary and adaptive. The mercantilist companies of the seventeenth century were very different enterprises from those of Microsoft, IKEA and Chevron. Companies that do not adapt and evolve will eventually die out. One way to think about the narrative thus far is to interpret it as a commentary on the evolution of MNC behaviour. To put the argument more subtly, what this narrative bears witness to is a metamorphosis in MNC behaviour. This is something that has been occurring since the Industrial Revolution. In this context Arena (2004: 59) talks about 'a continuous process of self-improvement'.

Many business leaders also have an interest in the environment and in conducting their businesses ethically. Indeed, their families and friends are as much affected by climate change as anyone else. Many are churchgoers and are passionately committed to a range of important causes. Some even volunteer their time and energy to helping others. Business leaders may form an identifiable group, but they are not all alike. To suggest, as some have, that they are somehow impervious to broader social trends is misleading. They read newspapers, watch television and attend conferences where such issues are regularly discussed and debated. Attend any mining or resource conference, and there are as many presentations on social and environmental issues as there are on the business side of the sector's activities.

The views of employees also impact on their managers. They make their views known in a variety of ways, including suggestion drop boxes and in team meetings. MNCs are not 'hard-shelled units', impervious to opinion. On the contrary, what has made them so successful over the last 100 years is that they are responsive to external social and political pressure. While one may doubt the motives of MNCs when it comes to addressing social and environmental issues, the fact that they are responding affirmatively to these pressures suggests an acute awareness of the relevant issues. Indeed, while critics bemoan the fact that some MNCs are greenwashing their image, an alternative interpretation is that this may be a better outcome than no response at all. A brief glance at the websites of some Chinese, Indian and Russian state-owned resource companies is quite a sobering exercise. Many of these are devoid of any reference to CSR or environmental sustainability. Indeed, the real challenge for anti-corporate activists is not neutering Western MNCs, but pressuring those companies and states who are not subject to the same level of popular and political scrutiny.

The Business Case for Ideational Change

The second reason for this ideational shift in thinking is that corporate managers can see that it makes good business sense to change their behaviour. During the 1950s companies like Standard Oil and Chase

Manhattan Bank used corporate philanthropy to further their business interests. As Vogel (2005: 18) points out, David Rockefeller noted at the time that a company needs to operate within a stable social and political environment if it is to flourish. 'Our urban affairs work is good for Chase Manhattan in a strictly business sense. Our efforts are aimed at creating a healthy economic and social environment that is vital to the existence of any corporation'.[36] In this sense, the business case is strategic in nature. An awareness of the social and environmental aspects of business affairs acts as a safeguard against the scrutinising eyes of critics; indeed, it may even help to 'outflank' them. This is a major theme in a number of recent books on reputation risk management (Alsop, 2004; Jackson, 2004; Larkin, 2003).

The business case can be looked at historically as well. In 1992, the Cadbury Committee produced the UK Corporate Governance Code (the Code). The document set out the core responsibilities of both shareholders and directors. Paragraph 2.5 nicely captures the intent of the Code.

> Corporate governance is the system by which companies are directed and controlled. Boards of directors are responsible for the governance of their companies. The shareholders' role in governance is to appoint the directors and the auditors and to satisfy themselves that an appropriate governance structure is in place. The responsibilities of the board include setting the company's strategic aims, providing the leadership to put them into effect, supervising the management of the business and reporting to shareholders on their stewardship. The board's actions are subject to laws, regulations and the shareholders in general meeting. (Financial Reporting Council, 2010)

The aim of the Code was meant to strengthen the governance structures of publicly listed MNCs in the UK – in areas such as finance, audit and compliance, remuneration, operations and risk management. The recognition of the need for a code came about after it was revealed that the CEO of Maxwell Communications, Robert Maxwell, financed risky acquisitions from resources in his pension funds. When he died unexpectedly in the Canary Islands, it became clear to auditors that his companies were insolvent. In addition, and around the same time, the Bank of Credit and Commerce International fell into bankruptcy and lost billions of pounds of shareholder and depositor funds. The development of the Code was seen as a step forward in tightening up corporate governance procedures to restore faith in the market. A key requirement of the Code was the need for MNCs to demonstrate to the Financial Reporting Authority (FRA) how they were compliant with it.

In 1999, the London Stock Exchange (LSE) set up a committee to further improve the internal controls of publicly listed companies. Referred to as the *Turnbull Report* or the *Turnbull Guidance*, it not only reminded boards of their obligations under the Code, but it also sought to improve internal controls and risk management procedures to ensure sound business practices. A related document and, in my view, no less important, is a practically focused publication called *Implementing Turnbull: A Boardroom Briefing* (Jones and Sutherland, 1999). This document was produced by the Institute of Chartered Accountants in England and Wales and was meant to supplement the *Turnbull Guidance*. What is most striking about this latter document is the extent to which it highlights the financial and strategic value of following the Code and the *Turnbull Guidance*. Some of the listed benefits include:

- early mover into new business areas;
- fewer sudden shocks and unwelcome surprises;
- achievement of competitive advantage;
- greater likelihood of achieving business objectives;
- better basis for strategy setting;
- higher share price over the longer term;
- lower cost of capital;
- reduction in management time spent 'fire-fighting';
- increased likelihood of change initiative being achieved; and
- greater focus internally on doing the right things properly.

There are three points to be made regarding these documents. First, they are evolutionary in nature. They chart the changing philosophy guiding business practice in the UK. Indeed, in the last two years there has been a further revision of the Code and the *Turnbull Guidance* in light of the GFC. Second, it demonstrates unequivocally that there are substantial benefits for MNCs that take self-regulation seriously. The overriding message of these documents is that good risk management and internal controls benefit the entire organisation. As Jones and Sutherland (1999: 6) explain, '[g]ood risk management has the potential to re-orient the whole organization around performance improvement'. It does this by improving the risk–return ratio, lessening a company's exposure to risk, and helping the company to cope better with external factors. This may have a flow-on effect on the quality of management as well. Finally, the underlying message of these documents is not simply that shareholder value should be protected, but that there is significant reputational value (and capital) for companies that operate ethically, above the minimum standard required by law.

The International Dimension of Corporate Reputation

Much of the recent literature on corporate reputation management shares something in common with their anti-corporate adversaries: an 'us and them' approach to understanding the relationship between MNCs and society. One is either an advocate of MNCs or their enemy. It is interesting that both sides use the term 'predator' to refer to their opponents. Korten describes MNCs as 'predatory' corporations (Korten, in Evans et al., 2002b: 15), while Peters (1999) describes anti-corporate activists as 'raptors' waiting to devour the reputations of poorly performing MNCs. The imagery is suggestive and powerful. It is also ideologically loaded and leads to something of a conceptual quagmire, with each side trading blows and counter blows. This is unhelpful in advancing our understanding of MNCs and the role that reputation plays in regulating their behaviour. Moreover, once MNCs are viewed through this dichotomous lens, we lose sight of the most important aspects of the corporate reputation in a globalising world; that is, the extent to which a company's reputation now constrains its behaviour to a considerable degree. While anti-corporate activists have seen the growing significance of the corporate reputation, they have largely missed the regulatory implications it has had. MNCs that want to build a strong corporate reputation are beginning to self-regulate. It is quite likely that reputation is a more effective means of constraining potentially damaging corporate behaviour than increasing government intervention in the market. There are a number of reasons for this. Globalisation may provide MNCs with a degree of operational freedom, but it also promotes the creation of global norms of behaviour in areas such as human rights, global environmental policy, labour conditions and so on. MNCs are being conditioned by these emerging trends. In a spirit of market competition, MNCs are also learning from each other. The view that a crisis can taint an entire industry is valid in this context. Moreover, because they operate in more than one jurisdiction at a time, they need to self-regulate in order to be efficient and able to service multiple markets. While a company may comply with local rules and practices and suffer no reputational loss in the host country, its operations may suffer reputational problems elsewhere, particularly in countries in which communities and individuals are more sensitive to social and environmental concerns. In other words, it is easier for MNCs to live up to a higher standard of behaviour than a lower one.

This happened to Coca-Cola in Belgium when it failed to remove tainted drinks from its outlets. The governments of Belgium, France and Luxembourg forced the company to remove the product. The reputational damage was not only felt in those three countries, but also in the US. The recall cost the parent company about US$200 million and the Belgium operation around US$103 million (Johnson and Peppas, 2003: 18). Revenues fell by 5 per cent and operating profit dropped by 6 per cent. In addition, the value of Coke shares fell by 1 cent per share. At the end of 1999, the company's profits had fallen by 31 per cent (Larkin, 2003: 107). As Ignatius (1999), a *Washington Post* reporter, noted at the time: 'The events last week show that the value of Coca-Cola's brand, built up over more than a century, can be shaken as suddenly and capriciously as the Thai Baht'.

Many years ago, Keohane and Nye (1977) wrote about 'mutual vulnerability' in the context of states becoming more interdependent. Their point, at the time, was that while closeness had positive social, political and economic advantages, a problem in one country would now be felt in others. The GFC is the most recent example of this fundamental point. But it applies equally well to MNCs. Zyglidopoulous (2002: 146) refers to this as 'international corporate reputation side effects' and argues that 'the multinational will have to operate at the highest level of social and environmental responsibility if it does not want to cause damage to its reputation in any of the countries it operates in'.

CONCLUSION

This chapter began by examining the concept of corporate reputation. It explored the tripartite division between corporate image, corporate identity and corporate behaviour. I argued that, in the context of globalisation, corporate behaviour has become the key variable. The chapter then considered the significance of reputation risk. I argued that of all the risks modern MNCs face in doing business in a globalised world, reputation risk is potentially the most hazardous. I discussed Enron, Arthur Andersen and A.H. Robins in this regard. BP would have also provided an excellent example of the truth of this point. However, the overriding argument of the chapter is that an ideational shift is taking place among MNCs and that this is beginning to constrain their behaviour. I refer to this as 'disciplining' of MNCs. As the cost of failure increases, MNCs have realised that their Achilles heel is their reputation. I concluded the chapter by suggesting that self-regulation is an important goal for MNCs to aspire to. CSR is an important part of the process of corporate self-regulation, but it is not the full story. In the next chapter I look at the debate between those who see more state regulation as the answer to bad MNC behaviour and offer a critique of this position. I suggest that self-regulation is a viable approach to building a strong corporate reputation and is an essential goal for all MNCs to aspire to over the next decade or so.

NOTES

1. Donaldson and Preston (1995: 65–72) highlight three uses or modes of stakeholder theory. The first is to provide a description of a company and the significance of its various internal and external relationships. The second is instrumental. This allows the manager to think in terms of stakeholders in order 'to achieve corporate performance objectives'. The third use is normative, that is, to use stakeholder theory to consider the moral or ethical purposes of the corporation and how it should conduct itself in society. See also Clarkson (1995); Freeman et al. (2010); Freeman (2010).
2. According to Iyengar et al.'s (2011) analysis of 1842 companies, some of the factors that lead to a company being admired include democratic corporate governance, profitability and performance, and a relatively large workforce. For an analysis of the ontological dimensions of reputation, see Heil and Whittaker (2011).
3. The most famous statement of the futility of such attempts is Gadamer (2013; 2008). See also Ricoeur (1981); Hiley et al. (1992); Rabinow and Sullivan (1988).
4. Some of the earliest books to consider the ability of states to exercise control over MNCs are Penrose (1959); Kindleberger (1969); Vernon (1971).
5. On the history of the US auto industry see Rubenstein (2008); Tata (2013).
6. For a history of the idea of corporate image, see Furman (2010). Furman suggests that the corporate image has its roots in nineteenth-century British companies. The use of visual arts and furnishings at that time was commonplace in the UK. See also Abratt (1989).
7. See essays by Margulies; Albert and Whetten; Stuart; and Balmer and Gray in Balmer and Greyser (2003). See also Melewer (2008); Kitchen (2013).
8. Jackson (2004: 43) argues that reputation is similar to the way the Chinese think about 'face'. As he notes, there are two senses of face: *lian* and *mian-zi*. '*Lian* stands for society's confidence in the integrity of one's character. A person or firm can't operate successfully in the society if they have lost face. *Mian-zi* denotes distinction earned from having achieved success in life. Having attained high status, one acquires dignity and deserves respect'.
9. For a good overview of the issues associated with corporate citizenship see Scherer and Palazzo (2010); Crane and Matten (2010); Pies and Koslowski (2013).
10. A recent survey of the management literature dealing with reputation uses the term 'organizational reputation' and uses different terms to describe the attributes of corporate reputation. Lange et al. (2011: 155) refer to these attributes as 'being known', 'being known for something', and 'generalized favourability'.
11. Jackson (2004: 43) also highlights authenticity as a key feature of a strong corporate reputation. On 'authenticity' in contemporary philosophy see Taylor (1992; 2007).
12. On storytelling as part of constructing a business narrative see Denning (2000; 2011).
13. For a history of Nestlé, see Schwartz (2002).
14. For more detailed accounts of the controversy see Dobbing (1988); Prakesh Sethi (1994).
15. Partly as a result of the controversy surrounding Nestlé, The World Health Organization developed The International Code of Marketing of Breastmilk Substitutes in 1981. Yet there is some evidence that Nestlé continued to supply its product to doctors and hospitals free of charge in the developing world. See Fisher and Lovell (2006: 489).
16. The company was previously known as the Union Fruit Company.
17. Chapter 11 is a chapter of the United States Bankruptcy Code. It provides all companies with a right to restructure their business interests to avoid having to completely liquidate their assets.

18. See Taylor and Scharlin (2004).
19. Hillenbrand and Money (2007: 261–77) are right to highlight the difficulty in establishing whether, in fact, corporate social responsibility precedes and brings about strong reputations, or whether CSR is an inherent part of a strong reputation.
20. Many other large mining companies prefer the language of sustainability and sustainable development. Both Anglo-American and Brazil's Vale subsume CSR under the banner of sustainable development. On sustainability and natural resources see Edwards (2005: 75–96).
21. For an analysis of these standards see Prakash and Potoski (2006).
22. Contrary to this view, Windsor (2001: 41) argues that '[t]he corporate citizenship notion conflates citizen (which a firm cannot be) and person (which a firm can be, but only as a legal fiction)'.
23. The quarry is called the Orca Quarry.
24. These surveys take different forms. They can be conducted through face-to-face interviews, by telephone, direct mail and, most commonly now, through the Internet using software such as SurveyMonkey.
25. On measuring corporate reputation see Fombrun (1998); Van Riel et al. (1998); Fombrun et al. (2000b); Gardberg and Fombrun (2002); Bromley (2002); Wartick (2002); Helm (2005); Abraham et al. (2008).
26. In a case study on Shell, Innocent et al. (2011) note that there is a clear link between CSR and profitability. See also Waddock and Graves (1997). Mio and Fasan (2013) look at this issue through a case study of the collapse of Lehmann Brothers.
27. See Coombs (2007); Watson (2007). Journal articles on particular corporate crises include Thomsen and Rawson (1998); LaPlant (1999); O'Rourke (2001); Werre (2003); Johnson and Pappas (2003); Carroll (2009). On crisis management see Albrecht (1996).
28. Johnson and Johnson's reputation in Europe has recently come under fire. While the company has generally had an excellent reputation, this has been sullied by the news that the company bribed doctors in Europe and paid kickbacks to Saddam Hussein's regime in Iraq. See Gallu and Nussbaum (2011).
29. See Schnietz and Epstein (2005).
30. The Dalkon Shield is an intra-uterine type of contraceptive device.
31. Subsequently, American Home Products was purchased by Wyeth. Wyeth then merged to form Wyeth-Ayerst. In the following years, the company went through numerous mergers. The most notable was with Pfizer.
32. These may include a loss of quality employees, litigation from regulators, changes in the market behaviour of consumers and, in extreme cases, revenue shortfalls, liquidity crises and possible bankruptcy.
33. The affected states were Alabama, Florida, Louisiana and Mississippi.
34. It should be noted, however, that most modern states in the West are hybrids of sorts. The neoliberal state continues to have a place for significant welfare measures. Australia, New Zealand and Canada are 'hybrids' in this sense.
35. So activities such as drinking, smoking and drug-taking should be strictly avoided.
36. For a recent study of the link between philanthropy and corporate reputation see Morris et al. (2013).

3. Exploring the idea of a self-regulating corporation

What is the most appropriate way to deal with corporate malfeasance? Governments invariably use the threat of hefty fines and incarceration of senior managers in order to deter criminal behaviour. The failure of Bernard Madoff's Ponzi scheme means he will never be released from jail, and the suicide of his son two years after Madoff was sentenced suggests that individuals who defraud investors pay an inordinately high price for their crimes.[1] These cases are relatively clear cut. Madoff simply pleaded guilty to defrauding his clients. But what about the times when things are less clear cut? These are the ethical 'hard cases', where it is often difficult to prove wrongful behaviour or to decide whether wilful negligence, inadvertent misfortune or outright criminality is the root cause of a crisis. An MNC may simply overlook issues of public concern. Schwartz and Gibb's (1999: 59) notion of MNCs operating in the 'gray area' is a fitting description of the difficulties facing global MNCs today. They may, or may not, fully comprehend the consequences of their conduct while they are single-mindedly focused on their business activities.

But how are MNCs to be judged under these circumstances? How should they be sanctioned, and what is the best way to ensure they behave ethically in the future? The issue here is to determine the most suitable form of regulation to ensure that MNCs remain profitable while acting in a socially responsible manner. Generally speaking, anti-corporate activists argue that what is needed is more effective regulation of MNCs by national governments. More regulation will put people before MNCs and their profits. New, and more powerful, state regulation is the only leash capable of restraining these economic juggernauts.

This may not be the most effective strategy for improving or controlling MNC behaviour if, as was argued in the previous chapter, the importance of a strong corporate reputation is already beginning to discipline them. Consequently, stricter state-based regulation may be counterproductive, not least because it has the potential to undermine global economic dynamism and the development potential of MNCs. In this chapter I argue that the need to focus on the reputations of MNCs obviates the need for a (re)introduction of stronger command and control forms of state regulation. Instead, the chapter looks at the role of corporate self-regulation in building strong corporate reputations.

THE IDEA OF A SELF-REGULATING CORPORATION

The concept of regulation refers to 'the promulgation of an authoritative set of rules, accompanied by some mechanism, typically a public agency, for monitoring and promoting compliance with these rules' (Baldwin et al., 1998: 3). Regulations are enacted by government law-makers and enforced by bureaucratic agencies in order to maintain a productive society.

Dudley and Brito (2012: 77) argue that there are two families of regulation. The first are economic regulations. These are the regulations that govern the market. They include investment and labour regulations, control of the stock market, and regulations that guard against market failure. The second are social regulations. The latter include workplace health and safety, security and justice, and the environment.

The reasons for regulating societies are many and varied. But, at its most basic, governments regulate in order to collect the taxes necessary to promote state-wide development, economic growth and social harmony. Other benefits include correcting for market failure, improving equity, coordination, reducing criminal activity, and advancing the public good. Failed states are states that have lost the capacity to regulate their citizens (Ezrow and Frantz, 2013).

Regulations do not simply exist in isolation from one another. Economic regulation may improve economic performance, while at the same time improving the environment and vice versa. Consequently, regulation needs to be understood holistically. We can call this a regulatory architecture or a regulatory regime. The latter term is useful because the word 'regime' highlights the importance of the monitoring and compliance capability of regulation.[2]

One of the difficulties faced by developing countries is that their regulatory environments suffer from a lack of institutional capacity.[3] This might be due to a lack of experienced personnel, government funding shortages or a lack of political will. Effective regulatory regimes also develop within unique social and political contexts. They are influenced by such factors as language, culture and traditions, among other things. This is a country's 'institutional endowment' (Levy and Spiller, 1994: 205).[4] The key point is that institutions and regulatory frameworks evolve according to the particular institutional endowment of a country, and this, ultimately, determines the efficacy of its regulatory regimes, its capacity for reform, and its ability to attract foreign investment. As Levy and Spiller (1994: 202) note, 'the credibility and effectiveness of a regulatory framework – and hence its ability to facilitate private investment – varies with a country's political and social institutions'. For example, mining regulation in a number of countries in the Asia-Pacific region suffers from poor institutional capacity. This generally means that foreign direct investment levels in the sector are lower than in those countries with well-developed and stable regulatory environments (O'Callaghan, 2009; 2010). Yet regulatory regimes in developed economies, such as the United States, are not immune from these sorts of problems. The GFC was caused, in part, by poor regulation of the financial services sector (Omarova and Feibelman, 2008–2009). Similarly, part of the blame for BP's recent oil spill in the Gulf of Mexico has been levelled at the US Department of the Interior's Minerals Management Service (MMS), the regulatory body which is responsible for regulatory compliance of drilling operations in the gulf (Schmit, 2010). The official verdict of the inquiry into the spill suggested that regulatory capture by the oil and gas industry may have occurred.[5] Capture occurs when an industry gains enough political power to undermine the neutrality of regulatory agencies, or is able to reduce their effectiveness. Bribes and gifts to politicians and regulators are key ways in which capture takes place. In the case of the gulf oil companies, the co-chairman of the inquiry into the spill has suggested that 'there has been a history of cosy relationship between the regulator and the industry, largely driven by the fact that the same regulator responsible for setting and enforcing safety also is the agency that collects almost $20 billion a year in royalties' [sic] (O'Brien, 2011).

The most common form (or mode) of regulation is 'command and control' (Ogus, 1994).[6] The state makes laws which are then policed by various government agencies to ensure compliance. Command and control regulation is generally seen in areas where the government wants to ensure certain standards of behaviour are met. Issue areas such as food hygiene, weights and measures, pollution control, construction and consumer protection are all examples where governments seek to limit certain activities and set appropriate standards.

Until the 1980s, this form of regulation predominated. However, at the time, a number of scholars and policy makers began to question the efficiency of such techniques, and levelled a number of criticisms against command and control approaches to regulation. According to Australia's Office of Regulation Review (1998: E14–E15), the following are the most significant drawbacks with command and control:

- it may be standardized and inflexible. This means that it may not adequately deal with diverse conditions or with changes over time. This can result in the regulation becoming irrelevant. It may also impede technological progress and innovation;
- it may, over time, generate more and more regulation. For instance, more regulation is created to adapt the original regulation to a new situation or to close the gaps where compliance is not being achieved;
- there are potentially significant time lags inherent in making and amending legislation;
- legislation is not well suited for influencing the quality of complex services such as those provided by many of the professions;
- the perception by some people that legislative drafting is complex and difficult to understand may deter some of them from trying to comply;
- government budgetary costs are often higher with black letter law, and there may be less accountability for administrative costs, compared to other regulatory forms which utilize the resources of commerce and industry;
- compliance costs may be high as the law often does not reflect accepted commercial practices; and
- costs and delays associated with the justice system may mean poor access for those without means to pursue their legal rights.

The problems associated with command and control led to a shift in thinking by governments and the employment of new methods of regulation. This occurred first in the US and Great Britain in the 1980s, but became a feature of most advanced economies from the 1990s onward (Hodgson, 2006). The centrepiece of this shift has been the trend toward deregulation and privatisation.[7] It is within this context that the emergence of the idea of self-regulation needs to be understood. As Levi-Faur (2005: 13) notes, 'a new division of labor between state and society (e.g. privatization) is accompanied by an increase in delegation, proliferation of new technologies of regulation, formalization of inter-institutional and intrainstitutional relations, and the proliferation of self-regulation in the shadow of the state'.

The concept of self-regulation is not new. It probably has its roots in the trade guilds and religious organisations of the early Middle Ages. The practice of self-discipline has always been a central tenet of Catholic theology. Moreover, in the late Middle Ages, with the advent of Free-masonry, the practice of self-regulation helped its members to maintain a code of conduct that protected the secrecy of the order. In a more modern sense, the term serves to highlight a number of practices. First, it is often associated with health and well-being, where individuals impose restrictions on their lifestyle and behaviour to maintain good health. Second, the term also has currency in psychiatry, where the role of brain function and individual self-regulation is a key area of research (Vohs and Baumeister, 2010; Baumeister et al., 2005). Third, the term is often linked to professional bodies, as well as industry certification and licensing arrangements.[8] These are sometimes referred to as self-regulatory organisations (SROs). Regulation of securities markets are the most common form of SRO (Centre for Financial Market Integrity, 2007). In the context of MNCs, however, there are two forms of self-regulation that are of relevance. The first is industry self-regulation. The second is corporate self-regulation.

Industry Self-regulation

Industry self-regulation is a specific form of regulation set up to advance the collective interests of particular industry sectors (Lad and Caldwell, 2009). It is a body charged by its members with a degree of rule-making capacity. Its purpose is to govern the behaviour of its members by setting standards and managing compliance.[9] The motivation for industry self-regulation varies. Industries may see benefits from banding together. First, there may be an enhancement of their reputation over non-members (Lennox, 2006: 677). Second, it may be a way for MNCs to reduce their overall risk. Imposing certain limits on their own commercial practices may lead to efficiencies and, ultimately, increased profitability. Third, it may be a mechanism to control the exploitation of a particular natural resource. Ostrom's (1990) seminal work on how collective action can be achieved in order to deal with 'tragedy of the commons' problems is perhaps the most notable exploration of this idea. Finally, MNCs may benefit from submitting to industry self-regulation in order to forestall stricter regulation by governments. In each of these cases, it is a sense of enlightened self-interest that drives MNCs to submit to such a regulatory regime.

In recent years the number of these associations has grown dramatically, especially in industry sectors such as chemical production, nuclear power, electronic retailing, advertising and tourism. Omarova (2011: 413) has even argued that industry self-regulation of the financial services sector may be the best solution for avoiding future systemic risks to the global economy.

One of the earliest, and most striking, examples of industry self-regulation is the 'Responsible Care' programme developed by the Chemical Manufacturers Association (CMA) in the US. In response to a number of incidents and, in particular, the devastating Bhopal tragedy in India, the CMA decided that reform of the sector was crucial. It was necessary to restore confidence in the industry's capacity to keep the public safe, as well as to limit the possibility of tighter regulation being imposed on the whole industry by government (Delmas and Montiel, 2007: 9).[10]

Responsible Care is a code of conduct which covers three major themes: health, safety and the environment (HSE). The stated goals of the programme are to encourage open and transparent dialogue with stakeholders in the sector. It was first introduced in Canada in 1985 and then in the United States in 1988. Currently, 55 national chemical associations participate in the programme. Moreover, 150 of the world's largest chemical companies have signed agreements to participate in it (ICCA, 2011a; 2012). In the early 1990s, the programme produced a set of guiding principles.[11] These were regarded as the basis for entry into Responsible Care and were used to orient the industry along a more responsible path.[12] Since then, as more chemical MNCs have become signatories, a new global charter has been developed to deal with the changing expectations of stakeholders. The new charter now includes a commitment to sustainable development (ICCA, 2011a).

Etzioni argues that these types of initiative amount to very little. According to him (2009: 42), they are akin to 'the fox that is supposed to guard the chicken coop'. There is an information deficit which arises from the market. First, it is difficult to get the kind of information that consumers need to make informed choices. Second, MNCs routinely skew relevant information deliberately to deceive consumers (Etzioni, 2009: 42). For him, the key solution to this problem lies in 'filters'; that is, government regulation with 'teeth' (Etzioni, 2009: 43). These filters are necessary to ensure that consumers are not duped by industries keen to improve their bottom line.

Etzioni's (2009) view is an interesting example of a problem that bedevils much of the debate about self-regulation. It dichotomises regulation and self-regulation. To put it slightly differently: regulation and free market capitalism. It is as if these are the only two possibilities at hand. The difficulty with this framing is that it fails to recognise that regulation is located on a continuum of possibilities.[13] Australia's Office of Regulation Review employs the table shown in Figure 3.1 to highlight this continuum.

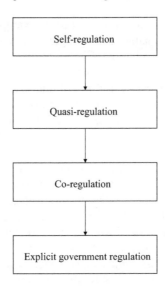

Figure 3.1   A simplified spectrum of regulation

Moreover, as Omarova (2011: 426) points out, as 'a matter of principle, the concept of industry self-regulation is not inherently incompatible with some form of direct government regulation'. Indeed, she suggests that the best governance model may be some combination of both government regulation and industry self-regulation. Part of the reason for this is that industry has a much better overview of the health of its sector than does government. Consequently, it is able to respond to challenges in a more timely fashion. Ayres and Braithwaite (1992: 3) make a similar point:

> Good policy analysis is not about choosing between the free market and government regulation. Nor is it simply deciding what the law should proscribe. If we accept that sound policy analysis is about understanding private regulation – by industry associations, by firms, by peers, and by individual consciences – and how it is interdependent with state regulation, then interesting possibilities open up to steer the mix of private and public regulation.

Arguments which dismiss forms of industry self-regulation as simply regulatory deception, as Etzioni (2009: 42) does, fail to understand the nature and multiple modes of regulation that are possible.

There is a growing body of literature which suggests that industry self-regulation can work to alter the behaviour of MNCs. King and Lenox (2000: 701) argue that there are three ways in which this can occur. The first is through informal, coercive means, such as embarrassing those MNCs who fail to live up to the standards of the association. The second is through codifying new sets of norms and values which the industry expects its participants to follow. The third is by providing members with information about current and future best practice. These bodies play an educative role in the sector's performance. Industry self-regulation, then, plays a crucially important role in improving the social and environmental performance of MNCs. Over time, these peak bodies have become de facto regulators of MNC behaviour in their particular industry sectors.

Corporate Self-regulation

Corporate self-regulation is not an alternative to other forms of regulation. It does not mean that industry self-regulation should give way to a renewed push for heavy-handed state regulation. And, it certainly does not mean that governments no longer have oversight of MNCs and the market. The concept of corporate self-regulation articulated here seeks to highlight the extent to which MNCs have the capacity to regulate their own behaviour, in line with other regulatory approaches and community expectations.

Corporate self-regulation takes seriously changing social, environmental and legal expectations, and manages these from within the organisation. Put slightly differently, a self-regulating corporation is one that takes all regulatory forms seriously, and perhaps, even advances beyond them.

Invariably, self-regulating corporations will draw their inspiration from many existing sources. These may include international institutions, stakeholders, industry bodies and NGOs. They may also draw on new management techniques and corporate governance thinking. Most importantly of all, a self-regulating corporation will filter all of this information and create a unique relationship with its stakeholders and with society more broadly. Most important of all, a self-regulating corporation is a leadership corporation. It will not hide among the pack. It will be a trailblazing corporation, pushing the boundaries of ethical behaviour and retooling the company in novel ways. A self-regulating corporation, then, will lead other companies into a new era of business practice.

What are the key characteristics of a self-regulating corporation? The business literature has already largely addressed this issue. Jackson and Nelson (2004) have come up with a set of principles to motivate this new type of corporation. According to them, the companies of the future will follow seven core principles. These include the view that the public good is at the forefront of a company's business. Second, understanding that people, both stakeholders and employees, are critical to corporate success. Third, business should benefit all those it touches, including employees and customers. This will take different forms depending on the target group, but should include development opportunities for as many stakeholders as possible. Fourth, it should also include the development of new stakeholder alliances. This not only expands business opportunities, but also cements the company at the forefront of managerial excellence. Fifth, successful companies are performance-driven. This means that they achieve greater success across commercial, social and environmental indicators than companies that perform less well. Sixth, as I noted in the last chapter, governance matters. Companies that self-regulate will have corporate governance structures that enable them to stay ahead of the 'pack' and fulfil these other obligations. Finally, this new kind of company will pursue 'purpose beyond profits'. As Jackson and Nelson (2004: 299) describe it:

> Together with principles and values, purpose is what a great company stands for and would stand by even if adhering to them resulted in a competitive disadvantage, missed opportunity, or increased costs ... Purpose, principles, and values are the bedrock of excellence. The manner in which they are articulated and implemented plays a key role in determining a company's strategic direction, its corporate culture, and the policies and incentive systems by which it operates and impacts the world.

There are numerous other works that we could point to that offer a similar picture of the kind of corporation that will be successful in the twenty-first century. Whether you call this an 'authentic company' (Fombrun and Van Riel), a 'supercorporation' (Moss Kanter), 'a civil corporation' (Zadek), an 'open corporation' (Parker), or a 'self-regulatory corporation', as the term is used in this book, the critical point is that for MNCs to prosper and have great success in the future, they will need to adapt their business model. The idea of a self-regulating corporation, while accepting the principles and values annunciated in many of these texts, stresses that it can only work if the inspiration comes from within the company. Just as governments have a regulatory regime that sets out the 'rules of the game' for various groups in society, MNCs of the future will need to develop their own architecture to put the principles, values and purpose into practice.

It is convenient to think that there is an ideal-type MNC out there. In truth, this is not the case. MNCs are diverse, have different internal cultures, and appeal to different stakeholders. It is important to think of corporate self-regulation as an ongoing process. In other words, there are degrees of corporate self-regulation. Some MNCs may be described as underdeveloped self-regulators. While they understand the importance of acting according to certain community standards and have adopted CSR, they may do no more than this. Jaffe and Weiss (2006: 915) make an interesting observation in this respect. Royal Dutch Shell's General Business Principles (2014) commits it to upholding applicable laws and regulations.[14] According to Jaffe and Weiss (2006: 915): 'This statement is vague. It only commits the company to not violating the law, but by using the term "applicable" they may, for example, employ child labor, where doing so is legal'. Of course, Royal Dutch Shell also has a statement of principle which commits it to upholding human rights (Royal Dutch Shell, 2011a; 2011b; 2011c). Presumably, this means that the company would not employ child labour as it would violate that commitment. But Jaffe and Weiss's point is valid. An underdeveloped self-regulating company would not necessarily feel the need to move beyond this position. In this instance, a company may equate corporate self-regulation with a commitment to abiding by the laws of the land and harmonising these with corporate priorities.

In regard to the criteria above, most MNCs appear to be underdeveloped corporate self-regulators. While almost all now practise some form of CSR, they do not appear to be moving beyond basic CSR commitments and embracing more proactive internal self-regulatory policies (Jenkins, 2001: 6). Many companies are now signatories to a variety of UN conventions. Shell has a stated commitment to reducing its emissions to levels set out in the Kyoto Protocol. The company has also accepted the UN's Universal Declaration of Human Rights as a benchmark for operating in the developing world. Levi Strauss has instituted a programme to ensure that under-age children do not work in the factories of its affiliates. However, it is in the area of environmental management that the clearest evidence is emerging that MNCs are beginning to self-regulate in a more sustained way. Christmann and Taylor (2001: 120) argue that the environmental performance of foreign corporations demonstrates that MNCs do not move heavily polluting industries to countries with weak regulatory environments. Not only do they argue that the environmental performance of foreign corporations exceeds that of local MNCs, but an increased attention to environmental management is also pushing them to self-regulate in order to remain competitive.

Similarly, Arora and Cason (1996: 413) argue that 'firms have an incentive to compete in environmental quality, and ... regulators can exploit this incentive to improve environmental performance – particularly in industries which have close contact with final consumers'.[15] This trend is visible in foreign firms operating in China, a country not well-known for its care of the environment. This is not because companies are being forced to comply with Chinese regulatory standards. On the contrary, it is because of the laxity of those standards and the difficulties of operating in the Chinese market that MNCs are acting in more environmentally responsible ways (Dean et al., 2009). Moreover, since large MNCs operate in multiple jurisdictions, it is much more efficient and easier for them to operate at a higher standard across the entire enterprise.

There is also evidence to suggest that MNCs in the automotive sector are beginning to self-regulate as well. Mikler's (2009) study of the car industry argues that there are four key areas where the industry is moving forward on environmental matters: the development of incremental technologies, petrol and diesel–electric hybrids, hydrogen fuel cells and alternative fuels. Mikler (2009) argues that this amounts to a 'greening of the car industry'. He notes that in the 1990s criticism of the car industry was rife. He cites Suzuki's (1993: 139) view that 'amid ... the suicidal demand for growth, happy stories are few'. A decade later, Mikler points out that Suzuki's view of the automotive industry has changed markedly. As he notes, 'Within the space of a decade, Suzuki's attitude had changed from pessimism to a decidedly more optimistic view of MNC perform-ance, with the car industry at the forefront of moves by big business towards environmental sustainability' (Mikler, 2009: 9).

From a corporate point of view, both industry self-regulation and corporate self-regulation are preferable to strong command and control forms of regulation for several reasons. First, self-regulation reduces the bureaucratic load on MNCs. This includes a reduction in the time dealing with inspectors and authorities. Second, greater clarity of the rules and standards can be achieved, especially in the case of internal corporate self-regulation, because those who implement the rules and monitor them have a stake in good outcomes. But, most of all, corporate self-regulation focuses attention squarely on organisational learning. This is especially important given that MNCs operate in multiple jurisdictions, and the capacity to self-regulate allows them to streamline and coordinate their activities. Consequently, corporate self-regulation is a market response to an increasingly competitive global business environment, and one more reliant than ever on a strong corporate reputation. At a time when MNC profits have soared and brand names have become important symbols of success, self-regulation is one of the many mechanisms by which MNCs are able to grow market share, enhance their competitiveness and protect their reputation.

Most critics of self-regulation would disagree with this analysis. They believe that MNCs are blindly motivated by greed and power and cannot be trusted to regulate their own behaviour. In this sense, Etzioni's (2009: 42) comment about the fox guarding the chicken coop is quite common in the literature. The fox, MNCs, will simply devour the chickens (consumers and citizens) when the hunger reflex (money and power) kicks in. What, then, is the critic's solution to the problem? How should MNCs be managed in the future? And, more importantly, what are the likely consequences for the global economy of such solutions?

THE ANTI-CORPORATE ACTIVIST SOLUTIONS TO EXCESSIVE CORPORATE POWER

Anti-corporate activists offer a number of suggestions about how to deal with corporate malfeasance. The first is to put them out of business if they break the law (Bakan, 2005: 157). This idea was most famously put forward in relation to the Union Oil Company (Unocal) in the late 1990s. Spearheaded by Robert Benson, a professor of law from the Loyola Law School in California, a coalition of more than 100 groups petitioned Governor 'Gray' Davis and Bill Lockyer, then California's Attorney General, to revoke the company's corporate charter. The grounds for the challenge were twofold. The first was the 1789 Alien Torts Law. This law basically gave non-US citizens the right to seek redress in US courts for breaches of international law which may have occurred outside the US. The second, and the punitive dimension of the challenge, was to invoke the corporate charter revocation laws to pave the way for the dis-establishment of the corporation.

The petition alleged that Unocal had violated the human rights of workers and villagers around its project sites in Myanmar, that they were responsible for ongoing environmental destruction, and that they had a poor occupational health and safety record.[16] According to Benson and his supporters, the company did not deserve to remain in business, as its continued existence was not in the best interest of the public.

The so-called charter revocation laws have existed in the US since the nineteenth century. They were originally put in place to assuage the fears of citizens over the growing power of early corporations. The argument which underpins these laws is that the existence of corporations rests on a conception of the public good (Bakan, 2005: 156; Benson, 2000). The view of anti-corporate activists is that if corporations continue to flout the law, and act in ways contrary to the will of the community, they are clearly not acting in the public good. Consequently, they should have their charter revoked by court order. The logic of this position is that if an MNC is put out of business by the courts, it will serve as a significant deterrent to other companies, and remove a substantial threat to the community.

No US MNC has been put out of business to date. Benson believed that his challenge in the California courts was symbolic, with little chance of putting Unocal out of business. Large corporations like Unocal have access to large amounts of capital and the best lawyers money can buy. As happened in subsequent suits against the company, Unocal settled out of court for an undisclosed sum. Moreover, it is unlikely that Republicans across the US would allow such an outcome to occur to a US multinational, as they would interpret this as undermining free enterprise and the 'sanctity' of capitalism. Even with the immensely destructive Deep Water Horizon oil spill in the Gulf of Mexico, there were no calls from the US or British Governments to put BP out of business. On the contrary, it is their profitability that has enabled BP to repair much of the damage. Under these circumstances, to put them out of business would be counter-productive to broader societal interests. This sort of reasoning would always come into play in determining the future of particular MNCs.

The second approach to dealing with corporate malfeasance is to call for much stricter regulation of MNCs worldwide. According to this view, better regulation is required not just to deal with corporate crime, but to restrict the power and global reach of MNCs. For example, Evans et al. (2002a: 218–22) have put forward a framework to better regulate MNCs in the mining sector. Their framework includes seven key ideas:

1. governments should strengthen the rights and capacities of civil society;
2. governments should stand up for the rights of their communities and civil society;
3. governments should allow civil society groups and communities to challenge mining companies' 'license to operate';
4. governments should no longer allow the international financing of mining;
5. the power of the state should be enhanced, and it should take the protection of their citizens more seriously;
6. directors should be made more personally responsible for the actions of their corporations;
7. shareholder powers should be democratized so that they can veto board decisions.

These ideas are quite standard demands among activists seeking to contest the power of MNCs. They would, for example, be equally applicable to forestry, the chemical industry and the oil and gas industry, any industry, in fact, where anti-corporate activists believe the rights of communities are being abused. Their view is that national governments and international institutions, such as the World Bank Group (WBG) and the International Monetary Fund (IMF), have erred in pursuing neoliberal strategies of deregulation, privatisation and globalisation. Consequently, imposing greater regulatory requirements on MNCs is seen as necessary to break the hold that MNCs have over people's lives.[17] Bakan (2005: 161) argues that: 'Government regulation should be reconceived, and relegitimated, as the principal means for bringing corporations under democratic control and ensuring that they respect the interests of citizens, communities and the environment'. The key to developing more robust regulation at both the national and international level, then, is to build strong civil society networks and action groups. Similarly, Clarke (1996: 307) argues that: '[t]he best hope for countering growing corporate domination lies in the building of social movements in which people reclaim their sovereign rights over TNCs and banks'.

These anti-corporate activists are sometimes seen as de facto regulators of MNCs (Zadek, 2001: 51–64). As national governments have 'de-regulated' their economies and empowered MNCs, civil society groups have stepped into the breach to try to (re)regulate them and constrain their power. Vogel (2005: 9) explains this important development: '[b]y applying pressure directly to companies, activists and organizations seek to foster changes in business practices that national governments and international law are unlikely or unwilling to bring about'.

When critics argue that there is a need for more effective regulation of MNCs, they generally mean a number of things. First, they deny that industry self-regulation works without an explicit enforcement regime monitored by governments. As King and Lenox (2000: 700) observe:

> If the industry cannot prohibit bad actors from becoming members of an association, these actors may join to disguise their poor performance (that is, adverse selection occurs). If the association cannot observe and enforce performance requirements, firms may adopt the outward form of the standard but shirk the real effort required (moral hazard occurs).

Second, they deny the capacity of individual MNCs to self-regulate effectively. In their view, it is a much weaker form of regulation than state-based regulation and is, therefore, less effective in controlling errant behaviour. Furthermore, the language of self-regulation is regarded as vague and imprecise. It often takes the form of motherhood statements which lack clarity and bite. Codes of conduct and CSR initiatives are viewed as symbolic statements made to impress a gullible public, but do little or nothing to alter behaviour. Moskowitz (2002: 4) pessimistically writes, '[l]ooking over the history of corporate social responsibility, I can see it has consisted of 95 percent rhetoric and five percent action'.

Perhaps the most problematic aspect of corporate self-regulation for anti-corporate activists is that it is voluntary. There is no enforcement or accountability mechanism available to punish breaches. Evans et al. (2002b: 222) argue that '[w]ithout credible minimum, mandatory standards of performance, credible monitoring and reporting and effective enforcement, self-regulatory regimes will not be the solution'. Similarly, Klein (2001: 479) asserts that self-regulatory codes of conduct are: '[a]wfully slippery. Unlike black letter law, they are not enforceable. And unlike union contracts, they are not drafted in cooperation with factory managers in response to the demands and needs of employees. Without exception, they were drafted by public relations departments in cities like New York and San Francisco'. In other words, MNCs are unlikely to punish themselves.

Third, anti-corporate activists want national governments to be more democratic and responsive to the demands of citizens, especially where decisions about MNCs are concerned. By this, they expect governments to listen to their citizens in order to have a say in the economic management of the state, rather than letting international institutions determine the nature of the global economic architecture. The inference here is that governments should serve their citizens' interests first, not those of large MNCs.

Finally, they want the international economic architecture dismantled and replaced with a system of self-sufficient national and local economies (Korten, 2006: 315–20). Korten (in Evans et al., 2002b: 16) argues that '[c]orrective actions are needed to eliminate international indebtedness, restore national ownership and control of productive assets, and balance exports and imports. A key step would be to close the World Bank, the IMF and the WTO, and restore the right of economic self-determination to people and their governments'.

IN DEFENCE OF CORPORATE SELF-REGULATION

There are three assumptions built into the above strategies. The first is that governments have the power to implement a more punitive regulatory regime against MNCs. The second is that social movements, on their own, have the capacity to force governments to 're-regulate' MNCs. The third is that command and control forms of regulation are superior to other forms of regulation. It is important to examine each of these points in turn.

Changing the Leverage of National Governments

Anti-corporate activists draw on a very strong conception of government to achieve their aims. The level of governmental power necessary to achieve this is likely to be a highly interventionist one, almost paternalistic. Indeed, they rely on a conception of government that has more in common with the way in which centrally planned economies were governed in the twentieth century. Stock markets would crash, and trade between economies would fall dramatically, thereby reducing the ability of consumers to buy from overseas markets. We would, in all likelihood, see a return of high tariff walls and protectionist behaviour. It is probably the case that such a reorientation of the global economy would see the world enter a new era of severe economic downturn, potentially much worse than the recent GFC.

There is also a tension in such arguments about national governments, which is rarely, if ever, resolved. National governments in the West are the main drivers of globalisation. They have supported and developed the international architecture that has allowed MNCs to flourish. Yet these same national governments are also berated by anti-corporate activists for failing to address adequately the serious environmental and social challenges that confront humanity. But who, then, will be responsible for developing and instituting a new regulatory agenda? Will it fall to the same elected officials who have presided over the neoliberal project? We are never told, nor are we provided with a detailed analysis of how these critics can at once stand outside of the mainstream political process, yet engender maximum policy change within it. O'Brien and Williams (2010: 428–9) argue that dramatic changes in the governance relationships between states have tended to occur only after large-scale wars. They identify only three occasions in the last two hundred or so years where this has happened: in the aftermath of the Napoleonic wars and after each of the two world wars. The last of these, World War II, brought into being the economic architecture and principles that continue, in one way or another, to govern the global economy today.

It is unlikely, then, that the kind of reforms that anti-corporate activists desire could occur without considerable global dislocation. Indeed, O'Brien and Williams (2010: 389) note that: '[l]arge scale changes in reforming or replacing existing global governance structures are unlikely unless there is a devastating crisis in the international system'. The end of the Cold War has made such a crisis less likely. This is because the threat of a new world war between states in the near future has lessened (Meuller, 2007; Doyle, 1997).

Of course, international relations (IR) is a realm where the unexpected is always a possibility. Very few academics, even specialists in Soviet studies, predicted the collapse of the Soviet Union in 1989 (Gaddis, 1992–93: 5). Such a collapse may lead policy makers to rethink the structure of the global economy and lead to the sort of economic reforms advocated by anti-corporate activists. However, a collapse of this proportion would lead to poverty and conflict. Put differently, the sort of agenda advocated by anti-corporate activists, if implemented, may actually plunge the international economic system into the sort of crisis that led to the outbreak of World War I and World War II. This is a sobering thought. At the very least, anti-corporate activists need to demonstrate how such a change in the governance structures of the global economy would not result in dire economic consequences.

The Transformative Potential of Anti-corporate Activism

The solution to the problem of corporate power relies on the transformative capacity of anti-corporate activists. But it is not clear whether civil society groups and activists have the power to drive a large-scale reform agenda. We live in a society where there is healthy competition between a plurality of competing interests (Dahl, 1973; Lipset, 1981).[18] The role of the government is often to mediate between these various interests. Just as there are opponents of corporate power, there are many individuals who have a more positive view of their role in society. These include employees, shareholders, consultants, and small businesses who supply MNCs with goods and services. It is difficult to envisage arguments that could convince such large numbers of people that dismantling their economy would be beneficial, especially if it led to high unemployment. Consequently, interest group competition will always act to constrain the capacity of anti-corporate activists to influence decision makers to the extent that they would like. Even anarchist Thomas Nail acknowledges this. He argues that there are problems within radical politics today, with the movement focusing too much on the critique of society and not enough on alternatives. As he notes (2010: 73–4):

> Radical politics today faces a two-fold challenge: to show the problems and undesirability of the current structures of exclusion and power, and to show the desirability and coherency of various alternatives that may take their

place. This paper argues that over the last 15 years, in particular, radical politics have been vastly more attentive to the former than to the latter and that what is now required is an appropriate shift in practical and theoretical efforts toward more constructive and prefigurative activities.

Despite this sober analysis, anti-corporate activists have clearly been successful in tackling single issue areas such as protecting endangered species, advancing gender equality, promoting gay rights and raising awareness of the problems associated with climate change. Yet it would seem that the protests at the 31st G8 Summit, held at Gleneagles in Scotland in 2005, did little to effect change in the G8 leaders' thinking. The G8 could not reach an agreement on global warming, despite the obvious pressure from tens of thousands of protestors.

Perhaps this is the reason why Frankel (1987: 238), a long-time supporter of the Left, is ambivalent about the effectiveness of political activists as agents of social change. According to Frankel, they have tried to develop a new kind of politics, but they continue to be plagued by bureaucratic tendencies, tensions between members and leaders, intolerance of dissenters, ideological divisions and funding crises. A particularly good example of this is the defection of Greenpeace boss, Patrick Moore, from the organisation in 1986. He is now one of the organisation's staunchest critics and supports the use of nuclear energy for generating electricity; something that has always been anathema to Greenpeace.

Marx understood how difficult it was to bring about a social revolution.[19] Even the proletariat failed to be a revolutionary force in the West. The proletariat no longer exists, nor does an easily identifiable 'agent of change' capable of taking their place. The Frankfurt School lives on in the academic literature as a reminder of the failure, not only of traditional Marxist thinking about the proletariat's capacity for revolution, but also of the failure of any other agent of change to materialise. In the late 1960s, Marcuse (2004) thought that French students could fulfil this role. However, the students failed to live up to his expectations. Moreover, socialist parties are increasingly marginal to mainstream political debate around the world. Some scholars think that a revitalised labour movement has potential in this regard (Armbruster-Sandoval, 2005; Schiavone, 2007). But the history of the labour movement is one of factionalism, internal power struggles and corruption.

Korten (2001: 309–11) points to a number of successful cases in which he believes anti-corporate activists (and other civil society groups) have made an important difference.[20] It is debatable whether the isolated examples he cites provide compelling evidence that a global revolution is underway or even possible. In the first place, it would require a high degree of cohesion among disparate groups and a single agenda. Yet, as was noted in Chapter 1, the main characteristic of these groups is that they are amorphous, fragmented and ideologically diverse.[21] Moreover, O'Neil (2004: 234) notes that they have their 'own internal and external dynamics of conflict and cooperation, playing them out on a global scale'. Finally, Scott (2005: 392) asserts that 'open collective protest is rare', even in localised settings. The sort of unified collective action that would be required to dismantle the architecture of modern capitalism and constrain MNCs is extremely underdeveloped.

Anti-corporate activists also have a negative view of the voting public in Western democracies. These are the people that they need to persuade about the righteousness of their cause. Ali and Barsamian (2005: 92) is right to argue that 'you cannot win unless you win over a majority, or at least a sizeable section of the population. We have got to win that consent to our side; that's the key'. But anti-corporate activists often appear to have distain for ordinary people, almost as much as they do for MNCs. Vidal (2003) declares, 'I don't know how anybody can buy this line, but people do. People are not very well-informed'. Moreover, Chomsky (2003: 95) speaks approvingly of Walter Lippman's description of people in a democracy as a 'bewildering herd'. On the one hand, then, anti-corporate activists seek to enlist people to their cause but, on the other, they lambaste them for their ignorance and lemming-like behaviour. As a popular educative strategy, this is unlikely ever to succeed.

Shortcomings with Command and Control Forms of Regulation

It is difficult to find any detailed exposition of just what increasing state regulation might mean in practice. Anti-corporate activists are often vague in their use of terms and provide little in the way of concrete details about their proposals. Many of their arguments are so general that they are of little use to policy makers to guide their thinking into the future, nor are they much use for academics interested in the fine print. Indeed, they fail to provide answers to a number of important questions. Some of the most important of the most relevant are listed below.

- How should national governments manage the transition from a global economic system to a national one?
- How should they manage the sharp increase in unemployment and the concomitant drop in living standards for the majority of their citizenry?
- How should they manage the backlash from shareholders, consumers and pension fund holders?

- How should national governments in the West reconstitute their now defunct manufacturing sectors?
- What should the millions of small manufacturing plants and sub-contractors in the less-developed world do to overcome their dislocation from these economic and regulatory changes?

Anti-corporate activists champion the plight of people in the less-developed world, and they are to be commended for this. Yet they never acknowledge the fact that most governments in the developing world are in favour of globalisation and the possibilities it brings for their people. In 2001, Ernest Zedillo, the former president of Mexico, and the person who guided Mexico out of its economic crisis, argued that 'leftists and rightists ... have joined forces to save the poor people of developing countries from development – that is, from prosperity and social justice' (cited in Moline, 2001).[22] According to Zedillo, globalisation provides the poor with new opportunities. It has an empowering effect. This is not the viewpoint of the Friends of the Earth International (FOEI). They agitate for local fence line communities around mining sites to reject applications by mining MNCs to operate on their tribal lands. They are an English NGO, operating in a number of countries around the world. It is hard not to draw the conclusion that they would rather the poor live in poverty than negotiate a royalty deal with a mining company that might improve their well-being.

When anti-corporate activists speak about the urgent need for national governments to impose more robust regulatory requirements on MNCs, they are generally referring to Western governments regulating Western MNCs. This is where anti-corporate activists are most vocal. But what about governments in the less-developed parts of the world? Here the situation is even more problematic for those seeking to force national governments to impose stricter forms of state regulation on MNCs. A major difficulty faced by these governments is a lack of public sector institutional capacity.[23] Many countries have decentralised their political structures and handed decision-making power to the local level. In the Philippines and Indonesia, for example, the existing regulatory environments are complex, open to interpretation and, at times, impossible to enforce (O'Callaghan, 2009; 2010). How stricter state regulation might work in this context is impossible to tell. Compounding the problem is a lack of adequate resources, financial and otherwise, for implementing a stricter regulatory regime. As Graham and Woods (2006: 879) point out, '[i]n developing countries, the limits of a government's capacity to regulate are even more striking. Regulators have fewer resources'. With an inevitable downturn in investment inflows, regulatory capacity would diminish even further.

Anti-corporate activists also do not engage with the regulatory literature. Yet there are serious debates among regulation scholars about the costs and benefits of more onerous state regulation. Presumably, anti-corporate activists want government regulators to be better funded, institute far-reaching reforms to corporate law, make management decisions more transparent, introduce much stricter auditing requirements, and force MNCs to develop more community-friendly compliance systems. Most of all, they argue for a new ideological direction for IR, one which moves the global economy away from neoliberalism and towards a more cosmopolitan world order, and one with a much greater redistributive function.

Scholars of regulation use the term 'regulatory state' to mark the shift in the way that states govern themselves and their citizens. Majone (1994) is the first to coin the phrase. He argued that the regulatory state had superseded the welfare state (Majone, 1997). The new term highlighted a new form of governance by states, first in Europe and then in other advanced Western economies (Lodge, 2008). States began to rely more on 'authority, rules and standard-setting', as opposed to an earlier emphasis 'on public ownership, public subsidies, and directly providing services' (Jordana and Levi-Faur, 2004: 8). Parker notes the important contradiction here. While deregulation, privatisation and the sale of public assets are regarded as the hallmarks of the new regulatory state, she does not believe that states have reduced the degree of regulation over MNCs, as anti-corporate activists claim. It may be true that governments have been using the rhetoric of deregulation and privatisation, but 'state regulation continues to be used more than ever before' (Parker, 2002: 12). Jordana and Levi-Faur (2004: 1) describe this as a paradox:

> [T]he institutional advance of regulation in the context of privatization and the neoliberal hegemony presents a paradox. In an era in which regulation has become synonymous with red tape, and deregulation has become a major electoral platform of the New Right, regulatory authorities have been created in unprecedented numbers and with unprecedented autonomy.[24]

This paradox is most apparent in the utilities sector, where governments have developed a raft of new legislation to ensure that utility MNCs continue to deliver services of an acceptably high standard. In most cases, this legislation includes harsh penalties in the event of a lengthy power outage, for example. But it is equally visible in the explosion in environmental legislation since the early 1990s. It is a challenge for anti-corporate activists to demonstrate, at least at a national level, that there has been a diminution of state regulatory authority over MNCs. Indeed, a more accurate description of what is occurring is that national governments have not abandoned the task of regulating MNCs, but rather that they have moved to regulate them differently, through standard-setting and the promotion of self-regulatory schemes. As was noted in the last chapter, Larner (2000: 11) attributes this to neoliberalism, which 'involves forms of governance that encourage both institutions and individuals to conform to the norms of the market'.

Sometimes the collapse of Enron is used to bolster the case for stronger government regulation of MNCs (Elliot and Schroth, 2002). Arguably, however, the opposite lesson should be drawn from the Enron case. Government regulators have shown that they are more than willing to hand out stiff penalties for breaches of regulation. The 24-year jail term and US$18 million in fines meted out to Enron's former Chief Executive Officer (CEO) is clear evidence of this (Eichenwald, 2005). In the current regulatory environment, governments have greater expect-ations of MNCs than ever before. This is partly because neoliberal governments expect MNCs to move towards self-regulation. Govern-ments use corporate failure to send a clear and unequivocal message to MNCs that they need to have adequate internal compliance and auditing systems in place or face substantial penalties. Arguably, the best way to achieve this is through corporate self-regulation.

The view that MNCs need to be more forcibly regulated by govern-ments, then, rests on a rather outdated view of the nature of the modern MNC. To suggest that they are single-minded profit maximisers fails to acknowledge a fundamental point. Just as there are many examples where profit maximisation is pursued single-mindedly, there are equally as many examples where this is not the case. One example is Interface Inc. (Anderson, 1998; 2000; 2009; 2010; Arena, 2004). Anderson's effort to turn his company into a sustainable enterprise is admirable, when it might have been cheaper to continue polluting the environment. After a fire burnt down his factory, Aaron Feuerstein (Seeger and Ulmer, 2001) continued to pay workers during the rebuilding phase. These, and other examples, show that MNCs can do the right thing and this should not be trivialised by an ideological agenda.[25] As I noted earlier, one indicator of this is the burgeoning literature highlighting this fact. Zadek (2001: 216) writes about his 'sceptical optimism' at the emergence of a civil corporation. Spar (1998: 8) notes that 'codes of conduct have already begun to be a significant factor in the pursuit of human rights'. She calls this the 'spotlight phenomenon', where stricter regulation of MNCs is unnecessary because when the spotlight is placed on a company, it forces them to improve their performance.[26] Similarly, Jaffe and Weiss (2006: 922) argue that corporate codes are having an impact on the problem of child labour: '[c]orporate codes, if optimally utilized, can make a tremendous difference in the area of child labor. These codes may also be used to address many other human rights and environmental issues'.

Some MNCs also recognise that actions speak louder than words. PepsiCo voluntarily left Myanmar (Burma) because of a concern that the military were violating human rights. Many large financial and banking institutions now apply the Equator Principles (EPs) as a condition of granting loans.[27] McDonald's refuses to buy beef or chicken that is fed antibiotics, and Ronald McDonald House has made a significant contribution to the lives of sick children. Timberland gives its employees a week's paid leave to work for their favourite charity. Other companies have voluntarily enforced prohibitions on the use of child labour and the logging of old growth forests. There is, then, evidence to suggest that many MNCs are taking social responsibility issues seriously, and actively beginning to self-regulate. To ignore this evidence is counter-productive to useful debate about the place of MNCs in society.

This emerging trend toward corporate self-regulation is mirrored in some of the popular business advocacy literature as well. The language used to describe this shift is often evolutionary. Terms like 'stages', 'phases' and 'steps' speak to the fact that the key insight in these texts is the acknowledgement that the corporate world is on an ethical journey. Neef (2003: 72–80) is one of the first authors to document this. According to him, companies go through a four-stage process in moving towards what he calls 'advanced CSR'. Stage one companies are purely reactive. They employ marketing-laden value statements and practise philanthropy, but do not engage in reporting on social, environmental or governance issues. Stage two companies enter the 'public relations phase' in that they begin to understand the need to protect their reputations. These companies practise 'soft' reporting and they tend to be compliance driven. Stage three companies enter the early CSR phase and are cognisant of the importance of CSR, making a clear commitment to ethical behaviour and practice. Stage four companies have ethics and risk management officers, undertake third party auditing, practise triple bottom line reporting, adhere to such initiatives as the UNGC, hold a strategic view of the purpose of their company that goes beyond profit, and stress the need to involve stakeholders throughout the company's supply chain. While Neef is right to paint the ethical journey of companies as an evolutionary one, his model does not draw on enough examples of companies that fit each of his stages. Indeed, he suggests that the American juice giant, Odwalla, fits stage one, but it is unclear how. He also suggests that there are a few stage four companies, but does not name any of them. Nor does he fully appreciate the implications of the journey he describes. Arguably his four-stage model stops at the water's edge. It is not advanced CSR that is the ethical end point for MNCs seeking to develop strong corporate reputations, but rather it is corporate self-regulation.

Parker (2002) recognises that CSR is only a part of the story. She argues that MNCs do indeed have the potential for corporate self-regulation and explores a range of ideas and themes to support her contention. This excellent book is a blend of both theory and practice; it not only sets out the theoretical issues that allow her to argue strongly that the idea of self-regulation should be taken seriously, but also sets out a range of practical strategies which would allow MNCs to self-regulate effectively. For Parker (2002: 50–55), three factors make effective self-regulation possible: external regulatory pressure, a commitment from management, and a team of self-regulation personnel. These three factors help to 'institutionalize purpose' in the organisation and create an environment where self-regulation is valued. By 'institutionalization of purpose', Parker means that 'policy is made an integral part of corporate objectives. Standard operating procedures are revised to make responsibility issues a part of everybody's job, and reward systems are changed so that managers are motivated to take responsibility issues into account' (Parker, 2002: 58). Once these conditions are met, effective self-regulation becomes possible.

Parker's work suggests that the view that modern MNCs are amoral profit maximisers is one-dimensional and simplistic. In her view, MNCs act on a range of other impulses and can behave well without excessive regulation or the threat of government sanction. In the context of industry self-regulation, I pointed out earlier that mechanisms of informal co-ercion, normative change and new information about best practice can all have a positive effect on the behaviour of MNCs. While these sorts of arguments are often made in relation to industry self-regulation, they are equally valid in relation to corporate self-regulation. What needs to be added to these arguments is an appreciation of the disciplining role that corporate reputation is having on MNCs. This is something Parker also understands very well. As she notes in relation to the development of compliance systems within companies, 'these results tend to confirm the primary importance of reputation and publicity as a motivator for compliance systems' (Parker, 2002: 94).

Parker's book contains none of the ideological and rhetorical flourish common to much of the literature critical of self-regulatory schemes. On the contrary, there is a healthy and dispassionate realism in the arguments, which significantly moves the debate forward. This realism is evident in the following passage: 'Corporate self-regulation is necessary to democracy. It is neither naive optimism nor a concession to market power to advocate reliance on corporate self-regulation as a matter of policy' (Parker, 2002: 292).

Parker has coined the term 'The Open Corporation' to describe companies that effectively self-regulate. In the latter chapters of her book, she goes into detail about the type of strategies that can make MNCs, as Parker notes, 'permeable to democracy'; that is, strategies that ensure that MNCs are open to broader societal interests. She describes three strategies that she believes lead companies to institutionalise responsibility. They are:

- *Strategy One:* Responsible corporate self-regulators use employees' cultures, values and self-identities to build organizational integrity. This is a '*bottom up*' approach to self regulation.
- *Strategy Two:* Responsible corporate self-regulators find it is strategic to take legitimate stakeholder perspectives and external values into account, by reporting information about self-regulation processes and performance to stakeholders, by consulting with stakeholders, and by giving those affected by corporate power the ability to challenge corporate decisions and actions. This is an 'opening-out' approach to self-regulation in which stakeholder concerns and values have become an external issue to be decisively addressed, not an externality to be ignored.
- *Strategy Three:* Responsible corporate self-regulators integrate into their routine management systems institutions and decision-making processes that ensure that the company becomes aware of, learns from and responds to social and legal responsibility issues. This is a '*systems approach*' to corporate responsibility which emphasizes the importance of internal discipline, justice, self-regulation and self-evaluation systems within the whole self-management of the organization. (Systems are so important for the integration of self-regulation management that both of the above two principles also include a systems element – systems for learning from disciplinary issues – and Justice Plans) (Parker, 2002: 197–8, italics in the original).

Parker (2002: 198) argues that these strategies 'can be read as a guide to the three best practice strategies necessary for managers and self-regulation professionals to institutionalize social and legal responsibility'. She goes on to stress that they are not a 'blueprint' and that 'responsible self-regulation' is not the accomplishment of the corporation alone (Parker, 2002: 198). It is found in the embrace of management with the values and concerns represented by internal and external stakeholders. Parker's tactic in the book is to tease out the implications of each of these strategies at great length. There are, however, other ways of unpacking what it means to be a self-regulating corporation, and that is by examining specific cases where companies have sought to find ways to achieve this same goal. And Parker is well aware of this. As she notes (2002: 198): '[e]ach organization must develop its own ways of engaging with employees, stakeholders and systems'. In the following three chapters, I look at three cases of well-known MNCs that have sought to become self-regulating corporations. These are Royal Dutch Shell, the Toyota Motor Corporation and Interface Inc. Each company has had its challenges in recent years, but has learned important lessons on the road toward corporate self-regulation. I suggest other companies seeking to become self-regulating corporations can learn a great deal from these three trailblazers.

CONCLUSION

Self-regulation does not mean that national governments abandon regulatory oversight of corporations. On the contrary, a self-regulating corporation is one that is cognisant of the demands of both government regulators and stakeholders. They are companies that understand their social and environmental responsibilities and the value of compliance and audit mechanisms in helping them to maintain a strong corporate reputation.

As noted earlier, this is an evolutionary journey for MNCs. Some will win, some will lose. Some will understand the shift in attitude and embrace it with a passion, others will not. The cases to follow tell the narratives of three MNCs that have worked hard to become self-regulating corporations. The readers will judge for themselves which has been the most successful in achieving this. My own view is that Interface Inc. has come the closest to this ideal. I treat this company's narrative last for this reason. It is, in my view, the best model of a corporation seeking to self-regulate. We can learn valuable lessons from Shell and Toyota as well. Each case offers a unique picture of the difficulties of MNCs becoming genuine self-regulating corporations.

NOTES

1. America's Securities and Exchange Commission defines a Ponzi scheme as 'an investment fraud that involves the payment of purported returns to existing investors from funds contributed by new investors'. New investors are attracted by the promise of higher than

     average returns on their investment. Ponzi schemes collapse when not enough new investors are found to pay returns to existing investors.

2. Eisner (1993: 1) defines a regulatory regime as 'a historically specific configuration of policies and institutions which structures the relationship between social interests, the state and economic actors in multiple sectors of the economy'.

3. Institutional capacity is defined here as the capacity of a country's institutions to promote development. A combination of, among other things, corruption, regulatory overlap and capture, slow approval time, lack of trained personnel and under-resourced administrative units often means that the regulatory regimes in particular industry sectors perform less well than those in developed countries. There may also be differences in institutional endowments across sectors as well, depending on particular government preferences.

4. In a similar fashion, North (1990: 36–53) distinguishes between formal and informal rules as key determinants of regulatory efficacy.

5. Mattli and Woods (2009: 10) define regulatory capture as 'de facto control of the state and its regulatory agencies by the "regulated" interests, enabling these interests to transfer wealth to themselves at the expense of society'. See also McNicholas and Windsor (2011), who describe the MMS as a corrupt regulatory agency.

6. This is also sometimes referred to as 'heavy-handed' regulation. See the Independent Pricing and Regulatory Tribunal of New South Wales (2006: 7.1.1).

7. See McCrudden (1999).

8. Such as those arrangements governing the building industry, forestry and manufacturing.

9. On the link between industry self-regulation and territory see Ronit (2001).

10. The Bhopal disaster is regarded as the worst chemical accident in history. At 5 minutes to midnight, a large amount of methyl isocyanate escaped from a Union Carbide plant in Bhopal, India. The accident killed around 4500 people and injured hundreds of thousands. See Lapierre and Moro (2002); Hanna et al. (2005).

11. These ten principles are listed in King and Lenox (2000: 700).

12. Prakash (2000: 203) concluded an assessment of the first decade of the programme by suggesting that it still had a long way to go and the CMA needed to 'acknowledge the deficiencies in Responsible Care and correct them'. These deficiencies include: (a) a communications gap with major stakeholders; (b) a lack of a verification system, once the voluntary codes are established; (c) a need to gain acceptance for the code from regulators; (d) an increase in legitimacy, such that the broader society is involved; (e) more publishable work needs to be carried out on the danger of chemicals to the public. Arguably, the deficiencies of 'Responsible Care' turn on ensuring that stakeholders are adequately informed about the relative danger to public health of the chemicals its members' companies produce.

13. See also Ayres and Braithwaite's (1992: 39) 'Enforcement Pyramid' for another example of the various ways of 'regulating'. Governments have various options open to them to regulate MNCs. Public–private partnerships are one example. It should be noted here that the focus on command and control forms of regulation is intentional, as it is the form of regulation most attractive to anti-corporate activists seeking to move beyond the neoliberal state.

14. Royal Dutch Shell (2005).

15. For a comparison between command and control and market instruments for making environmental policy, see Moran (1995).

16. The charges against Unocal were not simply relating to their activities in Myanmar. They also had a poor environmental record in the US as well. This was also used as a basis for trying to shut down the company in the US.

17. On the link between changes in the way states regulate MNCs and globalisation, see Braithwaite and Drahos (2001).

18. Lasswell (1958) once famously described politics as 'who gets what, when, how'. This 'distributional' notion of politics underpins much of the idea of politics as the interplay of a plurality of interests.

19. The most succinct statement of this can be found in the Communist Manifesto (Marx and Engels, 2011).
20. He refers to this as the 'global movement for a living democracy'.
21. Some of the groups Korten has in mind include America's Green Party, environmental justice groups, The Council of Canadians, and The Boulder Independent Business Alliance. As he (2001: 319) notes, '[t]hese and countless related initiatives are the proactive side of the living democracy movement, demonstrating the possibilities of local democratic control within a framework of commitment to creating healthy, ecologically sound communities that work for all'.
22. One of the staunchest supporters of globalisation is Ohmae (1995; 1994).
23. According to Cohen (1993: 26), public sector capacity building seeks to strengthen targeted human resources (managerial, professional and technical) in particular institutions and to provide those institutions with the means whereby these resources can be marshalled and sustained effectively to perform planning, policy formulation and implementation tasks throughout government on any priority topic.
24. Elsewhere, Levi-Faur and Jordana (2005: 7) note that '[n]eoliberalism preaches deregulation but paradoxically seems to expand and extend regulation'.
25. For other examples of this, see Holliday et al. (2002); Arena (2004).
26. What Spar calls the 'spotlight phenomenon' I would refer to as a reputation effect.
27. According to the Equator Principles website, '[t]he Equator Principles (EPs) are a credit risk management framework for determining, assessing and managing environmental and social risk in project finance transactions. Project finance is often used to fund the development and construction of major infrastructure and industrial projects. The EPs are adopted voluntarily by financial institutions and are applied where total project capital costs exceed US$10 million. The EPs are primarily intended to provide a minimum standard for due diligence to support responsible risk decision-making'.

Three case studies: in pursuit of corporate
self-regulation

4. Royal Dutch Shell's 'PR-led' approach to corporate self-regulation

When writers discuss the essence of a strong corporate reputation, they invariably point to the performance of companies such as The Body Shop and Timberland. For various reasons these companies are judged to have excellent reputations in the marketplace. As such, they make useful case examples of the way MNCs can grow and manage their reputations. Almost the exact opposite is the case with resource companies. For some people, they epitomise the ugly side of the modern global economy. They are large companies which are seen by many to lack accountability, have little regard for social and environmental values and often appear to be beyond the control of states.[1]

This chapter is the first of three cases that examine the link between corporate self-regulation and its ability to promote a strong corporate reputation. Royal Dutch Shell is one of the largest MNCs in the world. The statistics are impressive. In 2013, the company had revenues of US$451.23 billion and an income of US$26.87 billion (Royal Dutch Shell, 2013). It had an after tax profit of US$16.56 billion. The company spent US$44 billion on capital investment, US$1.3 billion in research and development, and US$156 million on voluntary social investment. Shell operates in more than 70 countries and produces 3.2 million barrels of oil a day (Royal Dutch Shell, 2013). The company also owns approximately 44 000 service stations and operates more than 30 refineries and chemical plants around the world. In 2013, Shell topped the Fortune 500 list. In 2015, the company dropped two places behind Walmart. Despite this, the company had revenues of US$431 344 billion and made a profit of US$14 874 billion.

Shell is one of the original 'Seven Sisters' and today is considered to be one of the six 'supermajors'.[2] Yet despite its long history, and these impressive statistics, the company has been dogged by controversy. It was the only company to remain in South Africa after sanctions were imposed on the country by the UN. In 1995, the company found itself embroiled in two severe reputational crises. The first was the proposed sea dumping of the Brent Spar oil storage facility in the North Sea, and later that same year the company was implicated, rightly or wrongly, in the execution of a high-profile Nigerian activist and eight of his colleagues. These incidents drew widespread criticism of the company and damaged Shell's reputation severely.

Coming on the heels of a number of major resource company disasters, Shell's problems were seen as emblematic of an industry sector that was seriously out of step with evolving societal values and expectations. Unfortunately, the Exxon Valdez spill in Alaska prepared the ground for Shell's unfortunate experience a decade later.

At midnight on 24 March 1989, the *Exxon Valdez*, one of the largest oil tankers in the world, struck a reef in Prince William Sound, Alaska. The single hulled super tanker hit the reef with such force that it ruptured a number of its tanks, spilling some 11 million gallons of crude oil into the Sound. So significant was this environmental disaster that a code of conduct designed to prevent such disasters happening again is now referred to as the 'Valdez Principles'.

At the time, the Exxon Valdez spill was the worst environmental disaster in American history, and one of the worst in the world. In terms of quantity, however, the spill was relatively small. In 1991, almost 500 million gallons of oil was released into the Persian Gulf. In 1999, the *Erika* sank and discharged 3 million gallons of heavy oil into the sea off the coast of Brittany in France.

What made the Valdez spill so significant was the relatively closed nature of the Sound, the richness of the wildlife in the area, and the failure of the company to mobilise a clean-up effort in time to prevent the spread of the oil when a storm arrived two days later.

Regardless of the size of the spill, it killed tens of thousands of birds, destroyed salmon and herring fish stocks, and decimated the local sea otter and seal populations. The spill also had long-term consequences for those people living around the affected area. Fishermen lost their livelihoods, locals lost a valuable source of food, and once vibrant towns, such as Cordova, began to wither away. By any account, this was a devastating accident.

The spill could have been contained easily, had the captain not attempted to free the vessel from the reef. This action only increased the amount of oil which spilled out of the ruptured tanks. Moreover, several hours passed before the captain reported the accident to local authorities, and the clean-up began some 14 hours after the spill. Another important factor exacerbated the dimensions of the problem: the super tanker had not been shadowed by an oil spill vessel into open water, despite this being mandatory federal law.

The cause of the accident is a matter of some conjecture. One view is that the captain was intoxicated and had left the bridge to 'sleep it off'. If this was the case, he would have been in no state to supervise the departure of the ship from the Sound. A second theory is that the helmsman either did not receive instructions from the third mate to turn back into the sea lanes after a manoeuvre to avoid floating ice, or that he did not follow the instructions correctly. As a consequence, the helmsman was unable to determine exactly where the reef was. A third view is that Exxon and BP were to blame (Palast, 2004, 365–79). Exxon had known for some years that they would be unable to contain a large spill in the Sound. But a drive toward cutting costs meant that the company was unwilling to invest in the necessary equipment and crews capable of responding to a large spill. Contrary to government regulation, Exxon systematically reduced the number of trained spill specialists at Port Valdez. They also falsified water quality test results to reduce the amounts of oil present in the Sound (Palast, 2004). This kept the operation out of the intrusive eye of government regulators. Palast further argues that BP knew of Exxon's inability to cope with a large oil spill. Rather than addressing the problem, it wilfully attempted to conceal the fact by harassing and intimidating alarmed employees.

Whatever the truth of the matter, the Alaskan government's inquiry into the accident pointed to the fact that the captain had left the bridge and did not supervise his crew properly as they tried to avoid substantial amounts of floating ice. During his trial, the jury cleared the captain of the charge of being intoxicated, partly because blood samples taken after the accident were not treated with appropriate care. Instead, he was convicted of negligence and fined a paltry US$5000. He was also required to perform 1000 hours of community service.

Despite trying to share the blame, there is little doubt that Exxon was primarily responsible for the disaster (Sullivan, 1989). Yet what compounded the company's problems was its poor crisis management in the days and weeks following the accident. As Beder (2002) observes, the Exxon Valdez spill has become something of a textbook case study in the public relations literature about how not to manage a crisis. It took Exxon's then CEO, Lawrence Rawl, six days to comment on the spill and three weeks to visit the site. When the director of Exxon's shipping division finally held a press conference, his upbeat assessment of the disaster was quickly contradicted by the accounts of members of the clean-up crew. Matters did not improve from there. When Rawl eventually agreed to a television interview, it became evident that he had not read reports detailing the clean-up operations. He stated that it was not the job of the Chairman to read such reports. In addition, a leaked internal memo from the local clean-up manager to Exxon executives suggested that the company would abandon the clean-up operation in

September, well before the job had been properly completed. Perhaps most astonishing of all, when an Exxon executive was asked how the company was going to pay for the clean-up, he responded by indicating that it would increase gas prices. In the eyes of the public, the media and concerned politicians in the US Congress, Exxon showed little or no remorse for the destruction it had caused to the environment and to the local economy.

In the end, the accident cost the company considerably. Some estimate the figure to be as high as US$16 billion (Larkin, 2003: 6). The company also lost market share and its stock price took a downward turn. Today, more than 20 years after the spill, the company is still on the defence over the accident. It appealed a US$4.5 billion judgment, and is likely to challenge a recent request from the US Department of Justice to pay a further US$100 million to clean up remaining pockets of oil in the Sound. In the latest chapter, a number of those who were involved in the clean-up are becoming ill with respiratory and other health problems. While is it difficult to prove the link to the clean-up operations, the so-called 'Valdez Crud' is a reminder of the costs to all stakeholders when a company does not do the right thing.

Partly, it is because of the industry's dubious history that Shell now attracts more attention from the media and anti-corporate activists than most other companies. Indeed, there are now more books and journal articles criticising Shell than possibly any other MNC, and certainly more than any other oil major. There is even an anti-Shell website that suggests that the company had been a supporter of the Nazis during World War II. To see the Shell logo situated next to a picture of Adolf Hitler demonstrates the depth of resentment some people have for the company.[3]

Nonetheless, there is probably no company in the world that has invested as much time, energy and money trying to rehabilitate its reputation. Since 1995, the company has developed an impressive reputation management strategy, which includes establishing commitments to both sustainable development and CSR. It has also accepted a range of international conventions, including the UN's Universal Declaration of Human Rights, the Kyoto emission reduction targets, and financed a multimillion dollar, not-for-profit foundation devoted to sustainability and poverty reduction (The Shell Foundation, 2011). In addition, the company is a founding member of the World Business Council for Sustainable Development (WBCSD) and is committed to the development of commercially viable alternative fuel sources. While Shell has been attempting to improve its reputation, its underlying motive is that the company wants to become a self-regulating corporation. It clearly understands that becoming a self-regulating corporation will reduce the level of criticism of the company, improve its community relations, save money, and build a strong reputation among its stakeholders.

Yet after a decade or more of effort, the company still attracts criticism. There are two potential answers that are explored in this chapter. The first is the gulf between their moral claims and their actions. Since 1995, the company has been fined numerous times for breaches of various laws. It has been found guilty of cartel behaviour and price-fixing, and has been accused of greenwashing its image.[4] These are hardly the sort of attributes that one would associate with a company that values a strong corporate reputation.

The second reason is that it has tried to rehabilitate itself through the use of public relations (PR). Indeed, Henderson and Williams (2002: 16) describe Shell's strategy as a 'PR-led' approach. This is a reference to the range of PR and marketing techniques Shell employs to communicate their values to a wider public and, in the process, attempt to build reputational capital. In this chapter, I focus on the weakness of 'PR-led' approaches to building reputational capital. I argue that, despite a remarkable improvement in Shell's social and environmental profile, the company has not sufficiently grasped the ethical dimension that underpins a strong corporate reputation, rendering its efforts as little more than 'spin'.[5]

This chapter is divided into four sections. The first section examines the two incidents that led Shell to understand the need to think about the value of its reputation in the marketplace. The second section analyses the main themes that the company embraced after a period of serious introspection. The third section considers the persistent charge of greenwash that has been directed at the company regularly. In the final section, I discuss the limitations of Shell's approach to becoming a self-regulating corporation, and question whether this particular strategy could ever fulfil its corporate ambitions to build a strong corporate reputation.

REPUTATION ON THE ROPES

1995 was undoubtedly Shell's *annus horribilis*. Two back-to-back crises, both handled badly, impacted the company's reputation significantly. Prior to that, the company's reputation was not strong. So these more recent crises added to their reputational problems.

Shell was the only foreign MNC to remain in South Africa after the UN imposed sanctions on the country. This was interpreted by many as a sign that Shell was a renegade MNC. Its duplicitous 'Neptune Strategy' only further reinforced this view in the eyes of the public. It is worth briefly covering these issues, as it helps to put the 1990s crises into perspective.

The 1980s, like the 1990s, were difficult years for Shell. The company came under immense pressure from politicians, religious groups and others to leave apartheid South Africa (Feder, 1987). While only about 1 per cent of Shell's revenue came from South Africa, the company's decision to remain was probably made for economic and strategic reasons. The international sanctions, and the decision of other oil companies to depart from South Africa, left Shell with a virtual monopoly in that country. At the time, Shell argued that it remained in South Africa to protect the jobs of its 7000 employees. Very few commentators accepted this rationale.

The decision to remain in South Africa proved a costly one for Shell. The company came under fire for supplying fuel and oil to the South African military, and for exporting South African coal into Europe, in violation of the UN sanctions. At the time, the company was viewed as a pariah.

Apartheid activists began calling for consumers to boycott Shell. Protests were held at Shell service stations in Great Britain and Europe. A city in the Netherlands even went as far as excluding Shell from supplying the city with oil because of its activities in South Africa. In a display of defiance, Shell subsequently sued the city.

After more than two years of boycotts, Shell employed Pagan International, a large American public relations firm, to counter the boycott. The company developed a 265-page document referred to as the 'Neptune Strategy'. The overall goal of the strategy was to weaken the boycott's effectiveness and ensure Shell's future market dominance in South Africa.

The 'Neptune Strategy' had three elements. The first was to investigate the 'personal characteristics' of those individuals leading the boycott, infiltrate their meetings, and tape their conversations in the hope of influencing them. Second, two well-known figures in the American government were employed to influence Union officials by focusing on Shell's post-apartheid plans (Lubbers, 2012: 64–77). Third, Pagan International set up a lobby group which was supposedly independent of Shell, but which endorsed the company's reasons for remaining in South Africa. The Coalition on South Africa (COSA) was launched in September 1987 and included US clergy and Black South Africans in its membership. COSA pointed out that Shell could play an important economic role in post-apartheid South Africa. This included educating and training black South Africans and the development of business links between Afro-Americans and black South Africans.

Someone from Pagan International leaked the 'Neptune Strategy' to the Interfaith Centre on Corporate Responsibility. The exposure led to Shell withdrawing its account and Pagan International eventually went into liquidation. However, the episode painted Shell as a deceitful and manipulative company with no sense of right or wrong. Indeed, it reinforced the general perception that Shell was a corporation without a conscience. According to one boycott leader, the 'Neptune Strategy' was a deliberate and deceptive attempt to 'divide and weaken the position of the religious community with regards to South Africa' (cited in Stauber and Rampton, 1995: 53).

Shell's decision to stay in South Africa was problematic from the start. No matter what sort of arguments they used to justify staying in the country, apartheid was an immoral and racist political system that had been universally condemned. To set out secretly to weaken the resolve of the international community, and anti-apartheid activists, showed extremely poor judgement. But it also highlighted the rather wilful nature of the company. This attitude seems to have prevailed into the 1990s as well, when Shell was challenged like no other contemporary MNC.

Brent Spar

With the conclusion of a pipeline from the Brent oil fields to an onshore oil terminal in Shetland, the Brent Spar oil storage facility had come to the end of its commercial life.[6] The Brent Spar:

> was unlike any other installation in the North Sea. It had a unique function: both to store oil, and to offload the oil from its storage tanks into tankers offshore. It was constructed as a huge floating buoy, fabricated from steel, and moored to the sea bed in the North Sea by six anchors. Its displacement was 66,500 tonnes, its floating draught 109 metres, its total height 137 metres and its dry weight 14,500 tonnes. (Royal Dutch Shell, 2008: 40)

The Brent Spar oil storage facility consisted of six separate segments and had a storage capacity of 300 000 barrels of oil. Clearly, disposing of an object of that size and weight was never going to be an easy task. In addition, the facility was reported to contain toxic substances, including oil sludge, and seawater, further adding to the problem of its disposal.

In 1992, Shell began to examine the best method of disposing of the facility, and a range of scenarios were explored, including towing it to shore and dismantling it. Shell's research suggested that this option would be a costly one, and would take approximately 360 000 hours to complete (Peters, 1999: 60). But this scenario was ruled out on the grounds that it could have serious environmental consequences for the shoreline, and there was a likelihood of fatalities occurring during the decommissioning. After three years of research, Shell concluded that towing the Brent Spar to deep water and sinking it was the best choice available to them.

Shell applied to Britain's former Department of Trade and Industry for a licence to dispose of the Brent Spar and gained the necessary approvals. In addition, Shell sought agreement from all those European countries who were signatories to the now obsolete Convention for the Prevention of Marine Pollution by Dumping from Ships and Aircraft.[7] From its perspective, the company had done all that was legally required to gain approval to sink the Brent Spar deep in the Atlantic Ocean. Shell's only mistake was not to engage environmental groups in the decision-making process.

On the eve of the decommissioning, along with a German television crew, Greenpeace flew four activists onto the structure by helicopter and began a protest campaign that attracted global attention. The NGO argued that sinking the structure was a mistake for a number of reasons. First, the arguments and data provided by Shell to the British Government were weak, if not spurious. Second, there was inadequate scientific evidence to determine the long-term impact on the marine environment. Third, as a matter of principle, companies should be responsible for dealing with their own waste. Fourth, the structure was filled with thousands of tonnes of 'toxic and radioactive sludge' (Wallace, 1995; Reddy, 1995).[8] Fifth, the decision to sink the Brent Spar was carried out in secret. However, most importantly, Greenpeace believed that if Shell were allowed to sink the Brent Spar at sea it would set a precedent for other companies looking for cheap and easy ways to dispose of unwanted assets.[9]

The consequences of the protests were significant (Bakir, 2005).[10] A number of Shell service stations in Germany were vandalised: two were fire-bombed, and one was strafed with bullets. In addition, Shell staff were threatened, and fuel sales in Europe fell. After ten days of relentless news and media coverage around the world, Shell released a brief statement on its homepage on the 20 June 1995, indicating that it would look for an alternative to dumping the Brent Spar at sea.

> Shell UK aborted the operation because the Shell position as a major European enterprise has become untenable. The Spar had gained a symbolic significance out of all proportion to its environmental impact. In consequence, Shell companies were faced with increasingly intense public criticism, mostly

in Continental Northern Europe. Many politicians and ministers were openly hostile and several called for consumer boycotts. There was violence against Shell service stations, accompanied by threats to Shell staff. (O'Rourke and Collins, 2008: 95).

Eventually, the structure was towed to a fjord in Norway and recycled as a roll-on, roll-off ferry terminal. The cost of decommissioning the Brent Spar oil storage facility was US$60 million (Royal Dutch Shell, 2008: 9).

The Brent Spar saga was like a runaway train. It took on a life of its own, beyond anything that Shell could have foreseen. European governments complained to Britain's Prime Minister, John Major. Newspapers and television stations around the world followed the story with interest. The scientific community debated whether ocean dumping was beneficial to marine life (Radford, 1995: 5). It was an event, and an issue, that polarised public opinion. Yet Shell did little to help its cause at the time. Its staff repeatedly tried to evict protestors from the platform by firing water cannons across the top deck of the Brent Spar. All of this was captured in video footage and used to good effect in the media. So impressive was the Greenpeace campaign that *The Economist* (1995: 18) magazine described the campaign as 'brilliant', while Schoon from *The Independent* (1997: 19) ran a story with the headlines 'David's great victory over Goliath'.

It is widely accepted that Shell's back-down was a victory for Greenpeace (Zyglidopoulos, 2002: 144). Yet even this did not reflect well on the company. After many months of convincing the British Government that ocean disposal was the best way to deal with the facility, and three weeks of defending this case in newspapers and television interviews, the company then suggested it could tow the platform ashore. This only served to strengthen Greenpeace's case, fuelling public suspicion that ocean disposal was an easy and cost-effective strategy for Shell. Furthermore, it embarrassed the British Government and its regulators, who believed that sinking the Brent Spar was the right thing to do. Indeed, so annoyed was the prime minister, John Major, that he referred to Shell as a 'wimp' for not following through with the sea-dumping (Sluyterman, 2010: 217).

The Execution of the Ogoni Nine

Despite the fact that there were a number of large oil companies operating in Nigeria at the time, Shell has been the main focus of attention among anti-corporate activists and local communities near its joint operations.[11] There are a number of reasons for this. The company is the largest oil producer in the country and has been there since 1953. Second, it has had a close association with the brutal regimes that governed the country. Third, Shell was, and continues to be, the main focus of local community anger.[12] Fourth, as noted earlier, the company has had a somewhat chequered history on the continent (Okonta and Douglas, 2003: 48).

In June 1995, while Shell was pondering the future of the Brent Spar, Ken Saro-Wiwa and eight fellow activists were arrested by the Nigerian military on suspicion of murdering four leaders of the Ogoni ethnic group.[13] Most observers, including Human Rights Watch, branded the subsequent trial a farce, and a gross violation of the rights of the accused. All nine were convicted, and despite pleas for clemency by Nelson Mandela and other political figures, were executed in November 1995.

Saro-Wiwa blamed Shell for the miserable conditions of his people, and for his incarceration. Two weeks before his arrest, he is reputed to have said, '[t]his is it – they are going to arrest us all and execute us. All for Shell' (Richardson, 2004: 166). Given the corrupt and brutal character of the ruling Abacha regime, Saro-Wiwa's indictment of Shell was probably unfair. Yet there is little doubt that Shell played its part in the Ogoni Nine case. The company invited police to protect its assets and paid the transportation costs and salaries of its security personnel. The police and military were directly responsible for serious human abuses against the Ogoni people (Bob, 2005; Okonta and Douglas, 2003). Moreover, it appears that Shell was completely disconnected from the communities around its sites and did not believe it had any responsibility for them. According to some accounts, Shell allegedly bribed witnesses to testify against Saro-Wiwa, and imported weapons for the Nigerian military (Manby, 1999: 295).[14]

However, Shell had clearly been responsible for some of the environmental problems in Ogoniland, although perhaps not on the scale some critics suggest. For example, a World Bank (1995: 5) report stated that oil pollution was not as damaging as untreated sewage, overuse of farmland and fishing grounds, and deforestation. Indeed, the report ranked oil pollution as a moderate priority. In addition, because the local Ogoni people were so angered by Shell's presence, sabotage of its assets was a continual problem for the company. But perhaps Shell's greatest mistake was consistently rejecting calls for the company to plead with the government to spare the lives of the Ogoni Nine, citing a company rule of not interfering in the domestic politics of the countries in which it operates. However, a month before the Ogoni Nine were executed, Shell did, in fact, write to the government.[15] The apparent indifference during the trial period gave prima facie credibility to claims that Shell was behind the executions or, at the very least, was unconcerned about the fate of the group (Project Underground, 2006).

Shell's suggestion that it had no right to be involved in the political affairs of the countries in which it operates shows a remarkable lack of understanding of the political aspects of doing business. There are a number of possible reasons for this. Shell failed to realise that its operations placed it squarely at the centre of Nigerian politics. As the largest generator of revenue for the government, Shell was supporting an undemocratic and abusive regime. The company's failure to pay heed to its stakeholders gave legitimacy to the regime and disenfranchised other important stakeholders, such as the local Ogoni community. Moreover, Shell's presence in the Niger Delta polarised the political environment of the country and led to the rise of the Movement for the Survival of the Ogoni People (MOSOP), of which Saro-Wiwa was one of the leading activists. By not addressing the social and environmental concerns of the Ogoni people, Shell alienated a key stakeholder group. Had Shell engaged in dialogue with affected communities, a better outcome may have eventuated; one that may have prevented the need for intervention by the Nigerian military, reduced the human rights abuses in Ogoniland, and prevented the execution of Saro-Wiwa and his colleagues. Ironically, in both its battle with Greenpeace and its problems in Nigeria, Shell's problems were largely political in nature.

SHELL'S ETHICAL TRANSFORMATION

Shell clearly realised the consequences of being involved in such acrimonious and public confrontations with stakeholder groups. The lack of 'fit' between its operating principles and its apparent actions, rightly or wrongly, exposed Shell to ridicule and its business suffered as a consequence. Indeed, in both these events the company appeared arrogant and out of touch with contemporary social and ethical values. In order to win back its reputation, it had to clearly demonstrate that it had changed its behaviour. According to Henderson and Williams (2002: 11), at the end of 1995 the Chairman of Shell Transport and Trading stated the following:

> The events of the past year demonstrated the degree of complexity in the multinational operations of Group companies and the need to gain broader understanding and acceptance of their activities. This is, in effect, the Group's license to operate ... We learned in 1995 that we need to have greater external focus if we are to create a better acceptance of the Group's business among

various audiences. Group companies must consult, inform and communicate better with the public.

The company's first attempt to repair the damage to its reputation was the publication of a report titled *Profits and Principles: Does There Have to be a Choice?* (Royal Dutch Shell, 1998).[16] *Profits and Principles* outlined Shell's 'new values' and provided a roadmap for implementing change across the organisation.[17] The key message that the report attempted to convey to its audience was that wealth generation and acting ethically in business were not incompatible goals. *Profits and Principles* signalled to stakeholders that Shell had developed a new business philosophy and had learned a valuable lesson from its previous mistakes.

Profits and Principles contains three core commitments. The first, and most important, is to sustainable development, that is, 'development that meets the needs of the present without compromising the ability of future generations to meet their own needs' (World Commission on Environment and Development, 1987: 43). Shell set out to invest in the development of alternative sources of power, such as solar, wind and biofuels.

Second, Shell has committed itself to a human rights agenda. This includes policies on the protection of the rights of its workers, a prohibition of the use of child labour and greater attention to the way its security forces dealt with local communities. The company now trains its security personnel in Nigeria. It has also devised a Human Rights Compliance Assessment Tool, and runs human rights seminars for staff and contractors working in politically sensitive locations (Royal Dutch Shell, 2011a; 2011b). Shell is also the first MNC to commit to the Universal Declaration on Human Rights.

The final component of Shell's 'new values' is a commitment to corporate social responsibility (CSR), particularly in the area of business integrity. This includes a commitment not to pay bribes or donations to political parties. The company has also instituted a global whistleblower hotline. This allows employees to report anonymously anything that might undermine the company's reputation. These new values and commitments are underpinned by a statement of General Business Principles. While Shell has had this document in place since 1976, it has undergone revision in recent years in order to take into account the company's changing values and priorities.[18] The latest revision of this document took place in 2014.

Shell understood that *Profits and Principles* was a work in progress. It laid the foundation for future efforts in these three areas. Since this initial publication, the company has devoted a great deal of time demonstrating to its stakeholders that it is able to live up to these new values. Some of its more recent initiatives include the establishment of a charitable foundation devoted to sustainable development and investment in renewables. Shell has recently partnered with Cosan, a Brazilian ethanol producer, in a deal reported to be worth around US$12 billion (Royal Dutch Shell, 2010; Financial Review, 2011). This makes Shell the world's largest producer of ethanol. It has banded together with a number of business organisations devoted to the issue of climate change and sustainable development. Most notably the WBCSD.

In addition to these important initiatives, the company has committed to transparency on environmental and social issues. At the time, this was an unprecedented move in the industry. Shell is now, arguably, one of the most transparent MNCs in the world. Perhaps the best example of this increased transparency is the publication of the company's environmental and social performance data sets. In Tables 4.1 and 4.2 selected environmental and social data between 2010 and 2013 are included and measured against the company's baseline 2004 performance. On almost all indicators, Shell's performance has been heading in the right direction.

Table 4.1   Selected figures from Shell's environmental performance data set

	2013	2012	2011	2010	2004
Direct greenhouse gases (GHGs) (million tonnes)	73	72	74	76	101
Carbon dioxide (million tonnes)	71	69	71	72	96
Methane (thousand tonnes)	120	93	133	128	192
Nitrous oxide (thousand tonnes)	1	1	2	2	2
Volatile organic compounds (thousand tonnes)	89	89	129	147	213
Freshwater withdrawn (million cubic metres)	198	203	209	202	No data
Hazardous waste disposal (thousand tonnes)	770	820	740	1048	421
Total waste disposal (thousand tonnes)	2835	3115	2590	2127	1135

Source: Royal Dutch Shell (2013).

The company has also made considerable progress in its social performance. Employee and contractor fatalities have fallen by two-thirds; the
use of armed security personnel has fallen; the company's gender profile
has improved, and the number of countries which are screened for child
labour has steadily risen. The reduction in both employee and contractor
fatalities is most impressive. An earlier sustainability report suggested
that many contractor deaths were due to road transport accidents. That
this number has dropped dramatically is a consequence of the company's
focus on these important indicators. It is also valuable to see a continued
increase in voluntary social investment.

Table 4.2   Selected figures from Shell's social performance data set

	2013	2012	2011	2010	2004
Fatalities (employees)	5	8	6	12	31
Fatalities (contractors)	5	5	5	12	29
Use of armed security (% of countries)	19	17	14	9	18
Gender equity in senior leadership (% women)	17.2	16.2	16.6	15.3	9.6
Gender equity in supervisory roles (% women)	28.8	28.1	27.3	26.3	20.7
Child labour (% of countries checked)	100	100	100	99	83
Estimated local procurement (% billions)	12	14	12	13	6
Voluntary social investment ($ millions)	159	149	125	121	106

Source: Royal Dutch Shell (2013).

Shell is quite open about the purpose of its ideational transformation. Its
annual reports are not compiled out of a universalist moral commitment
to the future health of the planet. Rather, it is because it makes good
business sense. According to Shell, committing to sustainable development has made the company more competitive and has added shareholder
value. It has also made the company think about present and future
efficiencies, created brand loyalty and added to the bottom line. As the
Shell (2011f) website notes: 'Our contribution to sustainable development comes from the choices we make about which projects to invest in,

from reducing the impact of our operations and from achieving the greatest benefits for local communities'.

This is the main reason why Shell has placed so much importance on its communications strategy. As a company spokesperson put it, '[w]e must communicate our values and demonstrate that we live up to them in our business practices' (cited in Balmer, 2003: 310). Shell's annual sustainability reports are critical in this regard, providing the company with an opportunity to highlight its strengths, demonstrate to various stakeholder groups that it is addressing their particular concerns, and is a vehicle for the company to meet criticism head-on. Yet, as noted earlier, the company has not been able to shake off claims that it has green-washed its image. I examine this issue in the following section.

THE PERSISTENT CHARGE OF GREENWASH

Over the last decade or so, Shell has continued to monitor and evaluate the success of its PR strategy in order to determine whether its ethical transformation has been successful in delivering reputational benefits to the company (Henderson and Williams, 2002: 25). It was buoyed by the initial survey results, which revealed that 67 per cent of respondents had a favourable view of Shell, 26 per cent were neutral, and just 7 per cent had an unfavourable view of the company. Other results indicated that respondents were satisfied with the way Shell communicated through the press and television. But, according to Henderson and Williams (2002: 23), the 'best test was an absence of criticism that the move was simply an expensive advertising campaign or "just PR"'. They argue that Shell's success in the survey was a result of a combination of factors including:

[a] commitment to a high level of research and evaluation to better understand audiences, test ideas and set measurable targets; giving time to consult staff in the countries where they operate in order to win local management support; putting a single team in charge of the effort to liaise with the PR agencies; and, crucially, a commitment from the Shell Group's leadership team to support the campaign.

Essentially, Henderson and Williams (2002) argue that Shell's success amounted to the triumph of substance over spin. However, this view is clearly not shared by anti-corporate activists. Since the launch of *Profits and Principles*, the company has been regularly accused of greenwashing its image.[19]

The idea of greenwash is an extension of what Mander (1970: 45) once called 'ecopornography'. He coined the term to draw attention to the nuclear power industry's multimillion dollar advertising campaign to promote nuclear power as a safe and environmentally friendly alternative to coal. According to him, the actions of these companies were 'pornographic' because they debased nature and desensitised people to the inherent problems associated with the nuclear fuel cycle. Since then, activist organisations have tirelessly pointed to the deceitful and propagandistic nature of corporate environmentalism. Even the *New York Times* (Deutsch, 2005) has noted that MNCs are increasingly spending more of their marketing budgets on environmentally oriented advertising.

The term 'greenwash' is employed by anti-corporate activists (and consumer groups) to highlight the fact that many MNCs attempt to conceal the real impact of their operations and their products on communities and the environment. Greenwash is about MNCs depicting themselves as environmentally friendly. They do this through significant public relations campaigns which seek to convince the general public of their good intentions, without actually reforming their business practices. Rather than actually taking responsibility for their pollution, MNCs use green imagery as a way of hoodwinking the public into believing that they care about environmental issues. A telling example of this is the Ford Motor Company's launch of the Ford Excursion, which coincided with Earth Day in 2000. The Excursion's advertising campaign had an environmental theme, despite the fact that the vehicle weighed over 4000 kilograms, and had a 166-litre fuel tank and a V10 diesel engine. The company clearly saw no incongruity between the car launch being held on Earth Day, its environment-themed advertising campaign, and its fuel inefficient automobiles.

It must be a great disappointment to Shell that it is regarded by many anti-corporate activists as one of the world's foremost exponents of greenwash. For example, in 2000, after three years of publishing sustainability reports, CorpWatch (2000) presented Shell with a Green Oscar. As they put it, 'Let's give credit where credit is due: When it comes to greenwash, Shell is simply superb'. Similarly, Multinational Monitor (2002) placed the company in its list of the top ten worst greenwashers. In 2009, the Advertising Standards Authority (ASA) in the UK upheld a complaint against Shell brought by the World Wildlife Fund for suggesting that its US$10 billion oil tar sands project in Canada was an investment in a sustainable energy future. This is the same year that the company backed away from research into renewable technologies such as wind, solar and hydrogen (Mcalister, 2016). Again, in 2011, the ASA (2011) upheld another judgment against Shell for misleading advertising relating to its fuel efficiency claims.

But is Shell really guilty of greenwash? The evidence appears to be compelling. First, Shell has enlisted the assistance of some of Britain's leading PR firms to promote itself as an ethical and sustainable business. Second, while the annual sustainability reports are critical in communicating Shell's values, it is hard not to get the sense that they are elaborate public relations documents, rather than an attempt to give an account of the company's actual performance.

Shell's use of photography in these documents is equally striking. Indeed, the images it uses in its annual sustainability reports are more suited to the ecotourism industry than a serious self-reflection on its social and environmental performance. It is impossible to find a negative image of any kind in the annual reports. There are no images of oil-soaked birds, spills, pollution around drilling sites, or pictures of the poor communities living on the fringes of company operations. The people and employees photographed appear to be healthy, clean, well-dressed and content. In contrast, Clark et al. (1999) offer a very different pictorial record of conditions in the Niger Delta to the idealised images of people and nature in Shell's annual reports. Third, according to Irvine (1989: 88) consuming in an 'environmentally-friendly' manner will not solve the earth's environmental problems. It needs a change in how we live. As she (1989: 88) argues, 'green consumerism may be a contradiction in terms'. In Shell's case, its core business, the production and sale of fossil fuels, is the primary cause of greenhouse gas emissions and climate change. Unless it stops producing oil altogether, it will never satisfy its critics that it is a sustainable company. Moreover, as previously noted, fossil fuels are finite; therefore, replacing them with renewable options, such as solar and wind power, while commendable, does not solve the fundamental problem that crude oil is unlikely to be available to future generations at current rates of consumption.[20] In other words, it is not sustainable development that Shell is referring to, but the substitution of new forms of power-generating capacity. Moreover, this does not address the problem of the future of the many thousands of products which are derived from crude oil.[21] It is difficult to imagine that if, and when, oil runs out, alternatives will be found for each and every one of the products that rely on oil for their manufacture. It is quite likely that future generations will not have access to a large number of the oil-derived commodities that we have at our disposal, even in our technological age. In essence, the point that environmentalists make is that we need to consume less and consume differently. Shell, like other oil and gas companies, is clearly not advocating that we buy less of its fuel or its many other petroleum-derived products.

The most vocal critic of Shell's ethical transformation is the environmental lobby group FOEI. Between 2002 and 2004, the NGO has singled out Shell for special attention, publishing three documents titled *The Other Shell Report* (FOEI, 2002; 2003; 2004). What is distinctive about these publications is that they deconstruct Shell's self-assessment of its environmental performance and progress in a systematic way. Moreover, the documents are written from the perspective of the fence line communities directly affected by Shell's operations. FOEI argues that these reports demonstrate the gulf between Shell's stated social and environmental commitments, and the daily life in the communities in which Shell operates. As FOEI (2004: 26) expresses it:

> Shell pays lip service to respecting human rights and promoting sustainable development whilst continuing with business as usual. In the ten years following the brutal killing of Ken Saro-Wiwa and 8 other MOSOP members – a time when Shell invested in rehabilitating its reputation – the company can point to few examples where it voluntarily and irrefutably corrected its environmental damage so that the land is restored, the air is healthy to breathe, and the water is clean.

There appears to be enough evidence from a range of different sources, then, to cast doubt on the veracity of some of Shell's claims to be operating ethically and sustainably.[22]

It would be quite appropriate for Shell to respond to these claims by pointing out that FOEI is a highly partisan and aggressive environmental group. Moreover, its glossy sustainability reports it produces are no different from those produced by almost all Fortune 500 companies. In fact, they pioneered this initiative. All this may be true, but it does raise the issue of Shell's capacity for self-regulation.

Perhaps the most convincing evidence of the difficulty of adhering to a regime of self-regulation comes from Shell's own internal problems over the last decade or so. On 27 April 2005, following an investigation into the deaths of two of Shell's workers on the Brent Bravo platform, Shell was fined £900 000 after pleading guilty to offences under health and safety legislation. According to the British Government's Health and Safety Executive, Shell 'admitted' to fundamental failures in health and safety management on the Brent Bravo platform. The court also ruled that the deaths were preventable (Macalister, 2006). Also in 2005, the US Environmental Protection Agency fined Shell and its joint venture partner, Equilon Enterprises LLC, US$16 500 for failing accurately to report the escape of Cyclohexane and MTBE to the Toxic Release Inventory Reporting System. The company also failed to inform the general public of the chemical releases (Environmental Protection

Agency, 2005). In January 2006, Shell agreed to a US$300 000 settlement in respect to allegations of 'fictitious' crude oil futures trading on the New York Mercantile Exchange. In September of the same year, the European Union's Competition Commission fined Shell €108 million for its involvement in a price-fixing cartel. The fine related to road bitumen supplies in the Netherlands. All members of the cartel were fined, but Shell's fine was the largest because, according to the Commission, it 'began and led the cartel' and was a 'repeat offender' (Europa, 2006b). In November 2006, the European Union's Competition Commission fined Shell a further €160 875 million for being involved in another price-fixing cartel. The fine, this time, related to synthetic rubber products. Shell's fine was increased by 50 per cent because it was, again, a 'repeat offender' (Europa, 2006a).

However, the most significant scandal to engulf Shell since the Brent Spar incident occurred in 2004, when the company admitted that it had been overstating its 'proved' oil reserves for a number of years (Cummins and Beasant, 2005). In Oman, Shell overstated its claim by 250 million barrels of oil equivalent (BoE) and, in Australia, by some 500 million BoE. According to Potter (2007), the company eventually revised its estimates down by over 20 per cent. The most damaging aspect of Shell's overstatement of its 'proved' reserves was that it was not merely a book-keeping error. It surfaced that the CEO of Shell's Exploration and Production Company, Sir Phillip Watt, had been overbooking reserves since at least 2000.[23] Indeed, after the scandal broke, an internal investigation found reserves overbooking in 100 of Shell's 300 largest oilfields (Farrell, 2004; Helman, 2006).

When Watt took over the stewardship of the entire company, he urged the new CEO of Exploration and Production, Walter van de Vijver, to continue the practice. However, Van de Vijver found it increasingly difficult to stay silent, as he indicated in an email to Watt: 'I am becoming sick and tired about lying about the extent of our reserves' (*The Economist*, 2004b). When news of the reserves overbooking broke, both Watt and Van de Vijver resigned from the company. Some estimates put the cost of the scandal at around US$700 million in damages and fines (Potter, 2007).

The regulatory authorities in Great Britain and the US could not establish whether the overbookings were a deliberate deception on Watt's part or an accounting error of epic proportions. Regardless of the source of the problem, or that the company was not replacing current production with new sources of supply, it demonstrated a significant error of judgement on Watt's part. Once Van de Vijver began to express concerns, it was Watt's duty as CEO to disclose the problem to shareholders and to the regulatory authorities.

The scandal was enormously damaging to Shell. After the announcement, the value of Shell Transport shares dropped by about 8 per cent, and the company's market value dropped by a similar amount (Taylor, 2006: 187). Indeed, Taylor (2006: 191) argues that, during the period of the overbookings scandal, Shell's share price declined by about 40 per cent, relative to other players in the sector. Furthermore, Shell was experiencing problems from within: a 2004 staff morale survey conducted internally found that fewer than half of its employees believed that it was a well-led company (Taylor, 2006: 190). Perhaps most significant of all, after almost a decade of dedication to rebuilding the company's reputation, it had again been sullied, and by Watt, the person who was the architect of the company's initial reputation revival.

Reflecting on the case of Enron and the other high-profile corporate collapses of 2001, Watt noted in the preface to the following year's annual report that, 'the corporate scandals of the past year underlined that good financial performance must be accompanied by the highest standards of governance. Shell's Business Principles and assurance process ensures we meet and maintain those standards' (Royal Dutch Shell, 2002; International Finance Corporation, 2005). Watt's resignation from the company demonstrates that he, and the company, were unable to live up to these high standards of governance in practice.

Sir Adrian Cadbury (Claessens, 2003: vii) defines corporate governance as being:

> Concerned with holding the balance between economic and social goals and between individual and communal goals. The corporate governance framework is there to encourage the efficient use of resources and equally to require accountability for the stewardship of those resources. The aim is to align as nearly as possible the interests of individuals, corporations and society.

This definition clearly demonstrates that one cannot separate internal and external behaviour. In some respects, Shell's attempts to restore its tarnished image in the wake of the Brent Spar confrontation with Greenpeace and the Ogoni Nine executions were as much about demonstrating a capacity for good corporate governance as they were about demonstrating to the public that it was genuinely concerned about social and environmental issues. This is one of the reasons why Shell has placed transparency at the forefront of its annual reports. Yet the overbookings scandal and other charges against the company in recent times show how great the divide is between ethical actions and its statements and ideals.

The essence of greenwash is the use of appealing social and environmental messages to influence the public into thinking that a company is environmentally friendly. If the company acts in ways counter to this, then the scandals, fines and legal breaches add substantial weight to claims that Shell has been engaging in a sophisticated greenwashing exercise, and is certainly not living up to its stated ethical principles. There is an irony at the heart of Shell's attempt to rehabilitate its reputation after 1995, then. What started out as a journey to restore its reputation has actually been a source of reputation risk for the company since that time.

THE LIMITS OF SHELL'S APPROACH TO BUILDING REPUTATIONAL CAPITAL

Despite its scandals and setbacks, Shell is a very different company today compared to what it was in 1995 when it found itself in crisis. The company has made record annual profits as a result of the resources boom, dissolved its duel ownership structure in 2005, and is more aware of its social and environmental obligations than it was when it sought to discredit anti-apartheid activists in the 1980s. In this sense, the company has made significant progress. This case study has sought to highlight the extent to which Shell's concerns about its damaged reputation led it to work through a process that it believed would help restore its reputation to health. The greatest achievement of anti-corporate activists (including Greenpeace) is to have compelled Shell to confront its past failings. However, as the more recent incidents demonstrate, Shell has not been entirely successful at managing its reputation. In the face of the over-bookings scandal, numerous regulatory breaches and suspicions that it has been greenwashing its image, the success of its reputation-building strategies has been blunted considerably.

Shell always viewed the challenge of building its reputation as primarily a public relations exercise (Henderson and Williams, 2002: 15). It employed some of the world's best PR professionals to help develop strategies to communicate its new business ethos to various stakeholder groups. For example, Ipsos MORI played a crucial intelligence-gathering role in the period immediately after the Ogoni Nine executions. Later, Fishburn Hedges was given a leading role in developing and improving Shell's reputation. However, it is arguable that a 'PR-led' approach was never going to lead to long-term reputational improvements. This is probably the reason why Shell has continued to attract greater criticism from anti-corporate activists than other large oil companies. Some of the reasons for this include a longstanding belief among critics of Shell, rightly or wrongly, that PR is more about spin than substance. Consequently, engaging PR firms to build reputational capital may actually have reinforced the assertion that Shell was greenwashing its image, undermining the very message it has been trying to communicate to stakeholders. Second, PR professionals are not experts in social and political matters. Shell may have been better served by seeking advice from ethicists, political scientists and sociologists. The contemporary global business environment is both complex and contradictory. The lack of understanding of international relations (IR), its actors and its dynamics is the area where reputations are now most vulnerable. Furthermore, employing PR professionals to develop reputational capital puts the emphasis in the wrong place. A strategy that relies heavily on advertising campaigns, television slots, glossy publications and interactive websites can yield only short-term reputational benefits.[24] Perhaps the most gaping problem with this strategy is that executives and employees play a largely passive role in building the company's reputation. According to Henderson and Williams (2002: 19), Shell's internal PR programme comprised workshops for brand executives to 'brief them on the strategy, receive input and comment and make any changes necessary' before the strategy went public. There is no place in this model for employees and managers to be reputation builders in a developmental sense. Kennedy's point noted in Chapter 2 continues to be valid today.

In 2000, Fombrun (2000: 90) described Shell as being portrayed in the media as 'patrician, slow moving, fat, rich, bureaucratic, and closed'. Two years later, after the company began to implement reforms, Fuller (2004: 20) argued '[f]or too long Shell has relied on its "culture", which it assumed was morally superior, to ensure good behavior. The test of its reforms – both internally and in its dealings with the outside world – will be whether its new systems pick up human failings before they infect the whole company'. Finally, Taylor (2006: 188) argues that one of Shell's main problems was that it lacked 'an ethical and compliant corporate culture'. There is something rather strange about a company that thinks that a public relations strategy can make it the world's most admired company, particularly when it is one of the heaviest polluters. This is either conceit or misguided idealism. The problem with a 'PR-led' approach is that it does not bring about the necessary ideational shift in values *within* the company. A shift in values must be meaningful to everyone in the organisation. Consequently, this cannot be accomplished by outsourcing it to marketing and PR consultants, even though they may be very skilled at what they do. Arguably, Shell's error is to assume that building reputational capital is an issue of effective communication strategies and clever marketing campaigns alone. Rather, such approaches must be combined with ethical action on the part of the organisation. While there is a place for PR professionals in helping a company to communicate its values and business principles to stakeholders, effective reputation-building needs to happen within the organisation. It is a ground-up task, not a top-down one. Put differently, a 'PR-led' approach to reputation-building will never make Shell a self-regulating corporation. But there is no doubt that the company has put in place the architecture to achieve this. Only time will tell whether it is successful in becoming one.

CONCLUSION

Shell is one of the first global MNCs to be challenged by the newly emerging business paradigm that we examined in Chapter 2. This paradigm 'demands' that MNCs act ethically towards the environment and the societies in which they operate, while remaining profitable. The twin disasters that befell Shell in 1995 highlighted the gulf between Shell's behaviour and these emerging imperatives. In a sense, Shell was caught with its pants down. It had no idea that the sea dumping of the Brent Spar and the trial of the Ogoni Nine would impact so negatively on its reputation. To its credit, it took the challenge seriously and made some important changes to its business model. Despite this, the company continues to be dogged by criticism.

One of the persistent criticisms of the company is that it is green-washing its image. I have argued in this chapter that there is prima facie evidence to support this claim. If we accept this, and take into account the continued legal breaches and the overbookings scandal, it is clear that Shell is not living up to its stated values. Part of the problem lies in a 'PR-led' approach to growing a strong corporate reputation. Such an approach may yield some short-term positive results, but it cannot deliver lasting ethical outcomes. The following case study examines the Toyota Motor Company. Like Shell, the company found itself embroiled in controversy in 2010. Moreover, it also handled the crisis badly, alienating key stakeholder groups.

NOTES

1. See Bakan (2005); Evans et al. (2002b); Gedicks (2001); Korten (2001); Moody (2005; 2007).

2. Enrico Mattei is credited with coining the term 'Sette Sorrelle' or 'Seven Sisters' in the 1950s. He used the term to refer to the seven biggest oil companies in the world and the close ties they had with each other, arguing that they were acting like a cartel. As head of ENI, Mattei wanted to ensure that Italy had its own independent oil supplies and sought to join the 'sisters', but was refused entry. The Seven Sisters were Jersey (Exxon), Socony Vacuum (Mobil), Standard Oil of California (Chevron), Texaco, Gulf Oil, Royal Dutch Shell, and British Petroleum. On the Seven Sisters see Yergin (2009: 483–7); Sampson (1975).

3. The site is run by Alfred and John Donovan (Donovan, 2010), two individuals who have run an anti-Shell campaign for many years.

4. In this sense, a cartel is a group of companies (usually producers) who collude to fix prices. Most governments regard cartel behaviour to be anti-competitive and, consequently, have laws in place to guard against such behaviour. On cartels see Connor (2008).

5. Public relations authors Healy and Griffin (2004: 33) refer to this as the strategy of 'tooting your own horn'.

6. The Brent Spar was also jointly owned by Esso, now ExxonMobil, in a joint venture called Shell Expro.

7. The convention is also referred to as the Oslo Convention. It has now been replaced by the Convention for the Protection of the Marine Environment of the North-East Atlantic. This treaty was signed in 1998. It is also known as the OSPAR Convention.

8. Many of these claims were exaggerated, as Greenpeace's apology to Shell some time later demonstrated.

9. What Greenpeace did not seem to consider at the time was the potential loss of life caused by breaking up the Brent Spar onshore or the potential for significant environmental damage to the coastline.

10. Bakir employs a social amplification of risk framework (SARF) to highlight the way that Greenpeace exploited the media and created a perception of the level of risk that the Brent Spar posed to the marine environment. The paper suggests that Greenpeace used three risk signals to convey their message. First, the Brent Spar was toxic. Second, Shell was a reckless polluting giant. Third, Shell was violating the moral sanctity of the deep ocean, and this would have repercussions for European society as a whole.

11. There is a large body of literature on Shell's activities in Nigeria. See, for example, Forrest (1993); Khan (1994); Frynas (1998); Omoweh (2005); Ariweriokuma (2008); Peel (2010).

12. This is especially the case with the Ogoni people.

13. See Osha (2007); Agbonifo (2009); Pegg (2000). On the role of oil companies in Niger Delta, see Okonta (2008); Okonta and Douglas (2003); Watts (2004).

14. Of course, Shell has vigorously denied many of these allegations. These denials are detailed in Okonta and Douglas (2003).

15. At the time Shell responded to a call from Human Rights Watch by denying that they had the right or the competence to intercede. As a senior Shell official in Nigeria replied: 'You have called Shell to get involved in, and to take a public stance on, several issues arising from the current situation – all of which are political. They are clearly issues where we as a commercial organization have neither the right nor the competence to get involved, and they must be addressed by the people of Nigeria and their government' (Human Rights Watch, 1999: 13). In November of that year, the Chairman of the Committee of Managing Directors of Shell in Nigeria did eventually plead for clemency for the Ogoni Nine, on humanitarian grounds. Unfortunately, the activists were executed a few days later (Hummels, 1998: 1403).

16. To prepare for the document, Shell undertook a series of interviews with politicians, government agencies, business leaders, NGOs and individuals from the media to gauge what expectations the public had of large multinational corporations, and business generally. The company also benchmarked itself against other similar companies. But arguably, the most important thing Shell did was to employ MORI (now Ipsos MORI), a UK public affairs and research company, to undertake a reputation survey of how Shell was perceived in the marketplace. According to Henderson and Williams (2002: 11), the

research was wide ranging and covered '7551 interviews with members of the general public in 10 countries; 1288 interviews with special publics in 25 countries, ranging from academics and investment fund managers to pressure groups, representatives of non-governmental organizations and journalists; and 583 questionnaires to senior Shell managers from 55 countries'.

17. Whatever else this document is, it is not a 'warts and all account', as the document claims. The Brent Spar crisis and the deaths of the Ogoni Nine receive only brief mention throughout the document. Nor does any external criticism of the company's behaviour during these events make it into the report. In fact, self-criticism only extends to saying that the company was not 'listening' to the community and was 'ill-prepared' for the public backlash against the sea dumping of the Brent Spar. And even here, the Shell report tries to put a positive spin on things. Yet the report is unique in corporate history, outlining in strong positive language the extent of Shell's commitment to change its behaviour.

18. Working from its three core values – honesty, integrity and respect for people – the company developed a number of operating principles to guide its business activities. These have been slightly modified since 1998, with the latest iteration coming in 2005. However, the business principles themselves are largely unchanged. They include: a commitment to being profitable; competing fairly in the marketplace; acting with integrity in its business dealings; acting within the law and complying with government regulations; a commitment to employee health, safety and security; a commitment to the environment; a commitment to contribute directly and indirectly to the well-being of the communities where Shell works; and ongoing dialogue and engagement with stakeholders. These principles are essentially the company's voluntary contract with society. Or, as Henderson and Williams (2002: 13) call it, Shell's 'licence to operate'.

19. See Laufer (2008: 165); Ramus and Montiel (2005).

20. The view that the world will run out of oil soon is generally referred to as 'peak oil'. Peak oil occurs when extraction and consumption outstrips the capacity of oil companies to replace their inventories. On peak oil see Deffeyes (2008). For a critique of peak oil hypothesis see Mirre (2013).

21. As Nielson (2005: 124) notes, '[t]housands of products depend heavily on crude oil: asphalt, plastics, fertilizer, medicines, insulation, glues, solvents, detergents, antiseptics, tyres, deodorants, shoes, dresses, pillows, boats, insect repellents, paint brushes, linoleum, wood filler, rubbish bags, TV cabinets, videotapes, CDs, film, loudspeakers, credit cards, telephones, sweaters, pantyhose, cassettes, toilet seats, life jackets, toys, contact lenses, car battery cases, hand lotion, fishing rods, water pipes, oil filters, and many more'.

22. See Doyle (2002); Cummins and Beasant (2005: 189–204); and Sluyterman (2010).

23. All international oil companies (IOCs) are required by law to publish their reserve holdings. During this period Shell over-stated its reserve holdings in order to maintain the price of its stock.

24. As King (2000: 6) notes, the spin doctor strategy is only able 'to provide them with short-term shifts in perception, rather than provide the multi-dimensional strategy needed to acquire reputational assurance'.

5. The rise and fall and rise of the Toyota Way

Orsatto and Clegg (1999: 264) argue that the automotive industry is 'the economic sector that is most emblematic of modern times and the polluting consequences of modernity'. Not only is it a major source of greenhouse gas emissions, it is also responsible for the release of other dangerous gases, referred to collectively as 'volatile organic compounds' (VOCs). Moreover, pollution from motor vehicles is linked to numerous health problems, particularly in the developing world. As Suzuki (1993: 138) argued some time ago: '[c]ar-generated air pollution degrades human health, causes premature death, and reduces crop yields'.

Putting to one side the health issues, the number of fatal motor vehicle accidents is staggering. According to a 2004 World Health Organization (WHO) study, approximately 1.2 million people died in car accidents globally that year, with about 250 000 in China alone (WHO, 2004: 3). The same study estimated that this figure will increase by approximately 65 per cent by 2020 (WHO, 2004: 35). The latest report from the WHO (2013) has revised the number of fatalities annually up to almost 1.24 million victims. The report also notes that 90 per cent of road deaths in the future will occur in low and middle-income countries.

The Organization of Motor Vehicle Manufacturers (OICA) published data points out that some 67 525 346 motor vehicles and 22 222 084 commercial vehicles were manufactured in 2014. Clearly, the footprint of motor vehicles on the world is enormous and, as developing countries such as Brazil, China and India experience accelerated economic growth, this number is sure to grow in the decades to come.[1]

Of all the major automotive companies, Toyota has been the most admired. The company's reputation for quality and safety, commitment to the environment, unique corporate philosophy, and streamlined manufacturing techniques, has set it apart from other car manufacturers. Indeed, while Ford, General Motors and Chrysler have been warding off bankruptcy for years, Toyota has continued to go from strength to strength.[2]

No company is immune from a crisis. It is a truism to say that the next corporate crisis is just around the corner for most companies. The first time Toyota had to manage a crisis was its battle with labour unions in

Japan in the 1950s. At that time, company president Kiichiro Toyoda sought to terminate a quarter of the company's workforce because of hard economic times. This move led to mass strikes in Japan and almost pushed the company into bankruptcy. Toyota and the Unions eventually negotiated a settlement. This allowed the company to release 25 per cent of its workforce, while at the same time guaranteeing the remaining workforce lifetime employment. In return, the company's employees agreed to more flexible work arrangements (Womack et al., 1990: 54). As part of the settlement, Toyoda resigned from the company. But it gave Toyota's management an opportunity to rethink aspects of the manufacturing process and the way in which it utilised its workforce. For the next five decades, the company would grow steadily, gaining the respect of its stakeholders and building a strong corporate reputation.

The chapter begins with an examination of Toyota's corporate philosophy and argues that the globalisation of Toyota has tested this philosophy markedly. I argue that transplanting The Toyota Way globally proved more difficult than the company realised. In the next section, I examine the car recall crisis that enveloped the company in 2009–10. This dented Toyota's reputation considerably. Following that, the key reasons for this reputational crisis are considered. In the final section, Toyota's capacity for self-regulation is examined. I argue that the philosophy of continuous improvement (*Kaizen*) which the company has returned to after the crisis, cannot guard against further crisis, as some writers have suggested. The reality of serious and unforeseen risk events is an ever-present problem for senior managers in the automotive industry. These so-called 'Black Swan' risk events are discussed later in the chapter.[3] A focus on corporate self-regulation may provide Toyota with a means to reduce the possibility of such events occurring. I am not suggesting that continuous improvement is a problematic ideal, only that corporate self-regulation offers a way of future-proofing the company. This is because corporate self-regulation is concerned with social, political, environmental and regulatory factors, as opposed to largely technical ones.

GLOBALISING THE TOYOTA WAY

As I have discussed in an earlier chapter, most MNCs today have committed themselves to a CSR agenda. They do this in various ways, ranging from philanthropy to pledging adherence to various international codes of ethical conduct. For example, over 80 of the world's largest oil,

gas and mining companies are now signatories to the Extractive Industries Transparency Initiative (EITI). Once a company has decided that it
should subscribe to a particular code of ethical conduct, it tends to
impose those principles on its employees. But this practice may not be
the best way for a company to instil such values. As Warren (1993: 189)
noted some years ago: '[a]ll too often ethical codes are handed down to
employees from the executive above, and the importance of trying to
create a "community of purpose" within the company is ignored'. In such
instances, employees have little or no ownership in the ethical development (and conduct) of the company. What Warren is referring to is the
development of a corporate philosophy which all employees 'own' and
are proud to support. This, I suggest, is one of the key things that sets
Toyota apart from many other MNCs. Not only does it have particular
guiding principles like most companies, it went further and developed a
unique corporate philosophy and culture based around its employees,
especially in Japan. Over the last 25 years, this philosophy has developed
and has become more sophisticated over time. Currently, it is referred to
as The Toyota Way.[4] It is a philosophy that is embraced by all employees
from the CEO down to the workers on the factory floor. As one US
advertising executive put it, The Toyota Way is 'almost like a religion'
(cited in Halliday, 2005).

Like Shell, Toyota has its roots in the last years of the nineteenth
century. The founder of the Toyota Industries Corporation, Sakichi
Toyoda, rose to success by designing and producing wooden looms that
were cheaper than those on the market at that time. Within a few years
Toyoda began to produce power-assisted looms that were technically
superior to their competitors. In 1937, the company turned its attention to
the production of automobiles and established the Toyota Motor Company.[5] Due to Japan's impending entry into World War II, the Japanese
Government would not allow the company to produce passenger vehicles.
Instead, it was forced to manufacture trucks in order to contribute to the
war effort. The company did produce a 'Type A' six-cylinder engine in
1934 and built several prototype cars during the war. It was not until after
the war ended that it was able to return to its goal of becoming a
world-class car manufacturer (Womack et al., 1990: 49).[6]

The two individuals most responsible for Toyota's initial success are
Eiji Toyoda and Taiichi Ohno (Ohno, 1988). Toyoda visited a Ford
production plant in 1950 and realised that there were inefficiencies in its
approach to mass production, something he believed Toyota could
improve on.[7] Ohno took these simple observations from Toyoda and
re-engineered every aspect of Toyota's manufacturing process. He understood the importance of a workforce that was flexible, experienced and

that could work in various parts of the assembly line. This approach came to be called the Toyota Production System (TPS).[8]

The TPS is a highly refined and sophisticated just-in-time approach to manufacturing. The key notion behind the TPS is eliminating waste or *muda*.[9] Ohno identified eight types of waste in the manufacturing process:

1. *muda* of transportation;
2. *muda* of motion;
3. *muda* of over-production;
4. *muda* of untapped employee potential;
5. *muda* of defects, scrap;
6. *muda* of inventory;
7. *muda* of waiting; and
8. *muda* of over-processing.

In order to reduce waste, Ohno redesigned the factory floor to make manufacturing processes more efficient and enable innovation in the supply chain. Moreover, the workforce was continually challenged to innovate and improve their skills.

A second feature of the TPS is *jidoka*. This refers to highlighting and visualising problems as they occur.[10] The aim of *jidoka* is to ensure a reduction in the time required to repair faults at the end of the assembly line. The term literally translates as 'intelligent automation' (Liker et al., 2008: 327). In practice, the TPS is the application of a scientific method to problems associated with mass-production. Spear and Bowen (1999: 98) note that the 'TPS creates a community of scientists. Whenever Toyota defines a specification, it is establishing sets of hypotheses that can then be tested. In other words, it is following a scientific method'.

The Toyota Way is essentially the philosophical articulation of the manufacturing principles established by Toyoda and Ohno. Since that time it has become part of the company's psyche and culture, and is something that all employees have a stake in. The Toyota Way, according to Liker et al. (2008: 13) has now superseded the TPS and is 'quite different in its emphasis'. The Toyota Way was first articulated in 2001 and comprises two philosophical pillars that underpin everything the company does, from informing its human resource management to driving its quality standards.[11] This is a broader focus than the TPS. It covers not just technical concerns, but issues of workforce management as well.

The first pillar is referred to as 'continuous improvement' and the second, 'respect for people'. While on the surface this seems a deceptively simple philosophy, in reality it is exceedingly complex. The company's former president and CEO, Katsuaki Watanabe, who has worked for the company for more than 40 years, declared that even he did not think he had a complete understanding of the philosophy (cited in Stewart and Raman, 2007: 80).

The three aspects of the 'continuous improvement' pillar are:

- *Challenge*: defined as forming a long-term corporate vision and meeting any challenges encountered with courage and creativity;
- *Kaizen*: defined as continuous improvement, with a drive for innovation and evolution;
- *Genchi genbutsu*: defined as go and see; that is, seek out the source in order to establish the facts, enabling informed decision making, facilitating consensus and efficient achievement of goals.

Pillar one represents the technical aspect of the company. In essence, these are key performance indicators that drive manufacturing excellence in the company.

The 'respect for people' pillar refers to the company's relationship with its employees, and stakeholders more broadly. This covers showing respect to colleagues, making an effort to understand colleagues, taking responsibility, and attempting to build mutual trust and teamwork, sharing development opportunities and improving individual and team performance.[12]

The Toyota Way's two pillars form the company's macro principles. A range of management principles flow on from each of these pillars. Liker et al. (2008: xxv) argue that The Toyota Way is both a philosophy and a corporate culture combined. The seeds of this philosophy and culture lie in a desire to see continual improvement in a manufacturing setting. This effectively means three things. The first is the elimination of waste from all aspects of the manufacturing process, including the production line and the supply chain, but also making employees more efficient. The second is ensuring that the company's employees are continually engaged in problem-solving, product development and personal improvement. The third is engendering a strong 'community of purpose' among all employees. By empowering employees within all parts of the company, The Toyota Way is a people-centred approach to corporate culture. As Liker (2004: 36) notes: '[t]he more I have studied the TPS and the Toyota Way, the more I understand that it is a system designed to provide the tools for people to continually improve their work. The Toyota Way means more dependence on people not less. It is a culture …'.

The outcome is an organic approach to manufacturing that is lean, able to produce high-quality products, with a workforce that is devoted to the company and proud of the quality of the products it produces. As Minoura's widely published quote puts it: '[a]n environment where people have to think brings with it wisdom and this wisdom brings with it kaizen' (Schermerhorn, 2012: C33).[13]

For most of the last 50 years, the TPS and The Toyota Way have been implicit in Toyota's approach to manufacturing and its people, and are responsible for taking the company from its humble beginnings to becoming the number one car manufacturer in the world in 2008. However, as the company began to diversify across different locales, it became clear that it needed to formalise its philosophy and culture, so that it would be understood by employees, in Japan and elsewhere. The first iteration of this took Toyota nearly a decade to produce. Cho (2001) notes in the final version of the document in 2001 that:

> [t]he rapid growth, diversification and globalization of Toyota in the past decade have increased the scope of our company's manufacturing and marketing presence throughout the world. Today, having invested authority and responsibility in a worldwide network of executives, we are preparing to operate as a truly global company guided by a common corporate culture.

As the company grew in size, reach, capacity and reputation, it needed to ensure that new employees in other countries understood and employed the principles of The Toyota Way, as effectively as Toyota's Japanese employees did. In order to achieve this, the company set up its Global Production Centre in 2003. The centre's two key functions are to educate employees on both The Toyota Way and the importance of quality assurance. According to a document on globalisation published by Toyota, the company needed to establish best practices and then spread this to affiliates around the world. To assist with this mission, nearly 2000 'coordinators' were trained, who have the role of ensuring that The Toyota Way is understood and practised in all of Toyota's plants (Stewart and Raman, 2007: 81). In addition, the company runs specialised training modules for foreign employees.

Toyota is acutely aware of the challenges it has faced in its journey to becoming the largest car manufacturer in the world. Former Toyota senior technical executive Koichi Ina (2012) notes: '[t]here are a number of hurdles that this globalization of production has to overcome. Among these the most important is quality assurance, which requires that "no

matter where Toyota vehicles are made, they have the same quality"
[sic]' (Paul and Kapoor, 2008: 264–5). Moreover, an analyst from JP
Morgan's Tokyo office noted that 'Toyota is growing more quickly than
the company's ability to transplant its culture to foreign markets. This is
a huge issue for Toyota, one of the biggest it will face in the decade
ahead' (cited in Dowling et al., 2008: 44). The question, then, is: how
well does an organic corporate philosophy and culture developed in
Japan translate into different cultural and corporate settings? This is an
issue I address later in the chapter. It is important now to examine the
reputational crisis that engulfed the company during this period of
expansion.

Toyota Hits a Reputational Speed Bump (2007–11)

Ever since Kiichiro Toyoda resigned from the company in the late 1950s,
Toyota's reputation has steadily improved. Making quality cars and
trucks had become a passion, if not an obsession, for the company. It is
no surprise that over the years Toyota has developed a standing in the
marketplace unlike any other automobile manufacturer, with the possible
exception of Mercedes Benz and BMW.

In 2014, the company was ranked by Fortune Global 500 as the 9th
biggest in the world, with revenues of US$256 billion, profits of US$18
billion, and assets of US$402 billion. While these financials are impres-
sive, the most outstanding fact is that in 2008 the company outperformed
General Motors in sales. This was the first time in 77 years that another
car manufacturer had beaten General Motors in the number of cars
sold.[14] Figure 5.1 highlights the sales figures of the major car manufacturers in 2008, when Toyota outsold General Motors.

The success of Toyota is partly due to the company's longstanding
reputation for building safe, reliable vehicles. Moreover, they can rightly
claim to be an environmentally sensitive manufacturer.[15] The Prius
hybrid-drive passenger vehicle, first sold in 1997, demonstrated to an
increasingly climate conscious public that Toyota is doing something
positive about global pollution and climate change. It is no coincidence,
then, that the Reputation Institute's annual Global Pulse survey found
that Toyota had the most respected reputation in the world that year
(Reputation Institute, 2008). While Google and Johnson & Johnson
ranked in the top five, the next best performing car manufacturer, Volvo
Bilar, had a reputation rank of 30. Moreover, in that year, the company
made US$19.9 billion profit. In addition, Toyota has also won the title of
the Japanese company with the best reputation in 2006, 2007 and 2008.

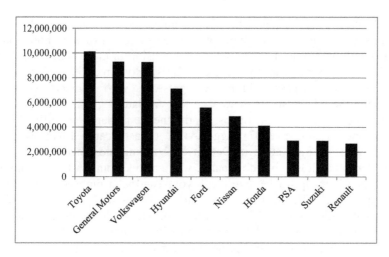

Figure 5.1   2008 motor vehicle sales by manufacturer

In 2009, *Business Week* estimated that the Toyota brand was valued at US$31.3 billion dollars, the 8th most valuable brand in the world.

Yet even as Toyota was being applauded as the most respected car maker in the world, signs were appearing that the company was about to have its reputation severely tested. In 2009, with the GFC in full swing, sales dropped by 1.3 million units and the company made a US$4.5 billion loss (Liker and Ogden, 2011: 25). This was the first loss in half a century. However, three other issues impacted heavily on the company's reputation. The first was its opposition to legislation requiring new fuel economy standards in California. The second was the massive recall crisis (there were two) after a number of road deaths. The third was poor crisis communication, not only from Toyota USA, but also from Akio Toyoda, the President of the company.

Toyota's Opposition to New Fuel Economy Standards in the US

In 2007, Toyota joined with Chrysler, Ford and General Motors to oppose the Californian Government's attempt to legislate a 30 per cent reduction in emissions over a ten-year period (Gallucci, 2012). Then, later in the same year, through the Alliance of Automobile Manufacturers, Toyota again sided with the Chrysler, Ford and General Motors in lobbying Congress to vote against legislation aimed at improving the fuel efficiency of newly manufactured cars. The Corporate Average Fuel Economy standards, if introduced, would commit car manufacturers to deliver a fuel economy standard of 35 miles per gallon by 2020. This would be a 10 miles per gallon improvement on current standards. The campaign to stop the passage of the legislation involved more than US$1 million worth of radio and TV advertising in those states with the highest sales of sport utility vehicles (SUVs) (Rosebro, 2007). Even after CAFE legislation passed through Congress, the auto industry continued to lobby the US President to weaken the standard.

Toyota's rationale for opposing the new standards is difficult to determine. Friedman (2007) suggests that it was because Toyota wanted 'to slow down innovation in Detroit on building more energy efficient vehicles, an area which it dominates, while also keeping mileage room to build giant pickup trucks, like the Toyota Tundra, at the gas-guzzler end of the market'. Friedman reasoned that Toyota could already meet the 35 miles-per-gallon standard in Japan and Europe, so lobbying against the standard in the US must have been to maintain their competitive edge.

It is true that Toyota was projecting a rise in sales in its SUV market and, consequently, it clearly wanted to protect this. Moreover, this class of vehicle would never achieve the new fuel economy standard. The Tundra had a 381 horsepower V8 engine that achieves a fuel economy of 14 to 18 miles per gallon.[16] The problem is that the SUV market will make an overall fleet fuel economy reduction of 35 miles per gallon very difficult to achieve. But the problem for Toyota was more profound than simply opposing legislation to protect a product line. By aligning itself with Chrysler, Ford and General Motors, Toyota weakened its reputation as an environmentally friendly car producer. Honda and Nissan did not join the lobby group. Indeed, they openly supported the new CAFE standards. Perhaps they sensed that joining the lobby groups was counterproductive. What is interesting is that, more than any other car manufacturer in the world, Toyota had built its reputation in the last decade on being an environmentally responsible manufacturer. The Union of Concerned Scientists (2007) even ranked Toyota second among US car makers for lowering greenhouse gas emissions across its fleet of vehicles. In opposing the new fuel economy standards, the company was clearly bringing itself to the attention of environmental groups and green consumers and consequently undermining its environmental credentials.

Road Deaths and Recalls

There is a chilling recording on YouTube of a 911 emergency call from a family travelling in a rented Toyota Lexus. Driven by an off-duty policeman, the car's accelerator pedal had become stuck, and one family member can be heard reporting the problem to the operator, desperately asking for their help. As the car sped through an intersection in San

Diego, it collided with another vehicle. Horrifyingly, the last words uttered by the caller were: 'we're approaching the intersection, we're approaching the intersection. Hold on guys. Pray, pray. Oh shoot. Oh, oh' (YouTube, 2010a; 2010b). At that moment, a loud thud can be heard on the recording, and the phone instantly goes silent. The car burst into flames and all the occupants were killed.

This was only one of a number of reports of unexpected accelerator problems with Toyota vehicles, going as far back as 1986. Safety Research and Strategy (2010), reported that there have been 3306 incidents of unexpected acceleration in Toyota vehicles including 1159 crashes, 469 injuries and 39 deaths. Other commentators suggest as many as 58 people may have been killed as a consequence of this fault. The cause of these accidents is still unclear. First, Toyota suggested that it was a problem with floor mats, in that the driver side floor mat would move out of position and jam the accelerator, causing the car to speed up without warning. A second possibility is that the electronic assembly that controls the acceleration was faulty.[17] While the company disagreed with these assessments, many external specialists believed they were the most likely cause of the company's problems (*Business Week*, 2010). In response, Toyota recalled about 8.5 million cars. At the time, this was the largest vehicle recall in US history. The recall occurred in two waves, as illustrated in Table 5.1.

The problem was not confined to the US, with the company recalling vehicles in China, Europe, Japan, South Africa and Australia. At the height of the recalls, shares in Toyota dropped by more than 7 per cent in Japan, as investors grew increasingly concerned about the profitability and reputation of the company (BBC News, 2010). The financial consequences of the recalls have been significant too. Dealers had to suspend selling some models, leading to a loss of unit sales. Sales staff at Toyota dealerships found themselves without an income. Production at some Toyota manufacturing plants was suspended, which led to temporary lay-offs. With the loss of sales, millions of dollars in government fines and settling a number of class action lawsuits, the total cost to the company will be prohibitive. The company also projected there would be lost sales of around 100 000 units. At the time, Toyota estimated the cost to be US$2 billion in the first quarter of 2010 alone (*The Guardian*, 2010b; Reuters, 2010).

As the crisis began to deepen, an internal presentation dated 6 July 2009 was made public by the National Highway Traffic Safety Administration (NHTSA). The presentation boasted that Toyota had negotiated favourable terms on the recall of some models. According to the presentation, US$124 million and 50 000 hours of work were saved by

Table 5.1   The two waves of motor vehicle recalls

Recall duration (years)	Model/make
First wave (floor mats)	
2004–09	Prius
2009–10	Venza
2006–10	RAV4
2009–10	Matrix
2008–10	Highlander
2009–10	Carolla
2005–10	Avalon
2005–10	Tacoma
2003–09	Runner
2007–10	Camry
2007–10	Tundra
Second wave ('sticky' accelerator assembly)	
2005–10	Avalon
2007–10	Camry
2007–10	Tundra
2008–10	Sequoia
2009–10	Corolla
2009–10	Matrix
2009–10	RAV4
2009–10	Venza
2010	Highlander

Source: Toyota (2011a; 2011b).

phasing in new safety regulations for side airbags, and US$11 million was saved by delaying a rule for tougher door locks (Thomas, 2009). While negotiation is a normal part of the working relationship between manufacturers and safety authorities, the release of the document in light of the deaths was damning. It demonstrated to the public that, contrary to Toyota's claims of putting safety first, it had compromised safety in order to save money.

Car manufacturers in the US are legally obliged to notify the NHTSA within five days of becoming aware of a safety defect in a vehicle. In February 2010, Ray LaHood, Head of the NHTSA, announced that it would investigate whether Toyota knew about the accelerator problem before the issue became public and, if so, how long it had known about the problem. In April that year the investigation revealed that Toyota knew of the defect four months before it became public. As a consequence, Toyota was fined US$16.37 million. This was the largest fine ever handed out to a car manufacturer in the US (NHTSA, 2010). Toyota could have challenged the fine in court, but it promptly accepted liability and paid it (CNN, 2010).

The damage to Toyota's reputation has been significant. Every major US news service has carried stories about the recall. One daytime television programme had a segment titled 'Toyota's Deathathon', running every day for a week. In equally flamboyant language, Illinois Congressmen Bobby Rush suggested that Toyota cars had the potential to be 'killing machines' (Neufeld, 2011). One news story (Jones, 2010) referred to Toyota as the 'Tiger Woods of motoring', inferring that the damage to Toyota's brand image was similar to that which followed revelations about Tiger Woods' infidelities.

Poor Crisis Communication

Effective communication is a necessary condition for the success of any business venture. But it is especially the case during a crisis. While it is not necessary to delve into the crisis communications literature here, two principles stand out. The first is the timeliness of the response and the second is the authenticity of the response. We saw in an earlier chapter how the President of Exxon's response to the oil spill in Prince William Sound was neither timely, nor did he come across as sincere. The American public were left with a similar impression of BP's boss, Tony Hayward, in the wake of the Deepwater Horizon disaster.

It is difficult to know why this is such a common problem among senior managers. It may be that they are complacent. They simply have not thought about the possibility of a crisis or how to handle it. It may be that a form of personal paralysis sets in. Or, possibly no one in authority within the organisation has expertise in handling a large-scale global crisis, so it falls to the CEO by default. Indeed, in the case of Toyota, it may be a combination of all these factors which led the company to deal with the crisis badly.

In Japan, Toyota's CEO and President, Akio Toyoda, was forced to apologise on national television and perform a ritual bow of remorse to the audience. Even the Japanese Government weighed in, suggesting that Toyota's crisis was not simply an isolated company issue, it was an event that undermined the entire Japanese automotive industry, and trust in

Japanese products more broadly (*The Australian*, 2010). Perhaps most embarrassing for Toyota was the highly publicised attendance of several senior executives at two days of congressional senate hearings to answer questions about the company's safety record. Toyoda is reported to have stated at the hearings, '[w]e are in the midst of a crisis and face big challenges ahead' (*The Guardian*, 2010a).

While the recall crisis was underway, the company began to devise a strategy to repair its reputation as a builder of high-quality, safe and reliable motor vehicles. The first glimpse of this strategy appeared in an article in *The Washington Post* by Toyoda (2010). The article begins with an apology. 'I am deeply disappointed by that [the crisis] and apologize. As the president of Toyota I take personal responsibility. That is why I am personally leading the effort to restore trust in our word and in our products'. Toyoda then outlined four things the company planned to do to rebuild trust in their products. First, the company would launch a review of their global operations and establish an Automotive Centre of Quality Excellence in the US. Second, it would establish an external safety advisory group to review operations. When the group reported, the company would make their findings available to the public and the company would respond to the findings promptly. Third, the company would investigate all customer safety complaints 'aggressively'. Finally, new structures would be put in place to improve the lines of communication with the NHTSA. Perhaps most notably is his renewed commitment to The Toyota Way. The following year the company re-launched its Global Vision 2020 as a response to the crisis. The purpose of this document was to further build on the company's earlier commitments.

HOW DID TOYOTA LOSE ITS 'WAY'?

Deconstructing the causes of a corporate crisis is a necessary activity, both for the company that weathered the storm, but also for other companies seeking to protect themselves under similar circumstances. It is also important for public relations and reputation specialists seeking to advise companies on how best to respond to future crises. The Toyota crisis is unique for four reasons. First, compared to its competitors, Toyota had one of the strongest brands in the world, and one of the best reputations. There are very few examples of companies that have had strong reputations and then have fallen so spectacularly. Second, few other reputational crises have impacted the national consciousness in the way that this impacted on the Japanese; it genuinely hurt Japanese pride. Consequently, the crisis has had a cultural impact. As Fujita argues:

'Toyota has failed to measure up to international standards; it's also failed to measure up to Japanese expectations' (VOA News, 2010). At a time when the Japanese economy has performed so poorly, and China has overtaken it to become the second largest economy in the world, Toyota was a company that all Japanese could be proud of. Third, given the high regard in which The Toyota Way has been held around the world, the crisis has undermined Toyota's (and Ohno's) core philosophy. Consider the hundreds of courses on lean manufacturing that are run regularly around the world, which tell of the almost perfect marriage between a corporate philosophy and a manufacturing system. Think of the countless hours Toyota's employees have spent learning about the exceptional qualities inherent in The Toyota Way. All of this was called into question. Finally, and perhaps most damaging of all, those devotees of The Toyota Way have had their ideals undermined. James Womack, President of the Lean Enterprise Institute, offers an insight into this kind of idealism: '[w]hat is reassuring for the country [US] is that if GM and Ford can't fix their problems, they will simply be replaced by new players in America, led by Toyota, who can' (Womack, 2006). The Toyota crisis, then, brought about a need for Toyota to re-evaluate many of its management and manufacturing practices.

What, then, are the causes of this crisis? According to Akio Toyoda (*The Guardian*, 2010a), the problem stemmed from the company's rapid growth trajectory:

> Toyota has, for the past few years, been expanding its business rapidly. Quite frankly, I fear the pace at which we have grown may have been too quick. I would like to point out here that Toyota's priority has traditionally been the following: First; Safety, Second; Quality, and Third; Volume. These priorities became confused, and we were not able to stop, think, and make improvements as much as we were able to before, and our basic stance to listen to customers' voices to make better products has weakened somewhat. We pursued growth over the speed at which we were able to develop our people and our organization, and we should sincerely be mindful of that [sic].

There is some truth to these assertions. Between 2004 and 2008, the company's profitability increased relative to that of Ford and General Motors, both of which suffered substantial losses during that period. Yet it now seems that Toyota's historical achievement has come at a high price, for the company and its reputation.

It is clear that such rapid growth, especially in the US, combined with further diversification into other markets, such as China and India, has increased Toyota's management challenges. The popular business press in the US highlighted three other factors that it believed contributed to the crisis. These are: (a) the company's management style and Toyota's corporate structure; (b) a cost-cutting drive from 2004 onwards; and (c) Japanese culture.

Corporate Management and Structure

Japanese firms have a unique approach to management. Abegglen (2006: 73–4) identifies three characteristics that he believes defines this approach. The first is the unique relationship between the company and the workforce and a communal approach to economic security. This is a relationship where employees are provided with lifetime employment in return for loyalty to the company and the brand. The second feature is a reward system which remunerates employees according to their seniority in the company. The third characteristic is a strong trade union system that enables all employees to be part of a single negotiating organisation. While this approach to management has clearly served the country well for the last 40 years or so, there are signs that the hierarchical and communal approach to management may no longer be in Japan's best economic interests.

The Japanese economy has been underperforming for more than a decade. Mitsubishi, Nissan and Mazda have experienced financial difficulties at different times over the years, and Sanyo has disappeared altogether. Toyota is simply the latest example of a more deeply rooted problem in the way Japanese companies manage their affairs in an era of globalisation. Specifically, commentators argue that Toyota has very hierarchical and outmoded management systems and structures, where problems tend to take time to filter up. This may be the reason why senior executives in Japan took so long to comment formally on the crisis. As Stewart (2010) put it, Toyota suffers from 'insularity and parochialism, and a hierarchical structure that discouraged innovation or input from others'. Put differently, there is a serious disconnect between The Toyota Way and the day-to-day running of the company. It was only after CEO and President Akio Toyoda received a call from the Japanese Prime Minister that the company responded publicly. Furthermore, this has led some critics to claim that Toyota lacks transparency. It is secretive and uncommunicative, and its vertical organisational structure limits contact with other suppliers and providers. The company is also highly bureaucratic. All key decisions are made by Toyota in Japan, making it challenging for the company to respond to a problem elsewhere in a timely fashion. In the case of the road deaths and recalls crisis, Toyota USA had to wait for Toyota Japan to provide the necessary guidance on how best to manage the crisis. Being such an insular company, Toyota's senior managers apparently failed to grasp the urgency of the situation.

Cost-cutting Drive

Another explanation for the crisis is that Toyota had been on a cost-cutting drive and this undermined the quality of vehicles rolling off the production line. Between 1999 and 2005, the company's former CEO and President Katsuaki Watanabe reduced global operating costs by $10 billion (Ohnsman et al., 2010). This was the first in a series of cost-cutting measures aimed at reducing expenditure on parts and production, and decreasing the time it took to get motor vehicles to market. This led to a loss of quality and a reduction in the company's capacity to solve problems at the assembly line. Indeed, one of Toyota's senior US managers claims that he had warned his Japanese bosses that vehicle quality was slipping (Ohnsman et al., 2010). Another example of this kind of problem is the company's approach to a pre-production problem with the 2002 to 2006 Lexus ES models. Despite complaints from American Toyota engineers about transmission problems with the models, the car went into production without the problem being addressed. Over the next few years, thousands of dissatisfied customers would bring about a lawsuit against the company, and a federal safety investigation would be launched into the transmission problems. It seems that Toyota's strategy was to try to reduce costs by limiting repairs only to those customers who issued complaints, ignoring those that did not (Bensinger and Vartabedian, 2010).

Japanese Culture

Another line of criticism is that Japanese culture is primarily at fault. There is a tendency in Japanese culture to avoid conflict and controversy, to defer to senior managers, to be reluctant to pass on bad news, and a historical defensiveness towards the outside world. As Seeger (2010) notes:

> Japanese corporate culture generally emphasizes harmony and tends to avoid publically [sic] addressing problems, preferring to manage them behind the scenes. Efforts at decision making and problem solving in Japanese firms rely on more consensual processes as opposed to directives from top management. Consensus is a time consuming process and may slow down the organization's response to a crisis.

There are two good examples of this. First, Toyoda's tardiness in dealing with the Japanese and American public as the crisis unfolded, demonstrating that he had little understanding of how to manage a crisis. The second relates to governance. As *The Economist* (2010a) pointed out at the time, Toyota's Board of Directors comprises 29 men, all of whom are Japanese. *The Economist* further notes '[t]here is a greater percentage of women on boards in Kuwait than Japan'. There is a large amount of evidence to suggest that boards that have a good gender balance perform better than those who do not. Similarly, a senior management team that comprises a number of international directors might also have helped to improve the company's crisis response. Indeed, from the perspective of this chapter, globalising Toyota, without globalising the Board, appears to have been a huge corporate governance issue.

All of the explanations are probably correct. Yet none answers the questions of why the crisis began in America and why The Toyota Way failed the company so spectacularly. I would argue that the source of the problem lies in the process of globalisation that the company has been going through over the last decade or so.

As noted in Chapter 1, globalisation is often presented as an idea that drives economic growth, wealth creation and innovation. In other words, it is a process that leads to beneficial outcomes and human flourishing. Some years ago, the former Australian Foreign Minister, Alexander Downer, echoed these sentiments: 'globalisation is an irreversible trend. It is happening. And it is good for all Australians, the region and the world' (cited in Firth, 1999: 275).

However, the picture is far more complex than this, at least from a business and manufacturing point of view. The challenges of operating and investing globally, across multiple jurisdictions, should not be underestimated. While globalisation may bring tangible benefits to companies, it also increases their exposure to risk. This makes foreign investment a difficult and complex business.

Toyota is not the first company to find that there are serious downside risks, not only with the globalisation of a production system, but with the corporate culture that underpins it. Indeed, the last 15 years are replete with examples of failure during an expansionary period. This book has offered a few interesting examples of this problem. As one of the largest, fastest growing companies in the world, it is inevitable that Toyota would suffer a risk event at some point. It is clear that the company has been overly confident in the capacity of The Toyota Way to deliver the rewards that it did for Toyota in Japan. The question is whether its indigeneity can sufficiently guide the company going forward. It may be for this reason that on 9 March 2011 the company (re)released a document titled 'The Toyota Global Vision 2020'.

TOYOTA'S CAPACITY FOR SELF-REGULATION: A WORK IN PROGRESS

'The Toyota Global Vision 2020' is both a healing document and a strategic one. It is a healing document in that it acknowledges the failings of the company during the crisis. It is a strategic document in that it looks to regaining the trust of its customers and stakeholders, and the eventual rehabilitation of its reputation.[18] The document commits the company to a number of things. The first is to continue to advance technologically and develop new modes of personal mobility. Second, to continue to build safe products that enhance people's happiness and well-being. Third, to continue to reduce waste and to minimise the environmental impacts of its products. Fourth, to develop new management structures. Finally, and perhaps most importantly, are those aspects of the document that deal directly with the handling of the crisis. It admits the company was slow to react once the crisis hit and that they did not listen to concerns of their customers. In response to the first point, Global Vision 2020 promises to give their regional centres of operation a greater degree of autonomy and decision-making capacity. In the event of a problem occurring, it can be dealt with quickly and efficiently, the document says. Global Vision 2020 also highlights the need for the company to listen to customer feedback in order for it to make quicker (and better) management decisions.

As with most vision statements, this is one that is not short of platitudes. Perhaps the most interesting of these is 'reminding us to "be kind and generous" and to "create a warm homelike atmosphere" ... [t]he smiles that we earn from our customers are our greatest reward'. By and large, though, the document looks to the future, while clearly learning some lessons from the past. Most emphatically, though, it continues the company's commitment to The Toyota Way, with its philosophy of continuous improvement.

During a crisis, much of the information comes from news outlets, magazines, radio and television, and other online sources, such as blogs. From an academic point of view such material is appropriate to recount the events. However, the intellectual commentary tends to emerge a year or two later, after academics have had a chance to digest the crisis, put pen to paper, and go through the normal peer review processes. This is what is now emerging in relation to the Toyota crisis.[19]

Perhaps the most significant intellectual contribution to the crisis and its aftermath is the book by Liker and Ogden (2011). Liker is a long-time Toyota scholar, so it is no surprise that this book is the first full-length manuscript to appear in print. The book follows a similar line of reasoning to a 2010 paper by Liker, suggesting that The Toyota Way is not undermined by the crisis. The original paper concludes that, despite the problems, The Toyota Way had the capacity to lead the company forward and 'if Toyoda is successful in leading Toyota to another level of customer responsiveness, we may have an even better model for excellence in the future' (Liker, 2010: 33). In other words, despite the crisis, the principles behind The Toyota Way have the capacity to revive the company's reputation for excellence, and perhaps catapult it to a higher level of service and safety.

The sub-title of the book hints at this possibility. It is 'Lessons for Turning Crisis into Opportunity'. The book (2011: v) charts the fortunes of Toyota from the Global Financial Crisis (GFC) through to the 2009–10 recall crisis. It presents a very sympathetic picture of the company and its woes, debunking a great deal of the media criticism. The main argument of the book is that the company lacked good communications skills at many levels. Communication channels between the various operations around the world were poor. As Toyoda (2010) himself notes, 'we failed to connect the dots between problems in Europe and problems in the United States'. Toyota's communication with their customers over their safety concerns was also poor in the period leading up to the crisis. Communication with the regulator was equally problematic and fraught.

According to Liker and Ogden (2011), there are a number of lessons that can be learned from the crisis. A corporate culture that seeks to blame one party or another will find it difficult to manage a crisis. Accepting responsibility for mistakes – whether the company is right or wrong – is critical to recovering and rebuilding long-term value. Even companies with the best corporate cultures can develop weaknesses. Finally, a globalising culture needs to balance localisation and globalisation in its communication and decision-making. They conclude (2011: 236) that the essence of turning crisis into opportunity is to understand that:

> [a] company that is simply trying to survive a crisis, to get back to the status quo ante, is never going to do better than that. A company that is dedicated to continuous improvement, to constantly moving the goalposts to a higher level of performance will expect much more from its crisis response. In fact, the crisis becomes less an obstacle to be overcome and more another tool in the arsenal of continuous improvement.

There is a teleological quality in this sentiment. Continuous improvement punctuated by crisis presents an opportunity to further improve the company's performance. What they seem to be saying is that a crisis is good for companies that focus on continuous improvement. Perhaps it has a jolting effect on management and allows time for self-reflection. This seems to be the sentiment of Jim Lentz, president of Toyota Motor Sales USA.

> As we went through this [crisis], and the water level dropped, we started noticing some of the rocks that had been there all the time, but they got kind of hidden by success and a big marketplace. So, I guess, in the long run, going through this is a good thing (Liker and Ogden, 2011: 235).

Coming on the heels of its first financial loss in 50 years, it is a matter of conjecture whether the recall crisis was 'a good thing' for the company. Perhaps the same outcome could have been achieved without the cost, disruption to business, loss of reputation, and damage to one of the world's most respected brands.

What the recall crisis calls attention to is the capacity of Toyota for corporate self-regulation. Toyoda's admission in front of the US Congress, and Lentz's view that there were issues (the rocks) lingering below the surface, is an admission that the company had fallen well short of the ideals encapsulated in The Toyota Way. Whether this was a consequence of arrogance, Japanese management style and the culture of the company, globalisation, or the company's fast-paced rise to the number one spot amongst the world's automakers, the point is that the company that expressed the ideals of quality, safety and reliability rose to prominence on the back of this mantra. In the end, it failed to deliver these qualities to its customers. It does not matter whether the media commentary was unfair or whether Congress used the crisis to enhance the standing of the Detroit Three. The point is that Toyota had the expertise, the culture and the positioning in the marketplace to have avoided these issues and we must not forget that people died as a consequence of its failure. Lentz suggested that the company focused too much on technological advancements. He is right. This is precisely what let the company down. Once the company's technological prowess was called into question, The Toyota Way lost its value and customers began to lose faith in the product and the message that accompanied it. I have no doubt that Liker (2010) is right about the crisis not invalidating 'its vaunted production system'. The crisis does, however, invalidate the company's capacity for self-regulation. As we have seen, corporate self-regulation is not about a production system, it is about understanding the interactions between politics, ethics and society. It is also about understanding that the regulatory architecture governing the industry is a minimum standard. One of the messages of the following chapter is precisely this. Interface, when challenged on its environmental credentials, quickly understood that the regulation of high-polluting companies in the US was ineffective to bring about a meaningful change to the climate. They learned to get well ahead of the status quo.

The idea of continuous improvement, which lies at the heart of The Toyota Way, is inherently dangerous. It is not that improving the company's behaviour and performance is a problem. It is that continuous improvement is simply not possible over time. At some point, a day of reckoning will come for all companies when they find themselves in trouble. Toyota's trouble occurred between 2008 and 2010. Unfortunately, the continuous improvement mantra is an unsustainable one. Like life, companies cannot count on the concept of continuous improvement to save them from crisis and reputation risk. Toyota would be well advised to tread cautiously here, despite the rhetoric of the many Toyota watchers.

The continuous improvement mantra is like a somatic drug. Once we interpret a crisis as an opportunity, Toyota's traditional narrative kicks in. This is how Liker and Ogden approach the issue. A crisis is an opportunity for improvement. I wonder how many companies would like to have an expensive crisis each year, if it meant an opportunity for continuous improvement. I suspect not many.

What is missing from the continuous improvement narrative is a deep appreciation of the unpredictable nature of risk. It is as if a return to the idealism of The Toyota Way is a solution to Toyota's current reputational woes. This is conjecture. I would have thought some political science savvy would have been a more valuable aid to the company now, rather than a simple return to their corporate first principles. After all, it was these same first principles that derailed the company in the first place.

Taleb's (2010) celebrated book confirms the persistence of this problem. The premise of the book is insightful. In the seventeenth century Europeans thought that all swans were white. It was not until naturalist John Latham first described the first black swan scientifically that this generally held view was proved false. This metaphor suggests that just because people hold a particular view based on available evidence does not mean that it cannot be falsified. The discovery of one black swan in Western Australia falsified hundreds of years of belief about the colour of swans in Europe.

Taleb uses this story to focus attention, not on what we know, but on what we do not know and what we cannot predict. He calls these 'Black

Swans' or 'Black Swan Events'. Black Swan Events have three characteristics. They tend to be outliers; that is, they tend to fall outside regular expectations. Second, they have extreme impacts. Third, human beings tend to develop – he says concoct – narratives to make the unpredictable predictable. As he summarises it: 'rarity, extreme impact, and retrospective (though not prospective) predictability' (2010: xxii).

It is important to note that Black Swan Events can be positive and negative. Taleb's point is that human beings crave predictability so they tell themselves comforting narratives. Consequently, they think about probabilities and risk and attempt to forecast or map the future. For example when governments bring down an annual budget, they do so on the *ceteris paribus* assumption that growth will continue at 3.5 per cent for the next three years, and make economic and social policy based on this number. Australia's Treasurer Joe Hockey's first budget forecast a particular level of revenue. What he did not factor in was a collapse in commodity prices, thus undermining his budget and the assumptions that underpinned it. Over the three-year cycle, he had to write off AU$25 billion in revenue.

Taleb, then, is arguing that we are far more likely to be impacted by random occurrences and have far less control of our lives, our economies, our businesses, and our future than we think. It is clear, too, that Taleb does not think much of statistics, economics, and the American social and political science that seek to model the social and political world on the natural sciences. Unpredictability is the norm, not the exception.

The simple point of relevance for Toyota and its future is that it has far less capacity to ward off another unforeseen crisis in the future. It is interesting that most of the commentary and academic literature on the Toyota crisis couches its arguments in damage to the brand, the need for image repair, crisis communication, the role of management and corporate governance. In other words, the predominant perspective is a business one. However, the moment the crisis began to bite, it became a political crisis. Regulators became involved and US Congress demanded explanations from the company. The Japanese government played a part in the politics as well. Individuals voted with their feet, and for a time stopped buying Toyotas. This, too, is a political act. And the politics was played out to good effect in the world's media.

Toyota has begun to rebound from the crisis. In 2014, sales numbers returned to about where they were in 2008. As Figure 5.2 demonstrates, Toyota again sold over 10 million vehicles.

What is missing from the continuous improvement narrative and Global Vision 2020, its sustainability reports and its CSR commitments, is an understanding that politics and the market cannot easily be

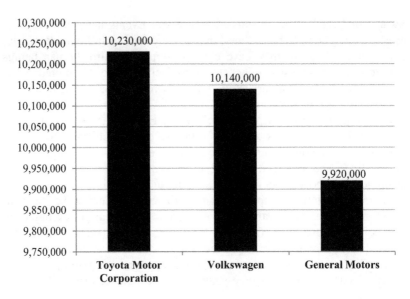

*Figure 5.2   2014 motor vehicle sales of Toyota, Volkswagen and General
              Motors*

separated. This is why corporate self-regulation has an important part to
play in rebuilding Toyota's reputation in the automotive industry and in
the community. To get the politics right means leading the industry in
advancing well beyond existing regulation, becoming climate neutral
and sustainable globally, and developing a viable path to zero waste. This
is the challenge for Toyota if it wants to become a self-regulating
corporation.

CONCLUSION

The chapter began by examining Toyota's corporate philosophy. Subsequently I looked at the problems that befell the company in 2007–10. The
next section examined some of the reasons given in the popular media for
the crisis. Some of the explanations included corporate management and
structure, a cost-cutting drive after 2004, and Japanese culture. All of
these explanations have some validity, but I argue that, even though the
company acknowledged that transplanting The Toyota Way globally was
a difficult task, it underestimated just how difficult this was going to be.

The final section began by looking at Toyota's efforts to rehabilitate itself after the crisis, in particular the launch of its Global Vision 2020, an updated version of an earlier document. The key feature of this document is that it had input from management outside of Japan. This suggests that the company is keen for it to be a global document, of relevance to the whole company. This lends further evidence to the suggestion that the company did not globalise well. Indeed, I noted the incongruity of the company globalising its manufacturing, without globalising its Board of Directors. Globalisation was not the gift the company thought it would be.

I also noted that the Global Vision 2020 returned the company's focus back to its continuous improvement narrative. I noted that Toyota's view, as well as Liker and Ogden's, has a teleological feel to it. In contrast, as argued above, it is Taleb's view that randomness and unpredictability are the norm. It is interesting that Taleb cites three characteristics: that a Black Swan event is an outlier, that it has enormous impacts, and that a rationalisation takes place after it. In many respects, this is exactly how to characterise the Toyota crisis and its response, if we think of Global Vision 2020 as the rationalisation. Ultimately, the continuous improvement narrative can only protect the company from a future crisis in a limited way. I concluded that the best way to think of the recall crisis is as a political crisis, not a technical one. This is where the idea of corporate self-regulation can be of most service to the company. It has regulatory, social, political and environmental dimensions. This is something The Toyota Way is at its weakest. Ultimately, Toyota is a work-in-progress on the corporate self-regulation front.

The next chapter examines the journey of Interface Inc. The company began by eliminating waste and this has allowed the company to pursue the goal of being climate neutral by 2020. There is an interesting irony here. Interface Inc.'s own journey begins with *muda*, something the company learned from Toyota.

NOTES

1. According to *The Guardian* (2010b), China produced 13.5 million cars in 2009, with the Chinese Government predicting annual growth in the car market of around 45 per cent. This is an increase of more than 6 million cars a year. Consequently, the car industry continues to face immense challenges in relation to climate change.
2. The 'Detroit Three' are General Motors, Ford and Chrysler.
3. Blacks Swans are unpredicable, random events, and are regarded as the norm, rather than the exception (Taleb, 2010).

4. Some of the most well-known literature on the Toyota Way are Liker (2004); Liker et al. (2008); Monden (2011); Morgan and Liker (2006); May (2007); Ohno (1988); Reingold (1999); Womack et al. (1990).
5. Prior to that the company was known as Toyota Industries.
6. On the history of the automobile see Glancey (2008); Kimes (2004).
7. Fordism is a manufacturing technique named after Henry Ford. The term was first used by Antonio Gramsci (2011) in his Prison Notebooks. Gramsci recognised that the model of manufacturing employed by Ford would lead to a complete change in how modern society functioned. As Harvey (1992: 125–6) explains: '[w]hat was special about Ford ... was his vision, his explicit recognition that mass production meant mass consumption, a new system of the reproduction of labour power, a new politics of labour control and management, a new aesthetics and psychology, in short, a new kind of rationalized, modernist, and populist democratic society'.
8. This is referred to in the US as Lean Manufacturing.
9. We shall see in the final chapter that this is also the starting point for Interface's 'climb up mount sustainability'. On *muda* see Hawken et al. (2008).
10. Just-in-time manufacturing is a manufacturing process where items are made to meet demand, not simply produced as surplus stock ahead of demand.
11. In an interview, Watanabe argued that he attached 'the greatest value and importance to quality; that lies at the root of my management style. It's critical for Toyota to keep making the highest quality vehicles in the world – the best products in every way, manufactured without any defects. Unless we enhance quality today, we can't hope for growth in the future' (cited in Stewart and Raman, 2007: 77).
12. Adapted from Liker et al. (2008). I would also like to take the opportunity here to thank Jeffrey Liker for some materials on Toyota. Of course, the views expressed here are entirely my own.
13. *Kai* means change, while *zen* means good. Together it equals continuous improvement.
14. In 2008, General Motors posted vehicle sales of US$4540 million, while Toyota posted sales of US$4818 million.
15. The Prius is a hybrid-drive vehicle with low emissions and excellent fuel economy.
16. Toyota has also recently redesigned its Land Cruiser, Lexus LX 570 and Sequoia, all of which have a 5.7 V8 engine and a six-speed automatic transmission.
17. All of the recalled vehicles had accelerator assemblies made in the US by a local company called CTS Corporation in Elkhart, Indiana.
18. Much of the same reasoning lies behind the publication of Shell's sustainability reports.
19. See Choi and Chung (2013); Fan et al. (2013); Heller and Darling (2012; 2011); Andrews et al. (2011); Quelch et al. (2011); Liker (2010).

6. Interface Inc.: a model of a self-regulating corporation?

Unlike Royal Dutch Shell and the Toyota Motor Corporation, Interface Inc. has never been the subject of a severe reputational crisis.[1] The company has never had to endure ongoing media attacks, serious government sanctions, or vocal complaints from anti-corporate activists. In many respects, Interface is a model corporate citizen, a poster child for a new approach to business that Jackson (2004) defined earlier in the book.

Interface is a relatively small company compared with the other two goliaths of industry. Interface's revenues of US$960 million in 2013 and US$1004 million in 2014 are modest by comparison. The relatively small size of the company has, probably, allowed it more easily to become a self-regulating corporation. The lessons that Interface has learned about its manufacturing processes, about how to reduce waste and innovate, and how to develop a strategy to become carbon neutral by 2020, has set a new benchmark in leadership, vision and cultural change within corporations.

The Interface Model (now called Mission Zero) is a 'eureka' moment in business conduct. The company offers a new way of thinking about the relationship between business and society; one that also takes seriously the environmental challenges that the earth faces. There are other examples of MNCs moving toward self-regulation. These include Unilever, Patagonia, Green Mountain Coffee Roasters, Stonyfield Farm, Timberland and Ecover, among others. Each of these companies is worthy of analysis as they progress toward self-regulation.

However, there are a number of reasons why Interface is a compelling case study. The first is the unique environmental and business philosophy of its founder and chairman Ray C. Anderson. Arguably, no business leader in America has done more to make people aware of the looming environmental crisis, and the need urgently to address it than Anderson.

He has written two books on Interface's journey towards sustainability, contributed to more than 100 books, given over 1500 lectures on the subject, has been interviewed on television and radio numerous times, and has co-chaired the Clinton Administration's Council on Sustainable

151

Development. In 2008, he was a member of an esteemed panel that delivered a 100-point Climate Action Plan to US President Barack Obama.

Anderson has also been the subject of a number of documentaries, including *The Corporation* (2004), *Big Ideas for a Small Planet* (2007), *The 11th Hour* (2007), *So Right, So Smart* (2009) and *I Am* (2011). In 1996, *Forbes* named him entrepreneur of the year and in 2007 *Time* named him a hero of the environment. That same year, *Elle Magazine* honoured him for his environmental work. He has also been awarded a number of honorary doctorates by universities across the US.

Second, the company began its journey toward self-regulation in 1994. At that time, it was probably the first company seriously to come to grips with the impact of its business operations on the environment. As McDonough (2007) notes, '[w]hat really set him apart was the fact that Anderson stood up early in a very public way with a commitment to making his business accountable'.

Third, Interface's employees are intimately connected to Anderson's environmental vision. Anderson tells a story of a visitor from another factory who voiced her scepticism about the company's drive toward sustainability. During a break in the presentations, she met an employee and they began chatting. After a few minutes, he said to her 'Ma'am, I don't want to be rude, but if I don't get this role of carpet to the next process right now, our waste and emission numbers are going to go way up' (Anderson, 2009: 170).[2] Anderson notes that after this brief encounter her scepticism faded. The internal programme that underpinned this approach is now called QUEST: Quality Utilizing Employees' Suggestions and Teamwork. In addition to QUEST, the company has also introduced specialised employee training programmes (called The Natural Step) and incentive schemes for improved environmental performance.[3] On the surface, at least, there appears to be a well-developed synergy between what Anderson wanted for Interface and the commitment of employees and stakeholders to embrace SD and make it their own.

Fourth, the company has become so well-known for its leadership in sustainability that it formed a separate consulting company to help other large MNCs think about their sustainability challenges. This company is called InterfaceRAISE. Anderson (2009: 167) notes that this name was chosen because they wanted to help other companies:

- reshape corporate cultures and *raise* awareness;
- measure progress toward sustainability and *raise* standards;
- uncover new opportunities and *raise* expectations; and
- inspire process and product innovation to *raise* profits.

The most high-profile client of InterfaceRAISE is Walmart, but laminate manufacturer Wilsonart has also used its services.

Fifth, the company is now globally recognised as a leading green innovator in all aspects of the manufacturing process, both upstream and downstream. Lampikoski (2012: 7) argues that Interface's innovations fall into two categories: product and service innovations and process and material innovations. In the first category, innovations include the development of climate-neutral carpet, carpet tiles that do not require glue in the laying process, a reduction in waste and the development of 100 per cent recycled product lines, and a lowering of the raw materials needed to produce its products. The latter category includes the development of new technologies to reduce yarn usage, product life cycle analysis, new and more efficient backing systems, and a recycling of tile backing systems. Perhaps the most surprising innovation is the linking of carpet manufacture to development outcomes in the Philippines. This product is called Net-Effects.

Finally, Anderson has been referred to as an environmental 'heretic', an eco-entrepreneur, a model of creative thinking about sustainable business practices, and a corporate evangelist for the environment. I know of no other business leader in the world with such a high profile. Indeed, long-time consumer advocate, Ralph Nader, has said that Anderson is 'the greatest educator of his peers in industry, and the most knowledgeable motivator, by example and vision, for the environmental movement' (Vitello, 2011).

The chapter begins by examining Interface's move towards corporate self-regulation. It focuses specifically on the business and environmental vision of Anderson. In the next section, I examine the development of Interface's strategy to become the world's first sustainable enterprise. In the final section I draw on the lessons from Interface's journey towards sustainability and argue that what makes Interface a model of a self-regulating corporation is that it looks beyond sustainability toward a decoupling of the company's manufacturing processes from nature. It is the first industrial company that looks beyond sustainability to a world where a company has zero impact on the environment, but one that actually creates more space for habitats, ecosystems, forests and species. In other words, this is a vision in which companies no longer need the environment to achieve economic success.

INTERFACE INC. ENTERS THE ENVIRONMENTAL DEBATE

Anderson founded Interface Inc. in 1973. Prior to that he worked at Callaway Mills, a Georgia-based manufacturer of textiles. In 1968, Callaway Mills was taken over by Deering Milliken, a manufacturer of carpets and floor coverings.[4] In the shuffle, Anderson went from being Vice-President Staff Manager at Callaway's to Director of Development at Milliken's floor covering business. In this role Anderson oversaw the development of a new business line: modular carpet tiles. As he notes (1998: 29), 'I took a leading role in helping Milliken bring carpet tiles to the United States from Europe. It was a major development project, and by 1972 Milliken was the established leader in the United States in this emerging niche market'.

At that time, modular carpet tiles were a relatively new product. Originally developed in the Netherlands, the product (and the technology for making them) was most successfully sold in Great Britain.[5] They were initially developed as a response to changes in office technology, as well as a trend towards open plan offices around the world. Locating the cables and power cords became a particular headache for managers of open plan settings. Modular carpet tiles gave offices the flexibility to reconfigure their spaces as necessary. They could simply rearrange the tile squares to suit different office layouts. This is something that could not be achieved with broadloom carpets. Reconfiguring an office with broadloom carpet meant pulling it up, disposing of it, and re-carpeting the whole area – a very expensive exercise. Moreover, carpet tends to wear most in high traffic areas such as doorways. Modular carpet tiles can be replaced easily in these areas. For Anderson, modular carpet tiles were a flexible, practical and aesthetically pleasing alternative to broadloom.

It is an understatement to say that Anderson thought they were a smart idea. As he notes, '[f]rom the minute I saw them, it was love at first sight (2009: 25–6). It was this love affair with modular carpet tiles that led Anderson eventually to leave Milliken to establish a specialised modular carpet tile business geared to US demand. Although Anderson does not say so, it is clear he had a vision of some day being a large player in this sector. Indeed, the company now proudly states on its website that it is the largest manufacturer of modular carpet tiles in the world.

In 1973, and after some initial legal and financial hurdles, Anderson established Interface as a joint venture with the European manufacturers of the patented modular carpet tile technology.[6] The first plant was established in LaGrange, Georgia. When the plant was established, the company had 15 employees and no orders. In 1978 sales had reached US$11 million. By 1983, the company listed on the NASDAQ exchange. By the mid-1990s, the company had a 40 per cent share of the global modular carpet tile market. At the turn of the century, the company had acquired more than 50 companies.

Today, Interface has operations in Asia, Australia, Canada, Europe, the Americas and the Middle East. The company has a sales presence in 110 countries and annual revenues of US$1 billion (The Ray C. Anderson Foundation, 2012; Hendrix and Lynch, 2016). In addition, it is the market leader in the Americas, Europe and Australia. Only in Asia is its market share smaller. Here the company comes in second to the Toli Corporation, a Japanese flooring and fabrics firm, with a long history in the region.

The company has also developed a number of well-known (and supported) brands including Cool Carpet, Interface FLOR, Interface Superflor, Biosfera and Net-Effects. Ninety-four per cent of the company's sales of FLOR and Superflor are through the world wide web (WWW) and through catalogue sales.[7] The company is also beginning to roll out specialised retail stores to sell modular carpet tiles directly to consumers. The company currently has 19 stores across the United States and Canada to sell FLOR. It is planning to open three more stores in 2015.

Anderson's contribution to the debate about business and the environment sets him apart from his peers. Unlike many other companies, Anderson did not embrace sustainability because it was a good public relations move, or as a means of placating anti-corporate activists. For him, the environment was the most pressing moral issue of our age. It was a challenge that required action, not simply open-ended and voluntary commitments. A rethink about the way Interface conducted its business was needed urgently. Not only did he challenge the business culture of Interface, its manufacturing processes and the company's attitude toward the earth, he challenged the very assumptions built into what he called 'the take, make, waste paradigm' of industrial capitalism – the paradigm that Interface had operated by 1973. Most significantly, he wanted Interface to become the first *restorative* company in the world after 2020 (my italics).[8] How did Anderson come to the realisation that his company was operating in a way that was so harmful to the environment?

The carpet industry is a heavily polluting one. The manufacturing process requires large amounts of energy, the carpet face is made from nylon, a petroleum by-product and, in the case of carpet tiles, the backing which gives stability to the tile is made from polyvinyl chloride (PVC). This, too, is a petroleum by-product. In addition, the majority of worn-out carpet either ends up in landfill or is incinerated, also requiring a great deal of energy. In 2011, the Carpet America Recovery Effort (CARE) estimated that some 3.8 billion pounds of carpet was discarded, with only 333 million pounds diverted from landfill (CARE, 2011). In 2013, 3.7 billion pounds of used carpet was discarded, with only 543 million pounds diverted from landfill. While this is a significant improvement on the 2011 data, it still only represents roughly one-sixth of the total amount of discarded carpet (CARE, 2013).[9]

The amount of resources used to manufacture carpets is also quite staggering. In 1995, when Anderson began to question his manufacturing processes, an audit of his company and its suppliers determined that they had extracted and processed 1224 billion pounds of natural resources (oil, gas, coal and so on) to generate US$802 million in sales. Of those exploited natural resources, some 800 million pounds were non-renewable. And, according to Anderson, two-thirds of that was simply burnt up in the various manufacturing processes (Anderson, 1998: 4). Moreover, carpet is one of the least biodegradable products in the world and is likely to stay in landfills for possibly thousands of years. Finally, the manufacturing process uses an enormous amount of water in dyeing and other related processes. Considering that 1.6 billion square yards of carpet were sold in the United States in 2007, it is clear that the industry has an extraordinarily large environmental footprint (Carpet and Rug Institute, 2012).

Early in the 1990s, the sales team at Interface were increasingly being asked by their customers what the company was doing for the environment. When they asked Anderson this question, his response was that the company had always abided by the law. This was all that Interface was required to do and Anderson believed his company had an exemplary record in this regard.[10] 'We were legal, in compliance – 100 percent' (Anderson, 2009: 9). Reflecting on the issue, Jim Hartzfeld from the Interface Research Corporation suggested to Anderson that they put together a task force to work through the issue.[11] Anderson approved this course of action. Later, however, Hartzfeld asked him to give a 'kick off' speech to the group and share his environmental vision. Anderson notes that he was very uncomfortable at the prospect of giving a speech on a topic he knew nothing about. 'The trouble was, other than obeying the law, I did not have an environmental vision' (Anderson, 2009: 10).

Fortuitously, a few days before the meeting of the task force, Anderson came across a book by environmentalist and businessman Paul Hawken. This small book profoundly changed Anderson's world view. According to Hawken (2005), the earth is in serious trouble. Species extinction is occurring at an alarming rate, the biosphere is being poisoned, forests are being plundered, resources are being depleted and the oceans are dying. Hawken's argument is that something has to be done quickly before the earth suffers ecological collapse. The reason for the plight of the planet, according to Hawken, is the industrial system that underpins our modern way of life.

Hawken did not deduce, as so many environmentalists do, that the world needs to deindustrialise.[12] Instead, he argued that the only institution large enough and wealthy enough to prevent ecological collapse is commerce itself. As Hawken (2005: 17) argues:

> Business is the problem and it must be part of the solution. Its power is more crucial than ever if we are to organize and efficiently meet the world's needs. … Commerce can be one of the most creative endeavours available to us, but it is not worthy of business to be the convenient and complicit bedfellow to a culture divorced from nature. While commerce at its worst appears to be a shambles of defilement compared to the beauty and complexity of the natural world, the ideas and much of the technology required for the redesign of our businesses and the restoration of the world are already in hand. What is wanting is collective will.

Anderson describes Hawken's message as a 'spear in his chest'. 'I read it, and it changed my life. It hit me right between the eyes. It was an epiphany' (Anderson, 1998: 29–30). Anderson drew a number of conclusions from reading Hawken's book. First, someday he and other captains of industry would be indicted as plunderers of the earth and probably be put in jail. Second, Interface had to make a 'mid-course correction'. The company could no longer manufacture in the same way, using the same petroleum-based resources and processes as it had done since 1973. In his view, industrial capitalism had to give way to a sustainable capitalism that takes nothing from the earth that it cannot replace. Third, it was not enough simply to follow the relevant government regulations. These rules and guidelines simply did not go far enough in dealing with the magnitude of the problem. Finally, Interface could become a leader in changing the way commerce thought about its relationship with nature, the earth, and importantly, its customers. 'With and through them (employees) we are energizing our whole company to step up to our responsibility to lead. Unless somebody leads, nobody will. That's axiomatic. I asked, "Why not us?" Their answer has become a tidal wave of change in our company' (Anderson, 1998: 43).

The 'kick-off' speech laid out Anderson's environmental vision. As he admits, he borrowed shamelessly from Hawken's book. The key messages in the speech were the following:

- modern industrial capitalism is destroying the earth
- there are three issues that need to be faced: what we take; what we make; and what we waste
- Interface takes oil (nylon, latex, bitumen, energy) from the earth to make its products, but the company does not put anything back into the earth. The company must work to ensure that it does not take anything from the earth that it cannot put back
- nothing the company takes from the earth should end up polluting it
- the company's manufacturing process wastes with impunity
- to be a steward of the earth makes good business sense
- sustainability is not a cost to be borne by the company, but an opportunity that will pay in the long run
- the new mission for Interface is to convert itself into a restorative enterprise worldwide.

The challenge he left the task force was to look at how the company could 'reclaim, reuse, recycle, conserve, adopt, and advance best practices' (cited in Arena, 2004: 7).[13]

According to Anderson, most of the members of the task force were nonplussed by the challenge he had laid out for them. It is easy to understand why. Here was the founder and chairman of a moderately large company who was asking employees to develop a new business model that would continue to see the company grow and make a profit, but which would not harm the earth. By any measure, this was a strange challenge, one that was likely to risk a hostile reception from some stakeholders, and that could potentially lead to unemployment for some of the company's workforce. So radical was Anderson's thinking at the time that stakeholders would have been right to question his fitness to lead the company into the future.

The task force accepted the challenge Anderson had set them, believing that it could be done by 2000. However, when they began to question all aspects of the manufacturing process, it became clear that this was going to take much longer. The starting point was tackling the problem of waste, something Anderson had learned from Hawken and others.[14] But these environmental gurus had learned this from Toyota. Essentially, reducing waste led to better efficiencies and this, in turn, paid for the other environmental initiatives that Interface subsequently embarked on.

Anderson chronicled Interface's journey in a 1998 book titled *Mid-Course Correction: Toward a Sustainable Enterprise: The Interface Model* and, again in 2009, in *Business Lessons from a Radical Industrialist*. The first book is a difficult one to categorise. It is largely autobiographical, with environmental philosophy, ethics and business issues represented in good measure. The book also addresses the technical challenges associated with moving his company toward sustainability. The message contained within its pages is both depressing and inspiring, as Anderson and his company wrestled with the enormity of the task. Ultimately, the argument of the book is that we need to have a new industrial revolution, one that moves us beyond the linear path of the take, make, waste paradigm. Anderson's body of work paves a new road for MNCs to travel. The second book is an updated version of the first. It is more polished than the first and offers a clearer picture of the parameters of what Anderson calls the 'Climb up Mount Sustainability'. The book is a very thoughtful one. After 15 years of studying industry and the environment, his knowledge base is far greater than that he utilised to produce the earlier work. The centrepiece of this latter work is a chapter titled 'Mission Zero' and the seven faces of the climb up Mount Sustainability.

Watson (2011) argues that Anderson is an 'evangelist' for corporate sustainability. I agree with this assessment. He suggests that the power of the Interface narrative is in three parts. The first is where Anderson is ignorant about the extent of the environmental problems and, once being made aware of it, owns up to his company's failings. This is the 'we comply with the law' Anderson. The second narrative is Anderson's wake-up call that he will someday be indicted as a plunderer of the earth. The third narrative is that his company must change its behaviour and help bring about a new industrial revolution.

Admitting guilt is not something that CEOs are very good at. I suspect that this is why Anderson became so admired. He confesses, in a heartfelt way, that his company has been on a collision course with nature since 1973 and decides to do something about it.

According to Watson (2011: 67), the uniqueness of Anderson's story is that 'most companies are not able, or are unwilling to publicise their past environmental indiscretions, they are not able to tell a story as authentic and inspiring as the one Anderson can tell about Interface'. But I would go further than this. I think there is an almost theological quality to the Anderson narrative. It is one of sin, conversion and redemption. Interestingly, at the end of *Mid-Course Correction* (1998: 188), Anderson concludes that: '[w]e found spirituality at Interface before we knew what to call it'. This is what makes the Interface narrative so unique and compelling.

What sort of 'environmentalist' was Anderson?[15] There is significant debate in the academic literature about how to tackle the environmental issues facing the earth. It is not possible here to articulate all the various positions or the nuances within them. However, the two dominant positions according to Dryzek (2005) are, Survivalism and Promethean Environmentalism (also sometimes referred to as ecological modernism).[16]

At its core, Survivalism is a paradigm about the looming insecurity of peoples as a consequence of humanity's profligacy with regard to the earth.[17] The survivalist narrative argues that the earth is fast reaching its 'carrying capacity' and overshoot is imminent. Carrying capacity refers to the extent to which the natural world can be exploited by human beings without it being degraded to the point where it can no longer support human life. Hardin's (1968) well-known description of the problem neatly illustrates what happens when the carrying capacity of a tract of land is exceeded.

Hardin describes a situation where a herdsman concludes he will benefit economically if he grazes an extra cow on the commons. Upon seeing this, other herdsmen follow his lead. In the end, there are more cows grazing the commons than it can sustain. Eventually the commons is destroyed and hardship follows for all the herdsmen. Hardin (1968: 1244) concludes:

> Therein is the tragedy. Each man is locked into a system that compels him to increase his herd without limit – in a world that is limited. Ruin is the destination toward which all men rush, each pursuing his own best interest in a society that believes in the freedom of the commons. Freedom in a commons brings ruin to all.

Similarly, Hawken (2005: 25) tells a powerful story of an event on St Matthew Island, off the coast of Alaska. It neatly captures the problem as survivalists see it. The island was a listening post during World War II. The Unites States Coast Guard shipped 29 reindeer to supply meat to the post in the event that supply ships could reach the island during the winter months. After the war, the station was abandoned. In subsequent years, with no natural predator, the reindeer population grew so large that the island's vegetation could not support them. By the early 1960s, some 6000 reindeer had starved to death.[18]

Survivalists draw a number of sobering conclusions from this evidence. The first is that the earth is in trouble and nature will not be able to support human beings indefinitely. Ecological collapse will occur at some point in the future, after we have exceeded the earth's carrying capacity. The second is that there are limits to growth. They believe we are reaching that limit now. The third is that if we do not alter our behaviour quickly, human survival will ultimately be threatened. Finally, there needs to be a radical rethink of our relationship to the natural world. We need to deindustrialise, give up the idea of growth as our guiding economic paradigm, and begin to preserve the world's scarce resources for our future and that of generations to come. Accordingly, the problem cannot be left to the market. It is the logic of the market that has caused the problem in the first place. The survivalist position, then, contains elements of apocalypticism, a desire to return to nature and a tragic, almost nightmarish, picture of the future of humanity if nothing is done.

Dryzek (2005: 35–7) points out that achieving this vision is less well articulated than their prognosis. Some writers over the years have suggested that women in India should be sterilized; others have suggested alternatives that border on authoritarianism; still others have put their faith in civil society and participatory democracy. However, at the heart of the survivalist agenda is the desire for a new world order which has a very different set of values than those which predominate today. Korten's recent work is a good example of this viewpoint. He argues that humanity needs to embrace the idea of an 'earth community' if it is to survive. As he (2006: 282) notes:

> [T]he work of the great turning requires us to free ourselves from the self-inflicted alienation and oppression of Empire as we create societies that support every person in connecting to life in ways that enhance the creative potential of both self and community so that all may enjoy the joys of Earth Community.

The survivalist imperative can be found in a wide range of topics. These include climate change, peak oil, opposition to MNCs, population growth and resource scarcity, to name but a few. It is clearly evident in Gore's (2006) *An Inconvenient Truth*, Gelbspan's (2004) *Boiling Point* and Greer's (2013) *Not the Future We Ordered: The Psychology of Peak Oil and the Myth of Eternal Progress*. The theme is also strongly evident in the work of think tanks such as the Club of Rome, the Sierra Club and the World Watch Institute.

Celebrities like Cameron Diaz (2007) have also aligned themselves with the survivalist position. Diaz has written the foreword to a book titled *The Green Book: The Everyday Guide to Saving the Planet One Simple Step at a Time*. She has also starred in a short five-minute film titled *Cameron Diaz Saves the World*. It is also a theme that Hollywood loves to exploit. *The Day After Tomorrow* and *Beasts of the Southern Wild* are two recent survivalist story lines. But there are literally hundreds of films in this genre, many of which have a message of ecological crisis at their heart.

Arguably, if the survivalist orientation can be summed up in one word, it is 'beyond'. This approach seeks to move us beyond, among other things, industrialism, the neoliberal global economy, coal, oil, growth and materialism. It is for this reason that Lewis (1992) once referred to the survivalist vision for the future of the planet as an Arcadian one. It is a vision that wants the human race to return to nature and live in harmony with it.

In stark contrast to survivalism, Promethean environmentalism has a more optimistic message about humanity's common future. It began as a critical response to the survivalist perspective, but it has now established itself as an important alternative to that view.

In ancient Greek mythology, Prometheus made human beings out of mud and gave them fire. The gift of fire allowed them to stay warm, cook food, forge metals and develop new technologies. In other words, fire helped human beings survive, flourish and progress. According to the myth, Zeus was so angered by Prometheus' exploits that he condemned him to be chained to a rock. As if this punishment was not enough, Zeus also commanded that a giant eagle pick at his liver day and night. Fortunately, Chiron the Centaur agreed to die in order for Prometheus to go free and Heracles (Hercules) came and broke his chains.

The significance of the mythic story of Prometheus for the environmental debate is that he looked forward to a time when human beings would reach their full potential. Fire was the first step in the evolutionary journey of human kind. By labelling certain environmentalists 'Prometheans', commentators are suggesting that there is such potential in human beings. They can solve many of the environmental problems that the planet faces, without the abolition of capitalism, or accepting arguments about the limits of growth.

Prometheans argue that growth cannot be forsaken because of the pessimistic story of the future that the survivalists tell. Arcadia is not the answer. While they regard our environmental problems as extremely serious, the solution is to be found in harnessing existing (and future) potential within humanity. Survivalists are about curtailing that potential. Consequently, the missing part of Hardin's parable is the ingenuity and creative nature of human beings. What might a Promethean response to Hardin's 1968 parable look like? Speculatively, it may read something like this:

After the herdsman decides to graze a cow on the commons, he realises that to graze more than one cow will increase his wealth. Upon seeing this, other herdsmen in the area decide that they might also achieve more wealth if they increase the number of cows that they graze on the commons. However, the commons starts to deteriorate. Empty patches of dirt start to appear, there is a discernible reduction in available grass for the animals to feed on, and the animals start to lose condition and, consequently, financial value in the market place. The herdsmen, seeing this, realise that over-farming the commons is likely adversely to affect them all economically. They decide rationally to reduce the number of animals grazing the commons, and work out a community plan for ensure the commons is available for years to come. By managing the number of animals grazing on the commons at any one time, they avert overshoot and collapse.

In other words, the herdsmen adopt a relative gains position. They understand that overgrazing will ruin them all, and they take steps to protect the commons. They also understand that in protecting the commons, they are protecting their own economic interests for the foreseeable future.

The Promethean position is primarily rationalist. Human beings are rational actors, with the capacity to solve problems and innovate. It is not placing limits on growth that will bring about the necessary environmental changes that bedevil humanity. The key solutions are to be found in more (and perhaps better) growth. As Nordhaus and Shellenberger (2007: 15) express it: 'Few things have hampered environmentalism more than its long-standing position that limits to growth are the remedy for ecological crises. We argue for an explicitly pro-growth agenda that defines the kind of prosperity we believe is necessary to improve the quality of human life and to overcome ecological crises'. They refer to this broad Promethean vision as 'the politics of possibility'. The driver of this politics is the link between investment and innovation. As they note, 'we must choose between a resentful narrative of tragedy and a grateful narrative of overcoming' (2007: 18).

The two positions stated here are ideal-types. In truth, many authors tend to accept parts of both narratives. Anderson is one of these. His views do not neatly conform to any one of the two positions outlined above. He accepts arguments about the carrying capacity of the earth and the problem of 'overshoot'. He talks openly in his books about species extinction, habitat loss, pollution and other environmental maladies of the modern world. So, in part, he accepts the survivalist prognosis of the plight of the earth. At the same time, he is firmly of the belief that business can, and must, be part of the solution. Anderson (1998: 9) argues that industry needs to have a *'truly revolutionary* industrial revolution' [italics in the original]. The problems with the first industrial revolution – unintended externalities, intensive reliance on finite fossil fuels, and industrial processes that are inherently wasteful and polluting – need to come to an end. The next industrial revolution must be built around the idea of sustainability and ensure it is achieved. 'I don't believe we can go back to pre-industrial days; we must go on to a better industrial revolution than the last one, and get it right this time'.

In various interviews, Anderson says he is fiercely competitive and wants every order he can win. Often he admits that he is a proud industrial capitalist. He also believes that the ingenuity of his people (and his suppliers) will get Interface up Mount Sustainability by 2020. The problem, of course, is getting enough companies to understand this revolution.

INTERFACE INC.: INVENTING THE NEXT INDUSTRIAL REVOLUTION

One of the complaints that anti-corporate activists make is that most MNCs employ CSR as a way of showing the public that they are good corporate citizens. Yet, in most cases, they argue that these commitments are smokescreens to hide the fact that they have done nothing meaningful for the environment or for the societies in which they operate. Interface Inc. is certainly not one of these companies. As it has placed sustainability at the core of its manufacturing capabilities, modified its systems and continued to turn a profit, its reputational capital has soared.

Certainly, much of this success has been due to the drive and vision of Anderson. But behind him are senior executives, executives, engineers, forklift drivers, machine operators, sales staff and suppliers. Interface's drive to Mission Zero is a team effort. All parties have willingly accepted Anderson's vision and worked hard to achieve it.

Hartzfeld suggested to Anderson that Interface could become the world's first sustainable enterprise in six years, by the year 2000. This was always going to be an impossible target to meet, given the technical challenges, the supply chain issues, the need to redesign products and convince stakeholders that this is a well-thought-out strategy to increase profitability. Nevertheless, I think we should read the original six-year target as an acknowledgement of the company's early enthusiasm for sustainability. Mission Zero, a plan which emerged a few years later, set a more realistic benchmark for the company to achieve its sustainability goals. The company is now committed to achieving this milestone by 2020.

Interface envisages Mission Zero to be an Everest-like mountain with seven faces, each face represents one of the challenges that the company faces in becoming environmentally neutral. The seven faces are:

1. Eliminate Waste: Eliminating all forms of waste in every area of business.
2. Benign Emissions: Eliminating toxic substances from products, vehicles and facilities.
3. Renewable Energy: Operating facilities with renewable energy sources – solar, wind, landfill gas, biomass, geothermal, tidal and low/impact/small hydroelectric or non-petroleum-based hydrogen.
4. Closing the Loop: Redesigning processes and products to close the technical loop using recovered and bio-based materials.
5. Resource-Efficient Transportation: Transporting people and products efficiently to reduce waste and emissions.
6. Sensitizing Stakeholders: Creating a culture that integrates sustainability principles and improves people's lives and livelihoods.
7. Redesign Commerce: Creating a new business model that demonstrates and supports the value of sustainability-based commerce (Anderson, 2010).

The Mission Zero target of 2020 is aggressive. There is no industrial company that has driven the sustainability argument harder than Interface. So what have the successes amounted to thus far?

At the beginning of his second book, Anderson talks about the 'carrot' that comes with sustainability. The carrot is essentially the benefits that have flowed to the company from its drive toward sustainability since 1996.[19] In the foreword, Anderson (2009, pp. xiv–xv) lists the company's achievements between 1996 and 2009:

- 80 percent reduction in the landfill waste per unit of production since 1996
- Water intake, down 80 percent per unit of production since 1996
- Total energy, down by 43 percent per unit of production since 1996
- With changing energy mix to include renewables, fossil fuel intensity reduced by 60 percent
- With verified offsets, net GHG reduced by 94 percent (absolute)
- 30 percent of global energy is from renewable sources
- 36 percent of total raw materials (by weight) is recycled or bio-based materials
- 100 percent renewable electricity in Europe (89 percent world-wide) in our factories
- 111 million square yards of climate-neutral carpet produced since 2003: 'Cool Carpet'
- 100 000 tons (200 million pounds) of reclaimed product via Re-Entry, our reverse logistics carpet reclamation program
- 200 million airline passenger miles offset by some 106,000 trees
- Overall footprint reduction, more than 60 percent

- Cumulative avoided waste costs totaling $433 million since 1994 – costs down, not up – waste elimination paying for the entire mountain climb.

Has the company made further headway since 2009? A 2013 press release reports on seven areas where the company has improved its environmental performance:

- The carbon footprint of the average Interface product is down 19 percent since 2008.
- 49 percent of total raw materials used by the company in 2012 were recycled or bio-based, including 36 percent of yarn and 51 percent of carpet backing.
- In 2012, Interface's recycling program diverted 15 million pounds of carpet and carpet scraps from landfill. Between 1996 and 2012, the company has recycled some 268 million pounds of carpet; that is a 94 percent reduction of waste to landfill.
- Energy use per unit of production is down 39 percent since 1996.
- Greenhouse gas emissions per unit of production from manufacturing facilities are down 41 percent since 1996.
- Water intake per unit of production is down 81 percent.
- Currently there are 48 registered EPDs for its products made in Europe, US, Australia and Thailand (Interface, 2013b).

More recently, at the March 2015 Investor Presentation, Interface has reported on four of its Mission Zero commitments (Hendrix and Lynch, 2016). Waste to landfill has now been reduced by 94 per cent. This is a 14 per cent improvement on Anderson's 2009 data. Renewable energy use has marginally increased to 35 per cent. The company sold its Bentley Prince Street broadloom business in California to Dominus Capital in order to concentrate its efforts in the carpet tile market (Interface Inc., 2012b). The difficulty for them is that the Bentley Prince Street plant was run on a 100 per cent renewable energy (solar). So the sale of this asset has retarded their renewable data slightly. In terms of their use of recycled and bio-based materials, the company remains at 49 per cent. Greenhouse gas emissions are down 71 per cent from the 1996 baseline. In addition, the company has planted 154 000 trees to offset business-related air travel and 64 000 trees to offset employee emissions commuting to and from work. Interface has also purchased and retired 38 000 tons of certified carbon offsets to cover the emissions of its vehicle fleet.

The story with Interface Europe is even more compelling, primarily because of higher levels of renewable energy that are available to them. But changes at their production facility at Scherpenzeel in the Netherlands have been impressive: 95 per cent of the company energy use is from renewable energy, GHG emissions are also down by 95 per cent, there is zero waste going to landfill and water usage is down by 95 per cent (Interface Europe, n.d.).

Metrics are an important indicator of the success of Mission Zero, but they are not without their problems. In some of the literature, it is unclear whether the presented data are an aggregate of all the operations' environmental footprint globally, or if they apply only to the US operations. Also there appear to be no metrics available beyond 2013. Even Hendrix and Lynch's recent Investor Presentation employs environmental data that is almost two years old. Yet the company says that it gathers this data quarterly. Moreover, metrics are only meaningful if they are accompanied by explanation. On page 32 of the same presentation, there is a graph with a trend line which highlights the fact that greenhouse gas emissions have dropped 71 per cent since 1996. Yet there is no explanation why emissions spiked between 2009 and 2012. It would be interesting to know what the value of the cumulative avoided waste costs now are. The company continues to suggest that it has made a convincing business case for sustainability. It would be useful to see this data published annually, if not quarterly.

The metrics noted above are, of course, only part of the Interface story. The company has undertaken a number of other environmental and social initiatives. All factories are certified as complying with the ISO 14001 environmental management standard. Many of the company's factories are also certified under the US Green Building Council's Leadership in Energy and Environmental Design (LEED) certification system, with four locations rated platinum (the highest rating) for energy efficiency and sustainability. Interface is also the first carpet company to introduce Life-Cycle Assessments (LCA) to determine the impacts of new materials and processes. It is also the first company to utilise Environmental Product Declarations (EPDs) to provide its customers with transparency regarding the environmental impact of its products.

The company has also made a number of technical innovations. It has introduced a new way of laying carpet tiles than does not require glue (and so is VOC free) in the laying process (Tac Tiles). It has developed a range of products that are made from 100 per cent recycled materials (Cool Carpet), developed a new backing system for the tile face which is also made with 100 per cent recycled material (Cool Blue), and there is a programme to recycle post-consumer products, including those of their competitors (Re-Entry 2.0). The company has also developed a carpet tile range based on the idea of biomimicry. The tiles are laid in a random pattern, as is seen in nature.

Perhaps their most powerful innovation is Net-Works™. This is a collaborative programme between Interface, the Zoological Society of London (ZSL), Italian nylon yarn maker Aquafil and local communities in central Philippines. The programme is designed to tackle the problem of discarded fishing nets around poor coastal communities. Not only are these nets dangerous to local marine life, but they are also an eye-sore on otherwise pristine coastlines. The programme pays locals a fee to bring the discarded nets to collection points. This gives them an income stream. After collection, the netting goes to Aquafil and it is put through their ECONYL regeneration system and recycled into new yarn. This is then reused by Interface in a new carpet tile range called Net-Effects.

Thus far, some 136 345 pounds of discarded netting has been collected. According to the Net-Works website, the programme has generated supplemental income equivalent to 213 259 meals (Net-Works, n.d.). The programme also has a positive social impact on local communities as well, as it is 'integrated with valuable community banking systems that support and strengthen the local, developing economy and provide new financial opportunities for residents' (Net-Works, n.d.). A second programme of this kind is soon to be set up around the Lake Ossa region in Cameroon, West Africa.

There may be other programmes/projects like this, but I have not come across one that seamlessly integrates local development goals and corporate goals. The environmental and social benefits are clearly evident, not only in the amount of discarded netting that is recycled into new carpet tile face, but also in the financial benefits that flow to local coastal communities. This is such a good example of the new industrial revolution that Anderson so often talked about.

Interface has never shied away from the difficulties in achieving its climb to the top of Mount Sustainability. The first challenge is to reduce its fossil fuel footprint. The key ingredient in all carpet fibres is nylon, a petroleum-derived product. But access to enough post-consumer product is limited and costly. The second challenge is keeping executives, employees and suppliers engaged with Mission Zero's goals. 'Sustainability fatigue' is something that can easily begin to undermine the company's efforts. The 'I am Mission Zero' YouTube videos are meant to deal partly with this issue. The third challenge is actually achieving a zero footprint on waste, energy use and emissions across the entire company. Once again, cost is an issue, as is the complex nature of many of its manufacturing processes.

Is the climb toward Mission Z achievable by 2020? With only five years to go, it is probably too early to tell with any certainly. First, technological innovation has not always kept pace with Interface's vision.

This has been acknowledged many times. As current CEO Hendrix notes, '[t]he real area that we struggle is in energy, and we need help. We've been trying to figure out how to get off the grid for a while, and it's just cost-prohibitive to do so' (cited in Randall, 2012). Second, and perhaps more significantly, energy transitions take decades to occur. US Vice-President Al Gore famously suggested the US could construct enough wind and solar plants to power America in ten years. However, noted energy expert Smil (2008) claims that this is a 'delusional' target and argues that it took 65 years to construct a system of thermal power plants and about 50 years for oil to capture a 10 per cent share of the global energy market. Hendrix seems to echo this sentiment, somewhat despondently. As he puts it, '[w]e need more solar energy. We need more hydro energy. We need more green energy out there' (cited in Randall, 2012). Finally, as one employee points out in a YouTube video titled InterfaceFLOR – Mission Zero (Interface Inc., 2009), as the company grows, the battle to get to, and stay at, 'zero' is likely to become even harder. How do we sum up the Interface journey toward sustainability?

I think there are a number of lessons that Interface has learned. These lessons will, ultimately, be subjective, as each of us takes a different lesson from their environmental journey. From my reading of Interface's journey, there are four important lessons the company has learned.

First, being sustainable is not just the morally right thing to do, it also makes good commercial sense. As Anderson notes, the sustainability effort 'has done more to lift the company's image than all the advertising we have ever done' (cited in Dean, 2007).

Second, the progress toward Mission Zero cannot be accomplished without the company partnering with other companies. The Interface–Aquafil relationship is a case in point. Without the ECONYL regeneration system, Interface would be using more virgin yarn than it currently does. This would make Mission Zero even more difficult to achieve. As the Vice President of Restorative Enterprise at Interface argues:

> [W]e recognize that a broader ecosystem of society lies beyond the boundaries of our business. In order to make meaningful progress, we need to rethink our value chains and find partners who will work with us to answer some of the world's most pressing social and ecological questions, while allowing us to create the best, most sustainable product. (Interface, 2013a)

Third, Interface began to develop a deeper understanding of the value of their employees in achieving Mission Zero. They realised that they are a major source of creativity and drive. As Anderson states in an interview, 'Our people are galvanized around a higher purpose. You can't beat it for attracting people and motivating people' (cited in Hymas, 2009). This higher purpose is embodied in the recent 'I am Mission Zero' videos (Interface Inc., 2012a). The brain-child of Erin Meezan, Vice-President of Sustainability at Interface, the videos are an excellent example of the strong relationship between the company and its employees. Perhaps the best example of this relationship is the way Interface treated its Australian employees after a fire destroyed its plant at Picton in New South Wales. The company continued to pay their wages for twelve months and arranged to keep employees busy with community service and work at its warehouse and distribution centre.

Fourth, the company has learned about the value of education to its business model. This takes three forms. The first is to educate stakeholders about the environmental challenges the earth faces, and the part that Interface can play as leaders on sustainability. This is evident in all Anderson post-1996 engagements, the company's 'Natural Step' induction programme, QUEST and many other activities. At all times, it has been an 'action-focused strategy'. The second is to educate their workforce about the company's environmental philosophy and what they can do to engage the community. The third is to highlight the problem of greenwash in the industry.

Fifth, Interface's emphasis is on becoming a restorative company through influence. By climbing Mount Sustainability, the company is developing a unique set of ideas, resources and experiences.

Finally, it uses a number of publications to educate customers about the uniqueness of Interface's products. There are two parts to this. The first is to continue to differentiate themselves in the marketplace. The second is Interface's fight against industry greenwash. The company has produced a number of documents to highlight their competitive edge in each of these areas. These include:

- *Mission Zero – The Power of a Challenging Vision* (Interface-RAISE, 2010a);
- *Embedded Sustainability: One Mind at a Time* (InterfaceRAISE, 2010b);
- *Just the Facts Guide: How to Choose the Most Sustainable Products and What to Ask the Manufacturers* (Interface, 2015b); and
- *Go Beyond* (Interface, 2015a).

The last two documents interrogate the 'easy facts', that is, the 'unsubstantiated marketing claims, exaggerations and half truths' in the carpet industry (Interface, 2015a: 22). Now that the company has established itself as a leader in the space, it is also working hard to maintain that competitive edge.

To conclude, Interface offers a powerful practical example of what can be accomplished with a vision and a truthful commitment to change. Even if we were to put aside the environmental driver of change in the company, its efforts are a game changer all the same. This is acknowledged in the *2014 Sustainability Leaders* survey. Between 2004 and 2014, Interface has ranked among the best three leaders on sustainability in the world. In 2007 and 2009, Interface was ranked as the top leader in sustainability globally (Global Scan/SustainAbility, 2014: 15).

INTERFACE INC.: A SELF-REGULATING CORPORATION?

The Interface Model is a newly emerging corporate form. Not only has it 'institutionalised purpose' throughout all parts of the company, it has a clear set of values, specific corporate, environmental and social goals and, perhaps most importantly of all, a timeframe to achieve them. It has also demonstrated a degree of leadership, unparalleled in the manufacturing industry.

At its simplest, the Interface Model can be distilled into three iterative ideas. It begins with discernible improvement in resource efficiency. This helps to lower costs and reduces environmental impacts. Second, the savings can then be reinvested into sustainable inputs, such as renewable energy, the use of recycled materials, and other technical innovations and processes. Third, it provides opportunities for commercialisation, capable of driving further resource efficiencies. As innovation occurs, the economic benefits grow and this improves all parts of the business. According to Lavery–Pennell (2014: 9), the serious application of this model could, in Europe alone, be worth as much as €100 billion in before-tax profits a year for manufacturers, lead to a 14.6 per cent reduction in greenhouse gas emissions, and create 168 000 new jobs.

This has been the experience of Interface as well. Wasting less and using resources more efficiently creates positive externalities for the business while reducing the negative ones. The end result of this iterative process is a more sustainable enterprise, one that gradually reduces its impact on the natural world.

What makes Interface a self-regulating corporation is not simply its environmental vision and commitment to the environment, it is also that it wants to become a restorative company after 2020. Anderson does not elaborate on this notion in depth, beyond saying it is about helping and influencing other companies on their own journey towards sustainability. I would argue that the obvious outcome of Anderson's thinking and the activities of the company to date, is much more profound than simply influencing others. It is a narrative about the need to decouple (or delink) the company's economic activity from its reliance on nature. This is what sets Interface apart from most other manufacturing companies. The process of decoupling means that we use nature less and, in time, may be able to reduce the human impact on the climate, biodiversity and habitat loss in both relative and absolute terms. Relative decoupling occurs when environmental impacts occur at a slower rate than overall economic growth. Absolute decoupling occurs when all environmental impacts decline, as the economy continues to grow. This is the path that Interface is following. It is an approach for both profitability and sustainability, as well as a strategy for reducing the relative and absolute environmental footprint of business on the planet. There are probably many ways for companies to decouple successfully. The Interface Model is one approach. The journey began in 1994. With intelligence, vision, innovation, willing partners, and a bit of luck, the company will be able to become restorative sometime after 2020. So, to date, this has been twenty-two projects.

Most companies today consider sustainability to be either a message they need to send to stakeholders, a compliance activity which costs money to implement, or something that is intrinsic to their business success. In a sense, and despite the rhetoric, it has become a status quo concept for business. By this I mean that sustainability is something that all MNCs now promote and accept as a key component of their social licence to operate.

The value of the Interface journey to the corporate world is demonstrating that a commitment to sustainability has had positive consequences for them and for the environment. What Anderson and Interface have done is peeked beyond the concept of sustainability and shown the myriad of benefits that come from relying less on the natural world to achieve economic success. Arguably, this is what makes Interface a genuine self-regulating corporation.

CONCLUSION

Interface is a unique MNC. In 1994, the CEO of the company challenged its employees to undergo an industrial revolution. To abide by the law was never going to solve the looming environmental crisis that confronted humanity. Consequently, and with a bit of inspiration from Paul

Hawken, the company developed a vision of how it could reform its operations and avoid harming the earth and the 6 billion people that draw sustenance from it. Eventually this became 'Mission Zero' and led to a pledge to be carbon neutral by 2020. The key concept driving reform is sustainability. Often a misused and abused idea, Interface took the sustainability challenge seriously, so seriously in fact that the company realised that only a complete rethink of all aspects of its business, from its supply chain to the amount of waste it creates during the manufacturing process, would suffice.

The company had many advantages over other similar companies at that time. First, it had the leadership and long-term commitment of its CEO, Ray Anderson. Without it, the company would, in all likelihood, still be manufacturing carpet the way Interface did in 1973. Anderson understood early that sustainability was actually good for business. Moreover, because Interface took the sustainability challenge seriously, it avoided the charge of greenwash and, over time, gained significant reputational capital with governments, the business sector, non-governmental organisations, and the purchasers of its products.

Interface illustrates well the gulf that now exists between those companies that still think and operate with an obsolete industrial paradigm (take, make, waste) and a new pioneering approach that seeks to decouple, as far as possible, industrial activity from environmental impacts. Whether this approach can be mimicked across other sectors is an open question. But there is no doubt that the Interface Model is a good one to follow for those companies seeking to become self-regulating corporations. The test is whether these companies are willing to take the leap of faith that Interface took in 1994. The lesson of the chapter, then, is that the rewards can be significant for those MNCs who are willing to become genuine sustainable enterprises. In this environment of instant communication, pretenders will quickly be found wanting, with potentially severe consequences for their corporate reputations.

NOTES

1. Hereafter referred to as Interface.
2. The story is told slightly differently in Arratia (2010).
3. On The Natural Step see Robèrt (2008).
4. Milliken is now a diversified manufacturing company. It makes chemical and packaging products, as well as flame resistant clothing, work wear and industrial textiles. The company also manufactures composite materials for military and industrial usage.
5. Broadloom is carpet that is manufactured in large rolls to a specified width and length. It is also sometimes referred to as 'wall to wall' carpet because it can be laid as a single piece in a room. The large size of broadloom is ideal for areas such as long hallways,

picture theatres, dining rooms and conference halls. In contrast, modular carpet tiles are small carpet squares, usually between 400 mm to 500 mm in size.

6. Two companies were formed in 1973. Carpets International – Georgia, Inc. and Carpets International – Georgia (Sales), Inc. In 1981, the two companies merged to form Interface Flooring Systems, Inc. in 1981. In 1987 the company name was changed again to Interface Inc.
7. In 2007, the InterfaceFLOR product range became climate neutral.
8. A restorative company is one that not only turns a profit but also helps to heal the earth. See Braungart and McDonough (2002). Anderson (2010) calls this the 'eighth face' of Mount Sustainability.
9. Interface Australia argues that 30 000 tonnes of carpet goes to landfill in Australia and New Zealand alone.
10. On the development of environmental regulation in the United States, see Hoffman (2001: 64–86).
11. At the time, Hartzfeld was a member of Interface's research company. Later, he would take over the job of managing InterfaceRAISE, the company's external consulting business.
12. By deindustrialisation I do not mean a process where there is a discernible reduction in manufacturing output or terms of trade. Rather, I mean a view put forward by some ecologists and environmentalists that human beings need to abandon capitalism and move to a more 'authentic' existence in harmony with nature. See Korten (2006).
13. There is an interesting reference in the speech to Kaizen and the notion of continuous improvement. What Anderson wanted from the taskforce was a strategy for continually improving their industrial practices toward sustainability.
14. See also Hawken et al. (2008).
15. I use the past tense here purposely because unfortunately Anderson died of cancer on 8 August 2011. The Ray C. Anderson Foundation is dedicated to his memory. See http://www.raycandersonfoundation.org/ (accessed 16 June 2016).
16. The survivalist position shares similarities to that of social ecology and deep ecology. On social ecology see Bookchin (1982); Bookchin and Foreman (1991). On deep ecology see Naess (2010); Bender (2003); Sessions (1995); Drengson and Inoue (1995). Others have termed it 'eco-pessimism' (Neumayer, 2001) or eco-radicalism (Rawcliffe, 1993). On ecological modernism or Promethean environmentalism see Stubbs and Cocklin (2006); Nordhaus and Shellenberger (2007).
17. Survivalism is also a theme in the international relations literature, where authors such as Klare (2002; 2012) point to looming crises that humanity must overcome in order to survive.
18. The original study of this collapse is Klein (1968). Anderson cited this story numerous times in various forums. For him, it is a metaphor for the potential for the ecological collapse of the entire planet.
19. 1996 is the company's original data collection point. This is referred as 'Ecometrics' by the company.

Conclusion: beyond sustainability and long live the night parrot

This book began in a critical conversation with anti-corporate activists. It praised their efforts to bring about change in the way that multinational corporations (MNCs) behaved in the social and environmental dimensions of their commercial activities. Anti-corporate activists understood early that there was a close link between corporate behaviour and the building of a strong corporate reputation. According to them, a failure to behave well impacted negatively on a company's reputation. The main mechanism for achieving this is the collective capacity of activists to politicise the reputations of MNCs. They have done this through open protest at corporate headquarters, setting up anti-corporate websites, highlighting the plight of victims of corporate behaviour, and by reacting angrily to corporate disasters. I used the social amplification of risk framework (SARF) to explain how anti-corporate activists have become adept at communicating the potential risks posed by MNCs. The result of this campaign is that MNCs are now acutely aware of the damage a well-organised activist campaign can do to their reputations. Three consequences flow from this insight. First, MNCs have begun to rethink the ways in which they interact with society. Second, they have seen the necessity of redesigning their corporate messages to demonstrate that they are – and can be – good corporate citizens. Third, they are redesigning the practical aspects of their businesses. This includes signing up to corporate charters, issuing sustainability reports, and undertaking special initiatives to reinforce their credentials on social and environmental matters. They are also adopting such initiatives as triple bottom line reporting, corporate social responsibility, and hiring specialist environmental and community engagement personnel to move this agenda forward. All these factors are substantially disciplining corporate behaviour.

At the conclusion of Chapter 1, I suggested that this represents a genuine ideational shift in thinking for MNCs and that, in the coming years, no company will be able to operate without taking responsibility for their social and environmental impact, or their need to add significant value to the communities where they operate. This is best understood as a demand that they move toward corporate self-regulation.

Chapters 2 and 3 represent the theoretical defence of this controversial proposition. Chapter 2 explores the concept of corporate reputation in detail. Corporate reputation is broken down into three concepts: the corporate image, the corporate identity and corporate behaviour. In the context of globalisation, I argue that the latter idea now takes precedence in discussions about how companies improve their relations with shareholders and the broader community. I focused particularly on reputation risk and argued that of all the risks faced by MNCs in their business activities today, reputation risk is the most significant. It has the potential to do the most damage. The chapter then put forward the argument that, as a consequence of globalisation, corporate reputation is now the chief driver of ideational change in MNCs. First, public sentiment matters to companies more than ever. Second, a strong economic business case can now be made for behaving well. Third, as the global economy has become more integrated, it has meant that companies can suffer a crisis in one country, and this can affect the share price in the United States, Japan and London.

Chapter 3 defends the idea of a self-regulating corporation. It examines a range of possible regulatory schemes, including command and control regulation, industry self-regulation and corporate self-regulation. It argues that corporate self-regulation does not mean that MNCs are left unregulated by the state, but that they are now being regulated differently. In addition, I defend the idea of a self-regulating corporation. I do this by challenging the anti-corporate activists' claims that states need to impose stricter state-based regulation upon MNCs. The emerging management and business literature appears to give some credence to the claim that meaningful corporate self-regulation is possible, maybe even a necessity in an era of globalisation. Indeed, MNCs that do not self-regulate are likely to be replaced by those that do.

The last half of the book examines three cases of MNCs that have sought to embrace corporate self-regulation. They are Royal Dutch Shell, the Toyota Motor Corporation and Interface Inc. The journey of each company has been very different. Royal Dutch Shell and the Toyota Motor Corporation have both endured a severe reputational crisis. Interface, on the other hand, has embraced sustainability unlike any other MNC. The lessons that can be learned from each case are instructive and are summarised here.

ENGAGING IN GREENWASH AND ENVIRONMENTAL PUBLIC RELATIONS EXERCISES CAN BE COUNTER-PRODUCTIVE

Engaging in greenwash (or bluewash) is unlikely to achieve anything positive in the long run. Indeed, it may even be counter-productive and lead a company in contradiction. If a company suggests that it is a good corporate citizen and then is found to have violated environmental regulation, health and safety laws, and other breaches, that company is likely to find itself being criticised for greenwashing its image. It also highlights the risks that companies run if they believe that public relations and marketing strategies result in them becoming good corporate citizens. It does not.

ADHERING TO CURRENT REGULATION IS NOT ENOUGH

It is no longer enough for companies seeking to build a strong corporate reputation to comply with existing legislation. Governments often set legislation at a minimum standard in order not to deter business or adversely affect the economy. However, this often means that the bar is set too low. This is especially the case with environmental legislation. Conservative politicians are generally sceptical about the veracity of climate science and, consequently, are unwilling to take the problem seriously. This means that the relevant legislation often lags behind community expectations. This presents an excellent opportunity for an enlightened company to profit by setting a higher standard for itself.

LEADING COMPANIES NEED AN ENLIGHTENED SOCIAL AND ENVIRONMENTAL CHAMPION TO DRIVE CHANGE IN THEIR BUSINESS

MNCs must become learning organisations, especially on social and environmental issues. Gaines-Ross (2003: 178–87) argues that good leadership must be thoughtful leadership. In her view, '[t]hought leadership encompasses the development of new ideas – ideas that keep a company at the forefront of change'. She gives a few examples of CEOs who have done this. She points to the enlightened efforts of J. Michael Cook, retired CEO of Deloitte & Touche, to employ more women in the company. He did this in the 1990s, at a time when women were severely underrepresented in the workforce. He also put in place strategies for the retention and advancement of women within the organisation.

While this kind of leadership is important, it needs to be broader than a single issue. The point Anderson understood very well is that is must be holistic across the entire organisation, address both the social and environmental impact of business in a tangible way, be something that all employees embrace, and be championed by the CEO and the board.

A MEANINGFUL CORPORATE VISION AND A REALISTIC STRATEGIC PLAN OF ACTION

A meaningful corporate vision is crucial, as it is the roadmap for achieving results. As we saw with Ray Anderson, the vision does not need to be original. He borrowed ideas from a range of sources and put them into practice in his company. What was unique in his vision was the level of commitment and passion he brought to challenges that his company faced in reducing its environmental impact.

But it must also be a realistic strategic plan of action. Open-ended statements in sustainability reports are inadequate for a self-regulating corporation. There has to be a tangible roadmap for achievement. It cannot be a promissory note for the future.

A SPECIFIED TIMEFRAME FOR ACHIEVEMENT OF SOCIAL AND ENVIRONMENTAL GOALS

One of the unique things about Interface is the fact that the company has set a timeframe for the climb up Mount Sustainability. As noted in the last chapter, it may not quite reach this goal by 2020, but the fact that it has set a timeline for achievement is important. This not only helps the company to orient itself toward the future, it helps to protect it against backsliding, and allows employees to be clear about where the company is heading and how well they are doing along the way.

DEVELOPMENT OF UNIQUE INITIATIVES TIED TO THE COMPANY'S INTERESTS

It is commonplace for companies to support causes. These may include, among other things, environmental causes, poverty alleviation programmes, and the protection of wildlife. Certainly, financial and other in-kind support is to be welcomed. Many volunteer organisations exist on a shoe-string budget, so support from a large benefactor is vital. However, it is not as clear-cut as this. A company donating funds to save the panda BHP Billiton) may be interpreted by the public as the company using a cuddly animal to bolster its image, rather than a genuine attempt to help an endangered species.

This is why Interface's 'Net-Works' is such an interesting initiative. Not only does it – in a small way – help protect the environment, it provides an income stream to poor villagers. Moreover, it dovetails with Interface's core business interests; that is, turning yarn into carpet that has no impact on the environment. This is clearly a win–win for all stakeholders. It is also less likely to be viewed as a public relations exercise. There is a technological dimension to this as well. It is more likely that significant technological advancements will flow to a company and its stakeholders, the closer it stays to its core business.

BEYOND SUSTAINABILITY AND THE NIGHT PARROT

Ever since the Brundtland Commission put sustainability at the centre of its famous report, the term has endured, and has now become part of the lexicon of MNCs, governments and individuals. For MNCs, the term is used to demonstrate to stakeholders that it is a good corporate citizen, but the term is also used to inform the future of business conduct. Yet the term is often abused, and this is why companies are often accused of greenwash. They are criticised for not doing anything concrete to reduce their emissions, change the way they act, or take less of the earth's finite resources. Sustainability has become a word of convenience, with few companies using the term as the Brundtland Commission intended. Perhaps the most liberal use of the term is in the oil and mining industries. It is commonplace to hear that mining can be sustainable or that oil extraction is a sustainable activity. Neither activity is, nor can be, sustainable in a meaningful sense. For example, rare earth elements are some of the scarcest minerals in the world. What is extracted of this type of mineral is being used in advanced technologies and in hybrid vehicles. In Australia, the Lynas Corporation sees no incongruity between its claim to be a sustainable enterprise and the fact that it is mining an extremely rare and dwindling range of minerals. That these may not be available to future generations seems to be of little consequence to the company. The same criticism can be levelled at most sustainability reports. They are as much a work of fiction as a marker of corporate performance. Consequently, their value to the companies producing them is largely problematic. The Friends of the Earth's critique of Shell's sustainability reports is a case in point.

The issues surrounding sustainability, then, are often coloured by half-truths, obfuscation, and are used as a self-congratulatory pat on the back. Moreover, the length of these documents is often a deterrent to reading them. Toyota's 2014 sustainability report is so large that the company has not provided page numbers. But the PDF tells us that it is 154 pages in length.

Despite this, the concept of sustainability must now be considered a status quo concept. It is something that all companies profess as a minimum position on the environment and how they should conduct business. They should be reusing, recycling, and reducing the size of their footprint on nature. However, what Anderson, Hawken and others are pointing out is that this status quo position is no longer a suitable place for companies to rest. The reason for this is that sustainability is no longer an end point: it is a means to an end. The end is the restoration of nature. MNCs that do not recognise this, and who think the language of sustainability will protect them from future reputation risk are mistaken.

The final lesson of this book is that Interface points the way forward. The self-regulating corporation of the future will not just be a paragon of virtue. It will not be a laggard on social and environmental matters, and it will not just comply with weak government regulation. It will understand that sustainability carries within it the seeds of the restoration of nature. MNCs that do not understand this are likely to have their reputations severely tested in the coming years.

The night parrot is a tiny green and yellow parrot that inhabits the interior of Australia. No one quite knows its range. It was first described by botanist John Gould in 1861. This little nocturnal parrot was feared extinct as the last known sighting was in the early 1900s. In the last few years, the bird has been documented and photographed by ornithologists. No one knows how many birds there are in the wild or the size of their habitat. As you can imagine, this is a significant event. There is apparently a colony in Western Queensland that is a closely guarded secret, in order to deter poachers. It has also been sighted in the Pilbara region of Western Australia.

The bird is the subject of predation, fire and drought. Its survival is a wonderful reminder of the surprises that our natural world extends to us. This little bird is not a regal Siberian snow leopard, a Sumatran orangutan, an African white rhinoceros or a majestic Bengal tiger. Indeed, it is a rather unexceptional little bird, but it has happily survived our modern world. C.S. Lewis once wrote a small book titled *Surprised by Joy*. I think most of those who have seen the night parrot will also have been as surprised by joy, as Lewis was when he converted to Christianity.

This secretive little parrot is a reminder of the fragility of the world we live in, the importance of our flora and fauna, and a hope that we, as a species, have a bright and healthy future. MNCs must play a critical role here. Hopefully, the night parrot can serve as a reminder of the need for MNCs to understand their responsibilities to the natural world and the importance of them becoming self-regulating corporations. Anderson is right. This is the only future we have. Long live the night parrot.

Bibliography

Abegglen, J. (2006), *21st Century Japanese Management: New Systems, Lasting Values*, Basingstoke: Palgrave Macmillan.

Abraham, S., B. Friedman, R. Khan and R. Skolnik (2008), 'Is publication of the Reputation Quotient (RQ) sufficient to move stock prices?', *Corporate Reputation Review*, **11** (4), 308–19.

Abratt, R. (1989), 'A new approach to the corporate image management process', *Journal of Marketing Management*, **5** (1), 63–76.

Advertising Standards Authority (2011), 'ASA ruling on Shell UK Ltd', accessed 4 January 2012 at https://www.asa.org.uk/Rulings/Adjudications/2011/10/Shell-UK-Ltd/SHP_ADJ_154707.aspx#.V0lHojJJl9M.

Agbonifo, J. (2009), 'Oil, insecurity, and subversive patriots in the Niger Delta: the Ogoni as agent of revolutionary change', *Journal of Third World Studies*, **26** (2), 71–107.

Albert, S. and D. Whetten (2003), 'Organizational identity', in John Balmer and Stephen Greyser (eds), *Revealing the Corporation: Perspectives on Identity, Image Reputation, Corporate Branding, and Corporate-Level Marketing*, London: Routledge, pp. 77–105.

Albrecht, S. (1996), *Crisis Management for Corporate Self-Defence*, New York: AMACOM.

Ali, T. and D. Barsamian (2005), *Conversations with Tariq Ali: Speaking of Empire and Resistance*, Melbourne: Scribe Publications.

Alsop, R. (2004), *The 18 Immutable Laws of Corporate Reputation: Creating, Protecting, and Repairing Your Most Valuable Asset*, New York: Free Press.

Amoore, L. (2005), *The Global Resistance Reader*, London: Routledge.

Anderson, R. (1998), *Mid-Course Correction: Toward a Sustainable Enterprise: The Interface Model*, Atlanta, GA: Peregrinzilla Press.

Anderson, R. (2000), 'The next industrial revolution', *Forum for Applied Research and Public Policy*, **15** (4), 23–8.

Anderson, R. (2007), 'Heroes of the environment – Ray Anderson', accessed 10 March 2015 at http://content.time.com/time/specials/2007/article/0,28804,1663317_1663322_1669929,00.html.

Anderson, R. (2009), *Business Lessons From a Radical Industrialist*, New York: St Martin's Press.

Anderson, R. (2010), 'Is Interface's sustainability strategy still relevant?', accessed 10 August 2012 at http://www.greenbiz.com/blog/2010/11/09/why-is-interfaces-climb-up-mount-sustainability-still-relevant.

Andrews, A., J. Simon, F. Tian and J. Zhao (2011), 'The Toyota crisis: an economic, operational and strategic analysis of the massive recall', *Management Research Review*, **34** (10), 1064–77.

Ang, S. (2009), 'Building intangible resources: the stickiness of reputation', *Corporate Reputation Review*, **12** (1), 21–32.

Annan, K. (1999), 'Kofi Annan's address to World Economic Forum in Davos', *World Economic Forum*, 1 February, accessed 29 April 2011 at http://www.un.org/press/en/1999/19990201.sgsm6881.html.

Arena, C. (2004), *Cause for Success: 10 Companies that Put Profits Second and Came in First*, Novato, CA: New World Library.

Ariweriokuma, S. (2008), *The Political Economy of Oil and Gas in Africa: The Case of Nigeria*, London: Routledge.

Armbruster-Sandoval, R. (2005), *Globalization and Cross-border Labor Solidarity in the Americas: The Anti-Sweatshop Movement and the Struggle for Social Justice*, London: Routledge.

Arnold, D. (2010), 'Transnational corporations and the duty to respect basic human rights', *Business Ethics Quarterly*, **20** (3), 371–99.

Arora, S. and T. Cason (1996), 'Why do firms volunteer to exceed environmental regulations? Understanding participation in EPA's 33/50 Program', *Land Economics*, **72** (4), 413–32.

Arratia, R. (2010), 'Embedding sustainability: one mind at a time', InterfaceRAISE, accessed 8 March 2015 at http://www.interface cutthefluff.com/wp-content/uploads/2010/05/EmbeddingSustainability. pdf.

The Australian (2010), 'Toyota President Akio Toyoda apologizes for faulty cars', 15 March, accessed 14 July 2010 at http://www.the australian.com.au/news/toyota-president-akio-toyoda-apologises-for-faulty-cars/story-e6frg6n6-1225827329343.

Ayres, I. and J. Braithwaite (1992), *Responsive Regulation: Transcending the Deregulation Debate*, New York: Oxford University Press.

Bakan, J. (2005), *The Corporation: The Pathological Pursuit of Profit and Power*, New York: The Free Press.

Bakir, V. (2005), 'Greenpeace versus Shell: media exploitation and the social amplification of risk framework (SARF)', *Journal of Risk Research*, **8** (7–8), 679–91.

Baldwin, R. and M. Cave (1999), *Understanding Regulation: Theory, Strategy, and Practice*, Oxford: Oxford University Press.

Baldwin, R., C. Scott and C. Hood (1998), *A Reader on Regulation*, Oxford: Oxford University Press.

Balmer, J. (1998), 'Corporate identity and the advent of corporate marketing', *Journal of Marketing Management*, **14** (8), 963–96.

Balmer, J. (2003), 'The three virtues and seven deadly sins of corporate brand management', in John Balmer and S. Greyser (eds), *Revealing the Corporation: Perspectives on Identity, Image, Reputation, Corporate Branding, and Corporate-Level Marketing*, London: Routledge, pp. 299–316.

Balmer, J. and E. Gray (2003), 'Corporate identity and corporate communications: creating a competitive advantage', in John Balmer and Stephen Greyser (eds), *Revealing the Corporation: Perspectives on Identity, Image, Reputation, Corporate Branding, and Corporate-Level Marketing*, London: Routledge, pp. 124–35.

Balmer, J. and S. Greyser (eds) (2003), *Revealing the Corporation: Perspectives on Identity, Image, Reputation, Corporate Branding, and Corporate-Level Marketing*, London: Routledge.

Banks, G. and C. Ballard (eds) (1997), *The Ok Tedi Settlement: Issues, Outcomes and Implications*, Canberra: Australian National University.

Barlett, D. and J. Steele (2008), 'Monsanto's harvest of fear', accessed 29 April 2012 at http://www.vanityfair.com/politics/features/2008/05/monsanto200805.

Barlow, M. and T. Clarke (2001), *Global Showdown: How the New Activists are Fighting Global Corporate Rule*, Toronto: Stoddard.

Barlow, M. and T. Clarke (2002), *Blue Gold: The Battle Against Corporate Theft of the World's Water*, London: Earthscan.

Barnet, R. and J. Cavanagh (1976), *Global Reach: The Power of Multinational Corporations*, New York: Touchstone Books.

Barnet, R. and J. Cavanagh (1995), *Global Dreams: Imperial Corporations and the New World Order*, New York: Touchstone Books.

Barnet, R. and J. Cavanagh (1996), 'The homogenization of global culture', in Jerry Mander and Edward Goldsmith (eds), *The Case Against the Global Economy and for a Turn Toward the Local*, San Francisco, CA: Sierra Club Books, pp. 71–7.

Barnett, M. and A.J. Hoffman (2008), 'Beyond corporate reputation: managing reputational interdependence', *Corporate Reputation Review*, **11** (1), 1–9.

Barnett, M., J. Jermier and B. Lafferty (2006), 'Corporate reputation: the definitional landscape', *Corporate Reputation Review*, **9** (1), 26–38.

Bartley, T. and C. Child (2010), 'Shaming the corporation: social movement pressure and corporate social responsibility', unpublished paper, accessed 25 November 2011 at http://www.vanityfair.com/news/2008/05/monsanto200805.

Baumeister, R., N. DeWall, N. Ciarocco and J. Twenge (2005), 'Social exclusion impairs self-regulation', *Journal of Personality and Social Psychology*, **88** (4), 589–604.

BBC News (2002), 'Ratner hopes to sparkle again', 27 May, accessed 1 May 2011 at http://news.bbc.co.uk/2/hi/business/2010949.stm.

BBC News (2010), 'Toyota set for global car recall', 28 January, accessed 5 January 2012 at http://news.bbc.co.uk/2/hi/business/8486401.stm.

Beder, S. (2002), *Global Spin: The Corporate Assault on Environmentalism*, London: Green Books.

Beiles, N. (2000), 'What Monsanto knew', *The Nation*, 29 May, accessed 29 April 2011 at http://www.thenation.com/print/article/what-monsanto-knew.

Bendell, J. and K. Kearins (2005), 'The political bottom line: the emerging dimension to corporate responsibility for sustainable development', *Business Strategy and the Environment*, **14** (6), 372–83.

Bender, F. (2003), *The Culture of Extinction: Towards a Philosophy of Deep Ecology*, New York: Humanity Books.

Bensinger, K. and R. Vartabedian (2010), 'Toyota took cost-cutting approach on Lurching Lexus Models, Records Show', *LA Times*, 23 May, accessed 10 March 2011 at http://articles.latimes.com/2010/may/23/business/la-fi-lexus-20100523.

Benson, R. (2000), *Challenging Corporate Rule: The Petition to Revoke Unocal's Charter as a Guide to Citizen Action*, New York: Apex Press.

BHP Billiton (2013), 'Annual environmental report FY13', accessed 14 April 2015 at http://www.oktedi.com/media-items/reports/environmental/annual-environmental-reports/208-2013-annual-environmental-report/file.

BHP Billiton (2014), 'Value through performance: annual report 2014', accessed 14 April 2015 at http://www.bhpbilliton.com/~/media/bhp/documents/investors/reports/2014/bhpbillitonannualreport2014_inter active.pdf?la=en.

Bob, C. (2005), 'From ethnic to environmental conflict: Nigeria's Ogoni movement', in *The Marketing of Rebellion: Insurgents, Media, and International Activism*, Cambridge: Cambridge University Press, pp. 54–116.

Bonini, S., D. Court and A. Marchi (2009), 'Rebuilding corporate reputations', *McKinsey Quarterly*, June, accessed 1 May 2011 at http://www.mckinsey.com/global-themes/leadership/rebuilding-corporate-reputations.

Bookchin, M. (1982), *The Ecology of Freedom: The Emergence and Dissolution of Heirarchy*, Montreal: Black Rose Books.

Bookchin, M. and D. Foreman (1991), *Defending the Earth*, Boston, MA: South End Press.

Bowes-Lyon, L-M., J. Richards and T. McGee (2009), 'Socio-economic impacts of the Nanisivik and Polaris Mines, Nanavut, Canada', in

Jeremy Richards (ed.), *Mining, Society, and a Sustainable World*, Berlin and Heidelberg: Springer-Verlag, pp. 371–96.

Boycott Nike (n.d.), accessed 8 August 2015 at http://boycott-nike.8m.com/.

Boyd, A. (2000), 'Extreme costume ball: a new protest movement hits the streets in style', *The Village Voice*, 18 July, accessed 29 April 2011 at http://www.villagevoice.com/2000-07-18/news/extreme-costume-ball/1/.

Braithwaite, J. and P. Drahos (2001), *Global Business Regulation*, Cambridge: Cambridge University Press.

Braungart, M. and W. McDonough (2002), *Cradle to Cradle: Remaking the Way We Make Things*, New York: North Point Press.

Briody, D. (2004), *The Halliburton Agenda: The Politics of Oil and Money*, New York: Wiley.

Bromley, D. (2002), 'Comparing corporate reputations: league tables, quotients, benchmarks, or case studies?', *Corporate Reputation Review*, **5** (1), 35–50.

Brown, W. (2004), 'At the edge', in Stephen White and J. Donald Moon (eds), *What is Political Theory*, London: Sage, pp. 103–23.

Brueckner, M. and R. Dyann (2010), *Under Corporate Skies: A Struggle Between People, Place, and Profit*, Perth: Fremantle Press.

Buchan, J. (2013), *Days of God: The Revolution in Iran and its Consequences*, New York: Simon and Schuster.

Buffett, W. (1995), *The Making of an American Capitalist*, New York: Broadway Books.

Business Week (2005), 'A milestone for human rights', 24 January, accessed 20 March 2006 at http://www.bloomberg.com/bw/stories/2005-01-23/a-milestone-for-human-rights.

Business Week (2010), 'The humbling of Toyota', 22 March, accessed 22 March 2010 at http://www.businessweek.com/magazine/content/10_12/b4171032583967.htm.

Carpet America Recovery Effort (2011), 'Annual Report', accessed 5 January 2012 at https://carpetrecovery.org/wp-content/uploads/2014/04/11_CARE-annual-rpt1.pdf.

Carpet America Recovery Effort (2013), 'Annual Report', accessed 5 July 2014 at https://carpetrecovery.org/wp-content/uploads/2014/04/CARE-2013-Annual-Report.pdf.

Carpet and Rug Institute (2012), 'Carpet and rug industry statistics', accessed 22 November 2013 at http://www.carpet-rug.org/carpet-and-rug-industry/carpet-and-rug-industry-statistics.cfm.

Carroll, C. (2009), 'Defying a reputational crisis – Cadbury's Salmonella scare: why are customers willing to forgive and forget?', *Corporate Reputation Review*, **12** (1), 64–82.

Carson, Rachel (2002), *Silent Spring*, Boston, MA: Mariner Books.

Castles, F., S. Leibfried, J. Lewis, H. Obinger and C. Pierson (2012), *The Oxford Handbook of the Welfare State*, Oxford: Oxford University Press.

Centre for Financial Market Integrity (2007), 'Self-regulation in today's securities markets: outdated system or work in progress?', accessed 16 September 2011 at http://www.investorvoice.ca/Research/CFA_Self-regulation_Oct07.pdf.

Cho, F. (2001), 'The Toyota Way 2001', accessed 30 July 2012 at http://www-personal.umich.edu/~mrother/KATA_Files/The_Toyota_Way_2001.pdf.

Choi, J. and W. Chung (2013), 'Analysis of the interactive relationship between apology and product involvement in crisis communication: an experimental study on the Toyota recall crisis', *Journal of Business and Technical Communication*, **27** (1), 3–31.

Chomsky, N. (2001), 'An evening with Noam Chomsky: the new war against terror', speech given at the Technology and Culture Forum, The Massachusetts Institute of Technology, 18 October, accessed 21 February 2008 at http://www.nadir.org/nadir/initiativ/agp/free/9-11/chomskywar.htm.

Chomsky, N. (2003), *What Uncle Sam Really Wants*, Berkeley, CA: Odonian Press.

Chomsky, N. (2004), *Hegemony or Survival: America's Quest for Global Dominance*, New York: Holt Paperbacks.

Christmann, P. and G. Taylor (2001), 'Globalisation and the environment: determinants of firm self-regulation in China', *Journal of International Business Studies*, **32** (3), 439–58.

Claessens, S. (2003), 'Corporate governance and development', accessed 9 July 2009 at https://openknowledge.worldbank.org/handle/10986/16395.

Clark, H. et al. (1999), 'Oil for nothing: multinational corporations, environmental destruction, death and impunity in the Niger Delta', *Trip Report*, September, accessed 31 May 2008 at http://www.essentialaction.org/shell/Final_Report.pdf.

Clarke, T. (1996), 'Mechanisms of corporate rule', in Jerry Mander and Edward Goldsmith (eds), *The Case Against the Global Economy and for a Turn Toward the Local*, San Francisco, CA: Sierra Book Club, pp. 297–308.

Clarkson, M. (1995), 'A stakeholder framework for analysing and evaluating corporate social performance', *Academy of Management Review*, **20** (1), 92–117.

CNN (2010), 'U.S. official: Toyota indicates it will pay $16.4 million fine', 19 April, accessed 3 March 2011 at http://edition.cnn.com/2010/BUSINESS/04/18/toyota.fine/index.html.

Cockburn, A., J. St Clair and A. Sekula (2000), *5 Days that Shook the World*, New York: Verso.

Cohen, J. (1993), 'Building sustainable public sector managerial, professional, and technical capacity: a framework for analysis and intervention', *Discussion Paper No. 473*, Harvard Institute for International Development, Cambridge, MA.

Connor, J. (2008), *Global Price Fixing*, New York: Springer.

Coombs, W.T. (2007), 'Protecting organization reputations during a crisis: the development and application of situational crisis communication theory', *Corporate Reputation Review*, **10** (3), 163–76.

Corpwatch (2000), 'Earth Day 2000 greenwash sweepstakes: Royal Dutch Shell', accessed 25 August 2015 at http://www.corpwatch.org/article.php?id=238.

Crane, A. and D. Matten (2010), *Business Ethics: Managing Corporate Citizenship and Sustainability in the Age of Globalization*, Oxford: Oxford University Press.

Crossley, N. (2002), 'Global anti-corporate struggle: a preliminary analysis', *British Journal of Sociology*, **53** (4), 667–91.

Culpepper, P.D. (2005), 'Institutional change in contemporary capitalism: coordinated financial systems since 1990', *World Politics*, **57** (2), 173–99.

Cummins, I. and J. Beasant (2005), *Shell Shock: The Secrets and Spin of an Oil Giant*, London: Mainstream Publishing.

Dahl, R. (1973), *Polyarchy: Participation and Opposition*, New York: Yale University Press.

Dahlsrud, A. (2006), 'How corporate social responsibility is defined: an analysis of 37 definitions', *Corporate Social Responsibility and Environmental Management*, **15**, 1–13.

Dale, J. (2011), *Free Burma: Transnational Legal Action and Corporate Accountability*, Minneapolis, MN: University of Minnesota Press.

Danaher, K. and J. Mark (2003), *Insurrection: Citizen Challenges to Corporate Power*, London: Routledge.

Dangl, B. (2007), *The Price of Fire: Resource Wars and Social Movements in Bolivia*, Edinburgh, WV: AK Press.

Davies, G., R. Chun, R. Vinhas da Silva and S. Roper (2001), 'The personification metaphor as a measurement approach for corporate reputation', *Corporate Reputation Review*, **4** (2), 113–27.

De Armond, P. (2000), 'Black flag over Seattle', *Albion Monitor*, No. 72, March, accessed 10 October 2014 at http://www.albionmonitor.com/seattlewto/index.html.

Dean, C. (2007), 'Executive on a mission: saving the planet', *New York Times*, 22 May, accessed 31 November 2008 at http://www.nytimes.com/2007/05/22/science/earth/22ander.html?_r=0.

Dean, J., M. Lovely and H. Wang (2009), 'Are foreign investors attracted to weak environmental regulations? Evaluating the evidence from China', *Journal of Development Economics*, **90** (1), 1–13.

Deffeyes, Kenneth (2008), *Hubbert's Peak: The Impending World Oil Shortage*, Princeton, NJ: Princeton University Press.

Delmas, M. and I. Montiel (2007), 'The diffusion of voluntary international management standards: Responsible Care, ISO 9000 and ISO 14001 in the chemical industry', ISBER Publications, Institute for Social, Behavioral, and Economic Research, UC Santa Barbara, accessed 1 September 2011 at http://escholarship.org/uc/item/8xh1j2fv.

Denning, S. (2000), *The Springboard: How Storytelling Ignites Action in Knowledge-Era Organizations*, New York: Butterworth-Heinemann.

Denning, S. (2011), *The Leader's Guide to Storytelling: Mastering the Art and Discipline of Business Narrative*, New York: Jossey Bass.

Department for Business, Innovation and Skills (2010), 'The impact of UK companies on the Millennium Development Goals', accessed 1 May 2011 at http://www.mmv.org/sites/default/files/uploads/docs/publications/UNGC_UK_Network_MDG_Report_June_2010.pdf.

Derber, C. (2014), *Corporation Nation: How Corporations are Taking Over Our Lives and What We Can Do about It*, New York: St. Martin's Press.

Deutsch, C. (2005), 'It's getting crowded on the environmental bandwagon', *New York Times*, 22 December, accessed 25 August 2011 at http://www.nytimes.com/2005/12/22/business/22adco.html.

Diaz, C. (2007) 'Foreword', in Elizabeth Rogers and Thomas Kostigen (eds), *The Green Book: The Everyday Guide to Saving the Planet One Simple Step at a Time*, New York: Three Rivers Press.

Dobbing, J. (1988), *Infant Feeding: Anatomy of a Controversy, 1972–1984*, The Hague: Springer Verlag.

Doe v. Unocal, accessed 29 April 2011 at https://www.earthrights.org/legal/doe-v-unocal.

Donaldson, T. and L. Preston (1995), 'The stakeholder theory of the corporation: concepts, evidence, and implications', *Academy of Management Review*, **20** (1), 65–91.

Donnelly, J. (2013), *Universal Human Rights in Theory and Practice*, Ithaca, NY: Cornell University Press.

Donovan, J. (2010), 'Royal Dutch Shell's Nazi secrets', accessed 25 August 2011 at http://royaldutchshellplc.com/2010/11/06/royal-dutch-shell-nazi-secrets-2/.

Doorley, J. and H.F. Garcia (2007), *Reputation Management: The Key to Successful Public Relations and Corporate Communication*, London: Routledge.

Dowling, G. (2002), *Creating Corporate Reputations: Identity, Image, and Performance*, Oxford: Oxford University Press.

Dowling, P., M. Festing and A. Engle (2008), *International Human Resource Management*, London: Thomson.

Doyle, J. (2002), *Riding the Dragon: Royal Dutch Shell and the Fossil Fire*, Vermont: Environmental Health Fund.

Doyle, Michael (1997), *Ways of War and Peace: Realism, Liberalism and Socialism*, New York: W.W. Norton.

Drengson, Alan and Yuichi Inoue (1995), *The Deep Ecology Movement: An Introductory Anthology*, Berkeley, CA: North Atlantic Books.

Drohan, M. and A. Freeman (2000), 'English rules', in Patrick O'Maera, Howard Mehlinger and Matthew Krain (eds), *Globalisation and the Challenges of a New Century: A Reader*, Bloomington, IN: Indiana University Press, pp. 428–34.

Dryzek, J. (2005), *The Politics of the Earth: Environmental Discourses*, Oxford: Oxford University Press.

Dudley, S. and J. Brito (2012), *Regulation: A Primer*, Arlington, VA: The Mercatus Center.

Dugan, I. (2002), 'Auditing old-timers recall when prestige was the bottom line – Andersen's Al Bows relished going over the books: CEO brought to account', *Wall Street Journal*, 15 July, A1.

The Economist (1995), 'Multinationals and their morals', **337** (7943), 2 December, accessed 10 December 2004 at http://web1.calbaptist.edu/dskubik/econ2.htm.

The Economist (2004a), 'From anarchy to apathy: anarchists seem to be having trouble getting organised. Let's give them a hand', **371** (8368), 3 April, accessed 29 April 2011 at http://www.economist.com/node/2553278.

The Economist (2004b), 'Another head rolls in the boardroom', accessed 3 January 2009 at http://www.economist.com/node/2608070/print.

The Economist (2010a), 'Toyota: accelerating into trouble', **394** (8669), 15, accessed 5 July 2011 at http://www.economist.com/node/15498249.

The Economist (2010b), 'Toyota's supply chain: the machine that ran too hot', **394** (8671), 74, accessed 5 July 2011 at http://www.economist.com/node/15576506.

Economist Intelligence Unit (2005), 'Reputation: risk of risks', accessed 2 May 2011 at http://www.acegroup.com/eu-en/assets/risk-reputation-report.pdf.

Eden, L. and M. Appel Molot (2002), 'Insiders, outsiders and host country bargains', *Journal of International Management*, **8** (4), 359–88.

Edwards, A. (2005), *The Sustainability Revolution: Portrait of a Paradigm Shift*, Victoria, BC: New Society Publishers.

Eichenwald, K. (2005), *Conspiracy of Fools: A True Story*, Louisville, KY: Broadway Press.

Eisner, M. (1993), *Regulatory Politics in Transition*, Baltimore, MD: Johns Hopkins University Press.

Elliot, L. and R. Schroth (2002), *How Companies Lie: Why Enron is Just the Tip of the Iceberg*, London: Nicholas Brealey Publishing.

Ellis, T. (2012), *The New Pioneers: Sustainable Business Success Through Social Innovation and Social Entrepreneurship*, Chichester: Wiley.

Environmental Protection Agency (2005), 'U.S. EPA fines Shell Oil of Bakersfield $16,500 for chemical reporting violations', accessed 25 August 2011 at http://yosemite.epa.gov/opa/admpress.nsf/748a5f366 9ca0b6c852570180055c8cb/19daf668a3f23687852570d8005e17e2!open document.

Equator Principles (n.d.), Equator Principles website, accessed 30 January 2012 at www.equator-principles.com.

Etzioni, A. (2009), 'The free market versus a regulating government', *Challenge*, **52** (1), 40–46.

Europa (2006a), 'Competition: commission fines producers and traders of synthetic rubber €519 million for price fixing', EU Commission Press Release Database, accessed 25 August 2011 at http://europa.eu/rapid/pressReleasesAction.do?reference=IP/06/1647.

Europa (2006b), 'Competition: commission fines 14 companies a total of €266.717 million for price fixing of road bitumen in the Netherlands', EU Commission Press Release Database, accessed 25 August 2011 at http://europa.eu/rapid/pressReleasesAction.do?reference=IP/06/1179.

Evans, G., J. Goodman and N. Lansbury (eds) (2002b), *Moving Mountains: Communities Confront Mining Globalisation*, London: Zed Books.

Evans, R., T. Quirk and A. Moran (2009), 'Back to the 19th century: Australia under a carbon pollution reduction scheme (sic) act 2009', accessed 24 February 2014 at http://www.lavoisier.com.au/articles/climate-policy/science-and-policy/backtothe19C.pdf.

Evans, G., G. Russell and R. Sullivan (2002a), 'An international regulatory framework?', in Geoffrey Evans, James Goodman and Nina Lansbury (eds), *Moving Mountains: Communities Confront Mining and Globalisation*, London: Zed Books, pp. 207–22.

Eviatar, D. (2005), 'A big win for human rights', *The Nation*, **280** (18), 20–22.

ExxonMobil (2007), 'Summary annual report', accessed 28 April 2011 at http://www.slideshare.net/earningsreport/ford-3q08-fixed-income-conference-call-presentation.

ExxonMobil (2010), 'Summary annual report', accessed 28 April 2011 at http://cdn.exxonmobil.com/~/media/global/Files/Summary-Annual-Report/news_pubs_sar_2010.pdf.

ExxonMobil (2013), 'Summary annual report', accessed 15 February 2015 at http://cdn.exxonmobil.com/en/shareholder-archive/~/media/Reports/Summary%20Annual%20Report/2013_ExxonMobil_Summary_Annual_Report.pdf.

Ezrow, N. and E. Frantz (2013), *Failed States and Institutional Decay: Understanding Instability and Poverty in the Developing World*, New York: Bloomsbury Academic.

Fagre, N. and L.T. Wells, Jr (1982), 'Bargaining power of multinationals and host governments', *Journal of International Business Studies*, **13** (2), 9–24.

Falk, R. (1999), *Predatory Globalisation: A Critique*, London: Polity Press.

Fan, D., D. Geddes and F. Flory (2013), 'The Toyota recall crisis: media impact on Toyota's corporate brand reputation', *Corporate Reputation Review*, **16** (2), 99–117.

Farrell, G. (2004), 'Shell says execs ignored warnings,' *USA Today*, 20 April, p. 01b, accessed 25 August 2011 at http://www.usatoday.com/money/industries/energy/2004-04-19-shell-cfo_x.htm.

Feder, B. (1987), 'Citibank is leaving South Africa: foes of Apartheid see major gain', *New York Times*, 17 June, accessed 8 February 2011 at http://query.nytimes.com/gst/fullpage.html?res=9B0DEFDB1730F934A25755C0A961948260&sec=&spon=&pagewanted=1.

Financial Reporting Council (2010), *The UK Corporate Governance Code*, accessed 10 August 2011 at https://www.frc.org.uk/Our-Work/Codes-Standards/Corporate-governance/UK-Corporate-Governance-Code.aspx.

Financial Review (2011), 'Shell, Cosan form $12bn ethanol deal', accessed 25 August 2011 at http://afr.com/p/business/companies/shell_cosan_form_bn_ethanol_deal_LA2P9Lo2N8Ha0KQs0WQ2BN.

Finnemore, M. and K. Sikkink (2001), 'Taking stock: the constructivist research program in international relations and comparative politics', *Annual Review of Political Science*, **4** (1), 391–416.

Firth, S. (1999), *Australia in International Politics: An Introduction to Australian Foreign Policy*, Melbourne: Allen and Unwin.

Fisher, C. and A. Lovell (2006), *Business Ethics and Values: Individual, Corporate and International Perspectives*, 2nd edn, London: Prentice Hall.

Flannery, T. (2009), *Now or Never: Why We Must Act Now to End Climate Change and Create a Sustainable Future*, New York: Atlantic Monthly Press.

Flynn, D. (2004), *Why the Left Hates America*, New York: Three Rivers Press.

Fombrun, C. (1996), *Reputation: Realising Value From the Corporate Image*, Boston, MA: Harvard Business School Press.

Fombrun, C. (1998), 'Indices of corporate reputation: an analysis of media rankings and social monitors' ratings', *Corporate Reputation Review*, **1** (4), 327–40.

Fombrun, C. (2000), 'The road to transparency: reputation management at Royal Dutch/Shell', in Majken Schultz, Mary Jo Hatch and Mogens Holten Larsen (eds), *The Expressive Organisation: Linking Identity, Reputation, and the Corporate Brand*, Oxford: Oxford University Press.

Fombrun, C. and C. van Riel (2004), *Fame and Fortune: How Successful Companies Build Winning Reputations*, New York: Prentice Hall.

Fombrun, C., N. Gardberg and M. Barnett (2000a), 'Opportunity platforms and safety nets: corporate citizenship and reputational risk', *Business and Society Review*, **105** (1), 85–106.

Fombrun, C., N. Gardberg and J. Sever (2000b), 'The Reputation Quotient^{SM}: a multi-stakeholder measure of corporate reputation', *The Journal of Brand Management*, **7** (4), 241–55.

Forrest, T. (1993), *Political and Economic Development in Nigeria*, Oxford: Oxford University Press.

Fortune (2015), Global 500, accessed 23 May 2016 at http://fortune.com/global500/.

Foucault, M. (1991), *The Foucault Effect: Studies in Governmentality*, Chicago, IL: The University of Chicago Press.

Frankel, B. (1987), *The Post-Industrial Utopians*, Oxford: Polity Press.

Freeman, Edward R. (2010), *Strategic Management: A Stakeholder Approach*, Cambridge: Cambridge University Press.

Freeman, Edward R., J. Harrison and A. Wicks (2007), *Managing for Stakeholders: Survival, Reputation, and Success*, New Haven, CT: Yale University Press.

Freeman, Edward R., J. Harrison, A. Wicks, B. Parmar and S. de Colle (2010), *Stakeholder Theory: The State of the Art*, Cambridge: Cambridge University Press.

Friedman, M. (1970), 'The social responsibility of business is to increase its profits', in Tom Beauchamp and Norman Bowie (eds), *Ethical Theory and Business*, 6th edn, New York: Prentice Hall, pp. 51–6.

Friedman, T. (2000), *The Lexus and the Olive Tree*, New York: Harper-Collins.

Friedman, T. (2007), 'Et tu, Toyota?' *New York Times*, 3 October, accessed 15 March 2014 at http://www.nytimes.com/2007/10/03/opinion/03friedman.html?_r=0.

Friends of the Earth International (2002), 'Failing the challenge: the other Shell report', accessed 25 August 2011 at http://www.h-net.org/~esati/sdcea/shellfailingchallenge.pdf.

Friends of the Earth International (2003), 'Behind the shine: the other Shell report', accessed 25 August 2011 at http://www.h-net.org/~esati/sdcea/shellreportFIN.pdf.

Friends of the Earth International (2004), 'Lessons not learned: the other Shell report', accessed 25 August 2011 at https://www.foe.co.uk/sites/default/files/downloads/lessons_not_learned.pdf.

Frynas, J.G. (1998), 'Political instability and business: focus on Shell in Nigeria', *Third World Quarterly*, **19** (3), 457–78.

Fuller, J. (2004), 'A triumph of form, now for the content: Shell's unitary answer to several questions', *Financial Times*, 29 October.

Fullerton, D. (2006), *The Economics of Pollution Havens*, Cheltenham, UK and Northampton, MA, USA: Edward Elgar Publishing.

Furman, D. (2010), 'The development of corporate image: a historiographic approach to a marketing concept', *Corporate Reputation Review*, **13** (1), 63–75.

Furrer, O. (2011), *Corporate Level Strategy: Theory and Application*, London: Routledge.

Gadamer, H-G. (2008), *Philosophical Hermeneutics: 30th Anniversary Edition*, Berkeley, CA: University of California Press.

Gadamer, H-G. (2013), *Truth and Method*, New York: The Seabury Press.

Gaddis, J.L. (1992/93), 'International relations theory and the end of the Cold War', *International Security*, **17** (3), 5–58.

Gaines-Ross, L. (2003), *Building CEO Capital: A Guide to Building CEO Reputation and Company Success*, New York: John Wiley and Sons.

Gaines-Ross, L. (2008), *Corporate Reputation: 12 Steps to Safeguarding and Recovering Reputation*, New York: John Wiley and Sons.

Gallu, J. and A. Nussbaum (2011), 'Johnson & Johnson will pay $70 million over bribery claims', *Bloomberg*, 9 April, accessed 5 May 2012 at http://www.bloomberg.com/news/2011-04-08/johnson-johnson-will-pay-70-million-to-resolve-bribery-claims.html.

Gallucci, M. (2012), 'California's landmark clean car mandate: how it works and what it means', accessed 7 March 2011at http://insideclimatenews.org/news/20120208/california-landmark-clean-vehicles-electric-cars-regulations-2025-fuel-efficiency-epa?page=4.

Gardberg, N. and C. Fombrun (2002), 'The global Reputation Quotient project: first steps towards a cross-nationally valid measure of corporate reputation', *Corporate Reputation Review*, **4** (4), 303–7.

Garnaut, R. (2008), *The Garnaut Climate Change Review: Final Report*, Melbourne: Cambridge University Press.

Gedicks, A. (2001), *Resource Rebels: Native Challenges to Mining and Oil Corporations*, New York: South End Press.

Gelbspan, R. (2004), *Boiling Point: How Politicians, Big Oil and Coal, Journalists, and Activists Have Fueled the Climate Change Crisis – and What We Can Do to Avert Disaster*, New York: Basic Books.

Gewin, V. (2002), 'Climate lobby group closes down', *Nature*, **415** (6872), 567.

Gibson, D., J. Gonzales and J. Castanon (2006), 'The importance of reputation and the role of public relations', *Public Relations Quarterly*, **51** (3), 15–18.

The Girl Effect (n.d.), 'The Girl Declaration', accessed 30 June 2014 at http://www.girleffect.org/the-girl-effect-in-action/girl-declaration/.

Glancey, J. (2008), *The Car: A History of the Automobile*, London: Carlton Publishing Group.

Global Scan/SustainAbility (2014), 'The 2014 Sustainability Leaders', accessed 1 April 2015 at http://www.sustainability.com/library/the-2014-sustain-ability-leaders.

Godin, S. (2005), *All Marketers are Liars: The Power of Telling Authentic Stories in a Low-Trust World*, London: Penguin.

Goins, S. and T. Gruca (2008), 'Understanding competitive and contagion effects of layoff announcements', *Corporate Reputation Review*, **11** (1), 12–34.

Gordon, J. (1997), The Ok Tedi lawsuit in retrospect', in G. Banks and C. Ballard (eds), *The Ok Tedi Settlement: Issues, Outcomes and Implications*, Canberra: Australian National University.

Gore, A. (2006), *An Inconvenient Truth: The Planetary Emergency of Global Warming and What We Can Do about It*, Emmaus, PA: Rodale Books.

Gotsi, M. and A. Wilson (2001), 'Corporate reputation: seeking a definition', *Corporate Communications: An International Journal*, **6** (1), 24–30.

Graham, D. and N. Woods (2006), 'Making corporate self-regulation effective in developing countries', *World Development*, **34** (5), 868–83.

Gramsci, A. (2011), 'Americanism and Fordism', *Prison Notebooks*, New York: Columbia University Press.

Greer, J. (2013), *Not the Future we Ordered: The Psychology of Peak Oil and the Myth of Eternal Progress*, London: Karnac Books.

Greer, J. and K. Bruno (1997), *Greenwash: The Reality Behind Corporate Environmentalism*, Sydney: Apex Press.

Grether, J-M. and J. Melo (2003), 'Globalization and dirty industries: do pollution havens matter?', *National Bureau of Economic Research*, Working Paper No. 9776, accessed 6 June 2011 at http://www.nber.org/papers/w9776.

Griffin, A. (2008), *New Strategies for Reputation Management*, London: Kogan Page.

Griffin, G. (2002), *Reputation Management*, London: Capstone Publishing.

Griffiths, M., T. O'Callaghan and S. Roach (2014), 'Multinational corporations', *International Relations: The Key Concepts*, London: Routledge, pp. 224–6.

Grosse, R. (2005a), *International Business and Government Relations in the 21st Century*, Cambridge: Cambridge University Press, Chapters 10–13.

Grosse, R. (2005b), 'The bargaining view of government–business relations', in Robert Grosse (ed.), *International Business and Government Relations in the 21st Century*, Cambridge: Cambridge University Press, pp. 273–90.

Grunig, J. (2003), 'Image and substance: from symbolic to behavioural relationships', in John Balmer and Stephen Greyser (eds), *Revealing the Corporation: Perspectives on Identity, Image Reputation, Corporate Branding, and Corporate-Level Marketing*, London: Routledge, pp. 204–22.

The Guardian (2010a), 'Timeline: Toyota's recall woes', accessed 29 January 2010 at http://www.guardian.co.uk/business/2010/jan/29/timeline-toyota-recall-accelerator-pedal.

The Guardian (2010b), 'China overtakes US as world's biggest car market', 8 January, accessed 8 January 2010 at http://www.guardian.co.uk/business/2010/jan/08/china-us-car-sales-overtakes.

Halliday, J. (2005), 'Relentless Toyota thrives on crisis', *Advertising Age*, **76** (8), 33–7, accessed 3 January 2011 at http://adage.com/article/toyota-report/relentless-toyota-thrives-crisis/102133/.

Hand, John and Baruch Lev (2003), *Intangible Assets: Values, Measures and Risks*, Oxford: Oxford University Press.

Handelsman, S. (2002), 'Human rights in the minerals industry', *Mining, Minerals and Sustainable Development*, January, accessed 6 June 2011 at http://pubs.iied.org/G00531.html.

Hanna, B., W. Moorhouse and S. Sarangi (2005), *The Bhopal Reader: Remembering Twenty Years of the World's Worst Industrial Disaster*, Sydney: Apex Press.

Hardin, G. (1968), 'The tragedy of the commons', *Science*, **162**, 1243–8.

Harmer, T. (2011), *Allende's Chile and the Inter-American Cold War*, Chapel Hill, NC: University of North Carolina Press.

Hartmann, T. (2007), *Screwed: The Undeclared War Against the Middle Class – and What We Can Do about It*, San Francisco, CA: Berrett-Koehler Publishers.

Harvey, D. (1992), *The Condition of Postmodernity: An Enquiry into the Conditions of Cultural Change*, Oxford: Blackwell.

Hawken, P. (2005), *The Ecology of Commerce: A Declaration of Sustainability*, New York: HarperCollins.

Hawken, P., A. Lovins and L. Hunter-Lovins (2008), *Natural Capitalism: Creating the Next Industrial Revolution*, Washington, DC: US Green Building Council.

Hawkins, M. (1997), *Unshielded: The Human Cost of the Dalkon Shield*, Toronto: University of Toronto Press.

Healy, R. and J. Griffin (2004), 'Building BP's reputation: tooting your own horn 2001–2002', *Public Relations Quarterly*, **49** (4), 33–42.

Heil, D. and L. Whittaker (2011), 'What is reputation, really?', *Corporate Reputation Review*, **14** (4), 262–72.

Heller, V. and J. Darling (2011), 'Toyota in crisis: denial and mismanagement', *Journal of Business Strategy*, **32** (5), 4–13.

Heller, V. and J. Darling (2012), 'Anatomy of crisis management: lessons from the infamous Toyota case', *European Business Review*, **24** (2), 151–68.

Helm, S. (2005), 'Designing a formative measure for corporate reputation', *Corporate Reputation Review*, **8** (2), 95–109.

Helman, C. (2006), 'Shell shocked', *Forbes*, **178** (3), accessed 25 August 2011 at http://www.forbes.com/forbes/2006/0814/092_print.html.

Henderson, D. (2009), 'Misguided corporate virtue: the case against CSR, and the true role of business today', London: The Institute of Economic Affairs.

Henderson, D. (2001a), 'The case against "corporate social responsibility"', *Policy*, **17** (2), 28–32.

Henderson, D. (2001b), *Misguided Virtue: False Notions of Corporate Social Responsibility*, London: The Institute of Economic Affairs.

Henderson, T. and J. Williams (2002), 'Shell: managing a corporate reputation globally', in Danny Moss and Barbara Desanto (eds), *Public Relations Cases: International Perspectives*, London: Routledge, pp. 10–26.

Hendrix, Dan and Paul Lynch (2015), 'Investor presentation', May, accessed 16 June 2016 at http://www.interfaceglobal.com/Investor-Relations.aspx.

Henisz, W. (2014), *Corporate Diplomacy: Building Reputations and Relationships with External Stakeholders*, London: Greenleaf Press.

Herremans, I., M. Herschovis and S. Bertels (2009), 'Leaders and laggards: the influence of competing logics on corporate environmental action', *Journal of Business Ethics*, **89** (3), 449–72.

Hiley, D., J. Bohman and R. Shusterman (1992), *The Interpretive Turn: Philosophy, Science, Culture*, New York: Cornell University Press.

Hillenbrand, C. and K. Money (2007), 'Corporate responsibility and corporate reputation: two separate concepts or two sides of the same coin?', *Corporate Reputation Review*, **10** (4), 261–77.

Hodgson, P. (2006), 'The rise and rise of the regulatory state', *The Political Quarterly*, **77** (2), 247–54.

Hoffman, A. (2001), *From Heresy to Dogma: An Institutional History of Corporate Environmentalism*, Stanford, CA: Stanford University Press.

Holliday, C., S. Schmidheiny and P. Watts (2002), *Walking the Talk: The Business Case for Sustainable Development*, San Francisco, CA: Berrett-Koehler Publishers.

Holtz, U. (2007), 'Implementing the United Nations convention to combat desertification from a parliamentary point of view: critical assessment and challenges ahead', paper presented at the Seventh Session of UNCCD's Parliamentarians Forum, Madrid, Spain, 12–13 September.

Hopkins, M. (2003), *The Planetary Bargain: Corporate Social Responsibility Matters*, Oxford: Earthscan Publications.

Howard, R. (2009), *Arctic Gold Rush: The New Race for Tomorrow's Natural Resources*, London: Continuum.

Huffington Post (2011), 'The sexiest PETA ads of all time!', accessed 1 December 2012 at http://www.huffingtonpost.com/2009/06/21/the-sexiest-peta-ads-of-a_n_217731.html.

Human Rights Watch (1999), 'The price of oil', New York: Human Rights Watch, **161**, accessed 25 August 2011 at http://www.hrw.org/en/reports/1999/02/23/price-oil.

Human Rights Watch (2012), 'World Report 2012: Burma', accessed 1 February 2014 at http://www.hrw.org/world-report-2012/world-report-2012-burma.

Hummels, G. (1998), 'Organizing ethics: a stakeholder debate', *Journal of Business Ethics*, **17** (13), 1403–19.

Hymas, L. (2009), 'Green-biz pioneer Ray Anderson says sustainability literally pays for itself', accessed 30 March 2015 at http://grist.org/article/2009-10-19-ray-anderson-sustainability-interview-book/.

Ignatius, D. (1999), 'A global marketplace means global vulnerability', *Washington Post*, 22 June, accessed 4 May 2011 at http://www.globalpolicy.org/globaliz/special/globvuln.htm.

Ina, K. (2012), 'Made by Toyota: aiming for global quality assurance', accessed 23 February 2015 at http://www.reliableplant.com/Read/3624/made-by-toyota-aiming-for-global-quality-assurance.

Independent Pricing and Regulatory Tribunal of New South Wales (2006), 'Investigation into the burden of regulation in NSW and improving regulatory efficiency: issues paper', accessed 13 September 2015 at http://www.ipart.nsw.gov.au/files/sharedassets/website/trim holdingbay/section_9_regulation_review_-_issues_paper_-_website_document.pdf.

Innocent, E., M. Samy, R. Bampton and A. Halabi (2011), 'The relationship between corporate social responsibility and profitability: the case of Royal Dutch Shell Plc', *Corporate Reputation Review*, **14** (4), 249–61.

Interbrand (2011), '100 best global brands 2011', accessed 15 February 2012 at http://www.rankingthebrands.com/The-Brand-Rankings.aspx?rankingID=37&year=368.

Interface Inc. (2013a), 'Looking beyond sustainability: Interface explores restorative enterprise at Greenbuild 2013', accessed 11 July 2016 at http://interfaceinc.scene7.com/is/content/InterfaceInc/Interface/Americas/Website%20&%20Content%20Assets/Documents/Press%20Releases/Greenbuild%202013/wc_greenbuild2013pr.pdf.

Interface Inc (2013b), 'Interface expands and adapts definition of sustainability with evolving eco and social Metrics', accessed 31 March 2015 at https://us.vocuspr.com/Newsroom/ViewAttachment.aspx?SiteName=interfaceIFrame&Entity=PRAsset&AttachmentType=F&EntityID=120183&AttachmentID=836625ad-11e1-40d3-bb8a-6fc761770f8e.

Interface (2015a), 'Go beyond', accessed 1 April 2015 at http://www.interfaceflor.com.au/files/files/pdf/sustainability/GoBeyond_Brochure.pdf.

Interface (2015b), 'Just the facts guide: how to choose the most sustainable products and what to ask the manufacturers', accessed 1 April 2015 at http://www.interfaceflor.se/web/sustainability/just_the_facts.

Interface Inc. (2008), 'The seven fronts (faces of Mt. Sustainability)', accessed 7 October 2009 at http://www.interfaceflor.eu/web/sustainability/mission_zero/seven_front.

Interface Inc. (2009), 'InterfaceFLOR – mission zero (2009)', accessed 30 March 2015 at https://www.youtube.com/watch?v=NrsK4Vn1ExY.

Interface Inc. (2012a), 'I am mission zero', accessed 30 March 2015 at https://www.youtube.com/user/IAmMissionZero.

Interface Inc. (2012b), 'Interface announces pending sale of Bentley Prince Street to Dominus Capital', accessed 28 March 2015 at https://us.vocuspr.com/Newsroom/ViewAttachment.aspx?SiteName=interfaceI

Frame&Entity=PRAsset&AttachmentType=F&EntityID=118904&
AttachmentID=4f2e0da9-7d5d-4fd2-8499-005fbf364464.

Interface Europe (n.d.), 'Interface Europe: our progress to zero', accessed 25 March at http://www.interfaceflor.co.uk/webapp/wcs/stores/ GetMediaBytes?mediaReference=63409.

InterfaceRAISE (2010a), *Mission Zero: The Power of a Challenging Vision*, accessed 5 May 2014 at http://www.interfacecutthefluff.com/ tag/interfaceraise/.

InterfaceRAISE (2010b), *Embedded Sustainability: One Mind at a Time*, accessed 5 May at http://www.interfacecutthefluff.com/tag/inter faceraise/.

Intergovernmental Panel on Climate Change (2007), 'IPCC fourth assessment report: climate change 2007', accessed 30 April 2011 at http:// www.ipcc.ch/publications_and_data/publications_and_data_reports. shtml#1.

International Business Leaders Forum (2011), 'The Millennium poll on corporate social responsibility', accessed 11 August 2011 at http:// www-dev.iblf.org/resources/general.jsp?id=85.

International Council of Chemical Associations (2011a), 'Responsible Care Global Charter', accessed 1 September 2011 at http:// www.cefic.org/Documents/ResponsibleCare/RC_GlobalCharter2006% 5b1%5d.pdf.

International Finance Corporation (2005), 'Toolkit: developing corporate governance codes of best practice', *Global Corporate Governance Forum*, Washington, DC: World Bank Group, accessed 25 August 2011 at http://www.ifc.org/wps/wcm/connect/topics_ext_content/ifc_ external_corporate_site/corporate+governance/publications/toolkits+and +manuals/toolkit2_codes_of_best_practice.

Irvine, S. (1989), 'Consuming fashions? The limits of green consumerism', *The Ecologist*, **19** (3), 88–9.

Iyengar, R., J. Kargar and M. Sundararajan (2011), 'Why are firms admired?', *Corporate Reputation Review*, **14** (3), 200–20.

Jackson, I. and J. Nelson (2004), *Profits With Principles: Seven Strategies for Delivering Value with Values*, New York: Doubleday.

Jackson, K. (2004), *Building Reputational Capital: Strategies for Integrity and Fair Play that Improve the Bottom Line*, New York: Oxford University Press.

Jaffe, N.R. and J. Weiss (2006), 'The self-regulating corporation: how corporate codes can save our children', *Fordham Journal of Corporate & Financial Law*, **11** (4), 893–922.

Jenkins, R. (2001), 'Corporate codes of conduct: self-regulation in a global economy', *Technology, Business and Society Programme*,

United Nations Research Institute for Social Development, No. 2, April, pp. 1–42.

Jewell, M. (2004), 'USA Inc: the corporate government tapestry of George Bush', in Clint Willis and Nate Hardcastle (eds), *The I Hate Corporate America Reader: How Big Companies from McDonald's to Microsoft Are Destroying Our Way of Life*, Cambridge, MA: Da Capo Press, pp. 127–39.

Johnson, Chalmers (2004), *Blowback: The Costs and Consequences of American Empire*, New York: Holt Paperbacks.

Johnson, V. and S. Peppas (2003), 'Crisis management in Belgium: the case of Coca-Cola', *Corporate Communications: An International Journal*, **18** (1), 18–22.

Jones, M. and G. Sutherland (1999), 'Implementing Turnbull: a board-room briefing', London: The Institute of Chartered Accountants in England and Wales, accessed 1 May 2011 at http://www.icaew.com/~/media/corporate/files/technical/research%20and%20academics/publications%20and%20projects/corporate%20governance%20publications/implementing%20turnbull.ashx.

Jones, S. (2010), 'Toyota now the Tiger Woods of motoring, recall to cost $US 80m a day', *Dow Jones Newswires*, 28 January.

Jordana, J. and D. Levi-Faur (2004), *The Politics of Regulation: Institutions and Regulatory Reforms for the Age of Governance*, Cheltenham, UK and Northampton, MA, USA: Edward Elgar Publishing.

Karliner, J. (1997), *The Corporate Planet*, San Francisco, CA: Sierra Club Books.

Kasperson, J., R. Kasperson, N. Pidgeon and P. Slovic (2003), 'The social amplification of risk: assessing fifteen years of research and theory', in Nick Pidgeon, Roger Kasperson and Paul Slovic (eds), *The Social Amplification of Risk*, New York: Cambridge University Press, pp. 13–46.

Kazin, M. (2002), 'A patriotic left', *Dissent*, **49** (4), 41–4.

Kegley, C. and S. Blanton (2009), *World Politics: Trends and Transformations, 2009–2010 Update Edition*, Florence, KY: Wadsworth Publishing.

Kegley, C. and E. Wittkopf (2004), *World Politics: Trend and Transformation*, New York: Palgrave Macmillan.

Kehr, J. (2011), *The Inconvenient Skeptic: The Comprehensive Guide to the Earth's Climate*, John Kehr Publishing.

Kennedy, S. (1977), 'Nurturing corporate images', *European Journal of Marketing*, **11** (3), 119–64.

Keohane, R. and J. Nye (1977), *Power and Interdependence: World Politics in Transition*, Boston, MA: Little, Brown Books.

Khan, S. (1994), *Nigeria: The Political Economy of Oil*, Oxford: Oxford University Press.

Killer Coke (n.d.), Killer Coke website, accessed 15 June 2013 at http://killercoke.org/.

Kimes, B. (2004), *Pioneers, Engineers, and Scoundrels: The Dawn of the Automobile in America*, Warrendale, PA: Society of Automotive Engineers Inc.

Kindleberger, C. (1969), *American Business Abroad: Six Lectures on Direct Investment*, New Haven, CT: Yale University Press.

King, A. and M. Lenox (2000), 'Industry self-regulation without sanctions: the chemical industry's responsible care program', *The Academy of Management Journal*, **43** (4), 698–716.

King, D. (1997), 'The big polluter and the constructing of Ok Tedi: eco-imperialism and underdevelopment along the Ok Tedi and Fly Rivers of Papua New Guinea', in G. Banks and C. Ballard (eds), *The Ok Tedi Settlement: Issues, Outcomes and Implications*, Canberra: Australian National University.

King, D. (2000), 'Stakeholders and spindoctors: the politicisation of corporate reputations', Hawke Institute Working Paper Series, No. 5, accessed 24 August 2004 at http://www.unisa.edu.au/Documents/EASS/HRI/working-papers/wp5.pdf.

Kitchen, P. (2013), 'Corporate identity antecedents and components: toward a theoretical framework', *Corporate Reputation Review*, **16** (4), 263–84.

Klare, M. (2002), *Resource Wars: The New Landscape of Global Conflict*, New York: Holt Paperbacks.

Klare, M. (2012), *The Race for What's Left: The Global Scramble for the World's Last Resources*, New York: Picador.

Klein, D. (1968), 'The introduction, increase, and crash of reindeer on St. Matthew Island', *The Journal of Wildlife Management*, **32**, 350–67.

Klein, N. (2001), *No Logo*, New York: HarperCollins.

Klein, N. (2002a), *Windows and Fences: Dispatches from the Front Lines of the Globalisation Debate*, London: Flamingo.

Klein, N. (2002b), 'Farewell to the "end of history": organization and vision in anti-corporate movements', *Socialist Register*, **38**, 1–13.

Klein, N. (2011), 'Occupy Wall Street: the most important thing in the world now', *The Nation*, 6 October, accessed 6 October 2011 at http://www.thenation.com/article/163844/occupy-wall-street-most-important-thing-world-now.

Kolk, A. and D. Levy (2004), 'Multinationals and global climate change: issues for the automotive and oil industries', *Research in Global Strategic Management*, **9**, 171–93.

Korten, D. (2001), *When Corporations Rule the World*, San Francisco, CA: Berrett-Koehler Publishers.

Korten, D. (2002), 'Predatory corporations', in Geoffrey Evans, James Goodman and Nina Lansbury (eds), *Moving Mountains: Communities Confront Mining Globalisation*, London: Zed Books, pp. 1–18.

Korten, D. (2006), *The Great Turning: From Empire to Earth Community*, San Francisco, CA: Berrett-Koehler Publishers.

Kurlantzick, J. (2004), 'Taking multinationals to court: how the Alien Torts Act promotes human rights', *World Policy Journal*, **21** (1), 60–67.

Lad, L. and C. Caldwell (2009), 'Collaborative standards, voluntary codes and industry self-regulation: the role of third-party organizations', *Journal of Corporate Citizenship*, **35**, 67–80.

Lampikoski, T. (2012), 'Green, innovative, and profitable: a case study of managerial capabilities at Interface Inc.', *Technology Information Management Review*, November, pp. 4–12.

Lange, D., P. Lee and Y. Dai (2011), 'Organizational reputation: a review', *Journal of Management*, **37** (1), 153–84.

Lapierre, D. and J. Moro (2002), *Five Past Midnight in Bhopal: The Epic Story of the World's Deadliest Industrial Disaster*, New York: Grand Central Publishing.

LaPlant, K. (1999), 'The Dow Corning crisis: a benchmark', *Public Relations Quarterly*, **44** (2), 32–3.

Larkin, J. (2003), *Strategic Reputation Risk Management*, Basingstoke: Palgrave Macmillan.

Larner, W. (2000), 'Neo-liberalism, policy, ideology, governmentality', *Studies in Political Economy*, **63**, 5–25.

Lasswell, H. (1958), *Politics: Who Gets What, When, How*, New York: Meridian.

Laufer, W. (2008), *Corporate Bodies and Guilty Minds: The Failure of Corporate Criminal Liability*, Chicago, IL: University of Chicago Press.

Lavery/Pennell (2014), 'The new industrial model: greater profits, more jobs and reduced environmental impacts', accessed 14 May 2015 at http://laverypennell.com/wp-content/uploads/2014/03/New-Industrial-Model-report.pdf.

Leech, G. (2001), 'Coca-Cola accused of using death squads to target union leaders', *Columbia Journal*, 21 July, accessed 1 May 2011 at http://colombiajournal.org/colombia73.htm.

Leith, D. (2002), *The Politics of Power: Freeport in Suharto's Indonesia*, Honolulu: University of Hawaii Press.

Lemke, T. (2000), 'Foucault, governmentality and critique', accessed 30 April 2011 at http://www.thomaslemkeweb.de/publikationen/Foucault,%20Governmentality,%20and%20Critique%20IV-2.pdf.

Lennox, M. (2006), 'The role of private decentralized institutions in sustaining industry self-regulation', *Organizational Science*, **17** (6), 677–90.

Levelle, M. (2014), 'Coast guard blames Shell risk-taking in Kulluk Rig accident', *National Geographic*, 4 April, accessed 24 April 2014 at http://news.nationalgeographic.com/news/energy/2014/04/140404-coast-guard-blames-shell-in-kulluk-rig-accident/.

Levi-Faur, D. (2005), 'The global diffusion of regulatory capitalism', *The Annals of the American Academy of Politics and the Social Sciences*, **598**, 12–32.

Levi-Faur, D. and J. Jordana (2005), 'The making of a new regulatory order', *American Academy of Political and Social Science*, **598**, 6–9.

Levy, B. and P. Spiller (1994), 'The institutional foundations of regulatory commitment: a comparative analysis of telecommunications regulation', *Journal of Law Economics and Organization*, **10** (2), 201–46.

Lewis, M. (1992), *Green Delusions: An Environmentalist Critique of Radical Environmentalism*, Durham, NC: Duke University Press.

Liker, J. (2004), *The Toyota Way: 14 Management Principles from the World's Greatest Manufacturer*, New York: McGraw-Hill Professional.

Liker, J. (2010), 'Japanese automaker's recall don't invalidate its vaunted production system', *Industrial Engineer*, May.

Liker, J. and T. Ogden (2011), *Toyota Under Fire: How Toyota Faced the Challenges of Recall and the Recession to Come Out Stronger*, New York: McGraw-Hill.

Liker, J., M. Hoseus and the Centre for Quality People and Organizations (2008), *Toyota Culture: The Heart and Soul of the Toyota Way*, New York: McGraw-Hill.

Lipset, S. (1981), *Political Man: The Social Basis of Politics*, Cambridge, MA: Johns Hopkins University Press.

Locke, R., M. Amengual and A. Mangla (2009), 'Virtue out of necessity?: Compliance, commitment, and the improvement of labor conditions in global supply chains', *Politics and Society*, **37**, 319–51.

Lodge, M. (2008), 'Regulation, the regulatory state and European politics', unpublished paper, accessed 16 September 2011 at http://aei.pitt.edu/7951/.

Lubbers, E. (2002), *Battling Big Business: Countering Greenwash, Infiltration, and other Forms of Corporate Deception*, London: Green Books.

Lubbers, E. (2012), *Secret Manoeuvres in the Dark: Corporate and Police Spying on Activists*, London: Pluto Press.

Lubin, G. (2010), 'BP CEO Tony Hayward Apologizes for His Idiotic Statement: "I'd Like My Life Back"', accessed 18 June 2016 at http://www.businessinsider.com.au/bp-ceo-tony-hayward-apologizes-for-saying-id-like-my-life-back-2010-6?r=US&IR=T.

Lupton, D. (1999), *Risk*, London: Routledge.

Luttwak, E. (2004), 'Rewarding terror in Spain', *New York Times*, 16 March, accessed 30 April 2011 at http://www.nytimes.com/2004/03/16/opinion/16LUTT.html.

Macalister, T. (2006), 'Shell safety under fire as Brent Bravo deaths judged preventable', *The Guardian*, 19 July, accessed 25 August 2011 at www.guardian.co.uk/business/2006/jul/19/oilandpetrol.news1.

Macalister, T. (2016), 'Shell says it will limit solar investment until it proves profitable', *The Guardian*, 26 May, accessed 27 May 2016 at https://www.theguardian.com/business/2016/may/26/shell-limit-solar-investment-until-profitable.

McCrudden, C. (1999), *Regulation and Deregulation*, Oxford: Oxford University Press.

MacDonald, K. (2011), 'Re-thinking "spheres of responsibility": business responsibility for indirect harm', *Journal of Business Ethics*, **99** (4), 549–63.

McDonough, W. (2007), 'Heroes of the environment: Ray Anderson', accessed 10 March 2015 at http://content.time.com/time/specials/2007/article/0,28804,1663317_1663322_1669929,00.html.

McKinsey and Company (2004), 'Assessing the Global Compact's impact', accessed 30 April 2011 at http://www.unglobalcompact.org/docs/news_events/9.1_news_archives/2004_06_09/imp_ass.pdf.

McNicholas, P. and C. Windsor (2011), 'The BP gulf oil spill: failed regulatory and corporate governance systems analysed through a regulatory capitalist lens', accessed 14 September 2011 at https://works.bepress.com/carolyn_windsor/15/.

Majone, G. (1994), 'The rise of the regulatory state in Europe', *West European Politics*, **17**, 77–101.

Majone, G. (1997), 'From the positive to the regulatory state', *Journal of Public Policy*, **17** (2), 139–67.

Makower, J. (1994), *Beyond the Bottom Line: Putting Social Responsibility to Work for Your Business and the World*, New York: Simon and Schuster.

Manby, B. (1999), 'The role and responsibility of oil multinationals in Nigeria', *Journal of International Affairs*, **53** (1), 281–301.

Mander, J. (1970), 'Ecopornography: one year and nearly a billion dollars later, advertising owns ecology', *Communication and Arts Magazine*, **14** (2), 45–56.

Mander, J. and E. Goldsmith (eds) (1996), *The Case Against the Global Economy and for a Turn Toward the Local*, San Francisco, CA: Sierra Book Club.

Manheim, J. (2002), *The Death of a Thousand Cuts: Corporate Campaigns and the Attack on the Corporation*, Mahwah, NJ: Lawrence Erlbaum.

Manheim, J. and A. Holt (2013), 'Contraband: activism and the leveraging of corporate reputation', in Craig Carroll (ed.), *Handbook of Communication and Corporate Reputation*, London: Wiley Blackwell.

Mani, M. and D. Wheeler (1997), 'In search of pollution havens? Dirty industry in the world economy, 1960–1995', Organisation of Economic Co-operation and Development, accessed 2 July 2004 at http://www.oecd.org/dataoecd/25/4/2076285.pdf.

Maplecroft (2012), '44% of global oil production taking place in countries with a "high risk" of resource nationalism – new report', accessed 5 April 2013 at http://maplecroft.com/about/news/resource_nationalism_index_2012.html.

Marcuse, H. (2004), *The New Left and the 1960s: Collected Papers of Herbert Marcuse*, London: Routledge.

Margulies, W. (2003), 'Make the most of your corporate identity', in John Balmer and Stephen Greyser (eds), *Revealing the Corporation: Perspectives on Identity, Image Reputation, Corporate Branding, and Corporate-Level Marketing*, London: Routledge, pp. 66–76.

Markwick, N. and C. Fill (1997), 'Towards a framework for managing corporate identity', *European Journal of Marketing*, **31** (5/6), 396–409.

Marx, K. and F. Engels (2011), *The Communist Manifesto*, Seattle, WA: CreateSpace International Publishing.

Mattli, W. and N. Woods (2009), *The Politics of Global Regulation*, Princeton, NJ: Princeton University Press.

May, B. (2005), 'Under informed, over here', accessed 6 June 2011 at http://www.guardian.co.uk/science/2005/jan/27/lastword.environment.

May, M. (2007), *The Elegant Solution: Toyota's Formula for Mastering Innovation*, New York: The Free Press.

Meadows, D., Jorgen Randers and Dennis Meadows (2004), *Limits to Growth: The 30-Year Update*, White River Junction, VT: Chelsea Green Publishing.

Meadows, D., D. Meadows, J. Randers and W. Behrens (1972), *The Limits to Growth*, New York: Universe Books.

Melewar, T. (2008), *Facets of Corporate Identity, Communication and Reputation*, London: Routledge.

Mertes, T. (2000), 'Tom Mertes on Naomi Klein, *No Logo*. Emblems of ownership: from branding hides to clothes, cattle to people?', *New Left Review*, **4**, July–August.

Meuller, J. (2007), *The Remnants of War*, New York: Cornell University Press.

Mikler, J. (2010), *Greening the Car Industry: Varieties of Capitalism and Climate Change*, Cheltenham, UK and Northampton, MA, USA: Edward Elgar Publishing.

Minerals Policy Institute (2000), 'BHP investigates ocean dumping for nickel mine', *Mining Monitor*, **5** (3), September, accessed 14 April 2015 at http://www.mpi.org.au/wp-content/uploads/2014/12/MINING_MONITOR_VOL5NO3.pdf.

Mining, Minerals and Sustainable Development (2002), 'Mining for the future – appendix H: Ok Tedi riverine disposal case study', accessed 14 April 2015 at http://pubs.iied.org/pdfs/G00561.pdf.

Mining, Minerals and Sustainable Development (n.d.), accessed 1 May 2011 at http://www.iied.org/mmsd-final-report.

Mio, C. and Fasan, M. (2013), 'Does corporate social performance yield any tangible financial benefit during a crisis? An event study of Lehman Brothers' bankruptcy', *Corporate Reputation Review*, **15** (4), 263–84.

Mirre, J.C. (2013), *The 'Peak Oil' Myth Debunked: There is Plenty of Oil for Another Century*, Seattle, WA: CreateSpace Independent Publishing.

Mirvis, P., B. Googins and S. Kinnicutt (2010), 'Vision, mission, values: guideposts to sustainability', *Organizational Dynamics*, **39**, 316–24.

Moline, M. (2001), 'Former President of Mexico talks globalization', *The Topeka Capital*, 4 May, accessed 23 August 2011 at http://findarticles.com/p/articles/mi_qn4179/is_20010504/ai_n11766552.

Monden, Y. (2011), *Toyota Production System: An Integrated Approach to Just-in-Time*, 4th edn, New York: Productivity Press.

Moody, R. (2005), *The Risk We Run: Mining Communities and Political Risk Insurance*, Dublin: International Books.

Moody, R. (2007), *Rocks and Hard Places: The Globalization of Mining*, London: Zed Books.

Moore, M. (2005), 'A letter to all who voted for George Bush from Michael Moore', accessed 9 May 2011 at http://www.opnlttr.com/letter/open-letter-george-w-bush-michael-moore.

Moran, A. (1995), 'Tools of environmental policy: market instruments versus command and control', in Robyn Eckersley (ed.), *Markets, the State and the Environment: Towards Integration*, Melbourne: Macmillan Australia, pp. 73–85.

Moran, T. (1974), *Multinational Corporations and the Politics of Dependence: Copper in Chile*, Princeton, NJ: Princeton University Press.

Morgan, J. and J. Liker (2006), *The Toyota Product Development System*, New York: The Productivity Press.

Morley, M. (2002), *How to Manage Your Global Reputation: A Guide to the Dynamics of International Public Relations*, New York: New York University Press.

Morris, S., B. Bartkus, M. Glasson and G. Steven Rhiel (2013), 'Philanthropy and corporate reputation: an empirical investigation', *Corporate Reputation Review*, **16** (4), 285–99.

Moskowitz, M. (2002), 'What has CSR really accomplished?', *Business Ethics*, **4** (3–4), 25–37.

Moss Kanter, R. (2009), *SuperCorp: How Vanguard Companies Create Innovation, Profits, Growth, and Social Good*, New York: Crown Business.

Mouawad, J. and D. Barboza (2005), 'In seeking Unocal, Chevron ruffles an Asian partner', 5 July, accessed 30 April 2011 at http://query. nytimes.com/gst/fullpage.html?res=990CE2DF1131F936A35754C0A9 639C8B63.

Muchlinksi, P. (2001), 'Human rights and multinationals: is there a problem?', *International Affairs*, **77** (1), 31–47.

Multinational Monitor (2002), 'Bad apples in a rotten system: the 10 worst corporations of 2002', accessed 25 August 2011 at http:// www.multinationalmonitor.org/mm2002/122002/mokhiber.html.

Nace, T. (2005), 'Fighting back', *Gangs of America: The Rise of Corporate Power and the Disabling of Democracy*, San Francisco, CA: Berrett-Koehler Publishers, pp. 197–218.

Naess, A. (2010), *The Ecology of Wisdom: Writings by Arne Naess*, Berkeley, CA: Counterpoint Press.

Nail, T. (2010), 'Constructivism and the future anterior of radical politics', in *Anarchist Developments in Cultural Studies:'Post-Anarchism Today'*, pp. 73–4, accessed 3 March 2014 at http:// www.Anarchist-Developments.org.

Nakajima, N. and W. Vanderburg (2005), 'A failing grade for our efforts to make our civilization more environmentally sustainable', *Bulletin of Science, Technology and Society*, **25** (2), 129–44.

Nakamura, L. (2003), 'A trillion dollars a year in intangible investment in the new economy', in John Hand and Baruch Lev (eds), *Intangible Assets: Values, Measures, Risks*, Oxford: Oxford University Press, pp. 9–47.

National Highway Traffic Safety Administration (2010), 'Secretary LaHood announces DOT is seeking maximum civil penalty from Toyota', 5 April, accessed 3 December 2012 at http://www.nhtsa.gov/ PR/DOT-59-10.

Neef, D. (2003), *Managing Corporate Reputation and Risk: A Strategic Approach Using Knowledge Management*, New York: Butterworth-Heinemann.

Net-Works (n.d.), Net-Works website, accessed 5 January 2015 at http://net-works.com/.

Neufeld, E. (2011), 'Lost in translation? Toyota and the recall scandal', in Parissa Haghirian and Philippe Gagnon (eds), *Case Studies in Japanese Management*, London: World Scientific, pp. 231–45.

Neumayer, E. (2001), 'Picking holes in a litany of loss', *Times Higher Education Supplement*, 16 November, accessed 5 June 2007 at www.timeshighereducation.co.uk/story.asp?sectioncode=26&story code=165814.

Nielson, R. (2005), *The Little Green Handbook: A Guide to Critical Global Trends*, Melbourne: Scribe.

Nordhaus, T. and M. Shellenberger (2007), *Break Through: From the Death of Environmentalism to the Politics of Possibility*, New York: Houghton Mifflin Company.

North, D. (1990), *Institutions, Institutional Change and Economic Performance*, Cambridge: Cambridge University Press.

O'Brien, K. (2011), 'Interview – Bob Graham', 4 Corners, Australian Broadcasting Commission, accessed 13 September 2011 at http://www.abc.net.au/4corners/content/2011/s3164554.htm.

O'Brien, R. and M. Williams (2010), *Global Political Economy: Evolution and Dynamics*, 3rd edn, London: Palgrave Macmillan.

O'Callaghan, T. (2007a), 'Anti-American heroes: the rhetoric of moral outrage', in B. O'Conner (ed.), *Anti-Americanism: History, Causes, Themes*, vol. 4, London: Greenwood Press, pp. 197–220.

O'Callaghan, T. (2007b), 'Disciplining MNEs: reputation risk in an era of globalisation', *Global Society*, **21** (1), 95–117.

O'Callaghan, T. (2009), 'Regulation and governance in the Philippines mining sector', *The Asia Pacific Journal of Public Administration*, **31** (1), 91–114.

O'Callaghan, T. (2010), 'Patience is a virtue: regulation and governance in the Indonesian mining sector', *Resources Policy*, **35** (3), 218–25.

O'Callaghan, T. and B. Spagnoletti (2015), 'Corporate social responsibility and development partnerships: re(de)fining the corporate social responsibility agenda?', in T. O'Callaghan and G. Graetz (eds), *Mining in the Asia-Pacific Region: Risks, Challenges and Opportunities*, New York: Springer.

O'Connor, B. (2007), *Anti-Americanism: History, Causes, Themes*, 4 vols, London: Greenwood World Publishing.

Office of Regulation Review (1998), *A Guide to Regulation*, Canberra: Commonwealth of Australia.

Ogus, A. (1994), *Regulation: Legal Form and Economic Theory*, London: Oxford University Press.

Ohmae, K. (1994), *The Borderless World: Power and Strategy in the Global Marketplace*, London: HarperCollins.

Ohmae, K. (1995), *The End of the Nation State: The Rise of Regional Economies*, London: HarperCollins.

Ohno, T. (1988), *Toyota Production System: Beyond Large Scale Production*, New York: Productivity Press.

Ohnsman, A., J. Green and K. Inoue (2010), 'The humbling of Toyota', *Bloomberg Businessweek*, 11 March.

Okonta, I. (2008), *When Citizens Revolt: Nigerian Elites, Big Oil and the Ogoni Struggle for Self-Determination*, Trenton, NJ: Africa World Press.

Okonta, I. and O. Douglas (2003), *Where Vultures Feast: Shell, Human Rights and Oil*, London: Verso.

Oldenziel, J. (2005), 'The added value of the UN norms: a comparative analysis of the UN Norms for business with existing international instruments', accessed 29 April 2011 at http://somo.nl/html/paginas/pdf/UN_Norms_report_news_2005_EN.pdf.

Olins, W. (2003), 'Corporate identity: the myth and reality', in John Balmer and Stephen Grayser (eds), *Revealing the Corporation: Perspectives on Identity, Image, Reputation, Corporate Branding, and Corporate-Level Marketing*, London: Routledge, pp. 53–65.

Olivera, O. and T. Lewis (2004), *Cochabamba! Water War in Bolivia*, New York: South End Press.

Omarova, S. (2011), 'Wall Street as community of fate: toward financial industry self-regulation', *University of Pennsylvania Law Review*, **159** (2), 411–92.

Omarova, S. and A. Feibelman (2008–09), 'Risks, rules and institutions: a process for reforming the financial industry', *University of Memphis Law Review*, **39** (4), 881–930.

Omoweh, D. (2005), *Shell Petroleum Development Company, the State and Underdevelopment of Nigeria's Niger Delta: A Study in Environmental Degradation*, Trenton, NJ: Africa World Press.

O'Neil, K. (2004), 'Transnational protest: states, circuses, and conflict at the frontline of global politics', *International Studies Review*, **6** (2), 233–52.

Opp, K-D. (2009), *Theories of Political Protest and Social Movements: Multidisciplinary Introduction, Critique, and Synthesis*, London: Routledge.

Orellana, M. (2002), 'Indigenous peoples, mining, and international law', *Mining, Minerals and Sustainable Development*, January, accessed 6 June 2011 at http://pubs.iied.org/pdfs/G00529.pdf.

Organisation Internationale des Constructeurs d'Automobiles (2013), 'World motor vehicle production: OICA correspondents survey', accessed 31 December 2013 at http://www.oica.net/wp-content/uploads/2013/03/worldpro2012-modification-ranking.pdf.

Organisation for Economic Co-operation and Development (2000), 'Guidelines for multinational enterprises', accessed 30 May 2011 at http://www.oecd.org/department/0,3355,en_2649_34889_1_1_1_1_1,00.html.

O'Rourke, J. (2001), 'Bridgestone/Firestone inc. and Ford Motor Company: how a product crisis ended a hundred year relationship', *Corporate Reputation Review*, **4** (3), 255–64.

O'Rourke, J. and S. Collins (2008), *Managing Conflict and Workplace Relationships*, 2nd edn, Mason, OH: South-Western Cengage Learning.

Orsatto, R. and S. Clegg (1999), 'The political ecology of organizations: toward a framework for analysing business–environment relationships', *Organization and the Environment*, **12** (3), 263–79.

Osha, S. (2007), *Ken Saro-Wiwa's Shadow: Politics, Nationalism and the Ogoni Protest Movement*, London: Adonis and Abbey Publishers.

Ostrom, E. (1990), *Governing the Commons: The Evolution of Institutions for Collective Action*, New York: Cambridge University Press.

Paine, T. (2009), *Rights of Man, Common Sense, and Other Political Writing*, Oxford: Oxford University Press.

Palast, G. (2004), 'A well-designed disaster: the untold story of the Exxon Valdez', in Clint Willis and Nate Hardcastle (eds), *The I Hate Corporate America Reader: How Big Companies from McDonald's to Microsoft are Destroying our Way of Life*, Cambridge, MA: Da Capo Press, pp. 365–78.

Paltridge, G. (2010), *The Climate Caper: Facts and Fallacies of Global Warming*, Texas: Taylor Trade Publishing.

Parker, C. (2002), *The Open Corporation: Effective Self-Regulation and Democracy*, Cambridge: Cambridge University Press.

Paterson, M. (2000), 'Car culture and environmental politics', *Review of International Studies*, **26** (2), 253–70.

Paterson, M. (2007), *Automobile Politics: Ecology and Cultural Political Economy*, Cambridge: Cambridge University Press.

Paterson, M. and S. Dalby (2006), 'Empire's ecological tyreprints', *Environmental Politics*, **15** (1), 1–22.

Paul, J. and R. Kapoor (2008), *International Marketing: Text and Cases*, New Delhi: Tata McGraw-Hill.

Peel, M. (2010), *A Swamp Full of Dollars: Pipelines and Paramilitaries at Nigeria's Oil Frontier*, Chicago, IL: Lawrence Hill Books.

Pegg, S. (2000), 'Ken Saro-Wiwa: assessing the multiple legacies of a literary interventionist', *Third World Quarterly*, **21** (4), 701–8.

Penniman, N. (2002), 'Where's the movement?', *The American Prospect*, 16 September, accessed 1 March 2005 at http://prospect.org/article/wheres-movement.

Penrose, E. (1959), *The Theory of the Growth of the Firm*, Oxford: Oxford University Press.

Perlman, J. (2004), *Citizen's Primer for Conservation Activism: How to Fight Development in Your Community*, Houston, TX: University of Texas Press.

Peters, G. (1999), *Waltzing with the Raptors: A Practical Roadmap to Protecting Your Company's Reputation*, New York: John Wiley and Sons.

Pierson, C., F.G. Castles and I.K. Naumann (2013), *The Welfare State Reader*, 3rd edn, Cambridge: Polity Press.

Pies, I. and P. Koslowski (2013), *Corporate Citizenship and New Governance: The Political Role of Corporations*, New York: Springer.

Plate, E., M. Foy and Krehbiel, R. (2009), *Best Practices for First Nation Involvement in Environmental Assessment Reviews of Development Projects*, Vancouver, BC, accessed 24 February 2014 at http://www.newrelationshiptrust.ca/downloads/environmental-assessments-report.pdf.

Polet, F. (2007), *The State of Resistance: Popular Struggles in the Global South*, London: Zed Books.

Potter, M. (2007), 'Royal Dutch Shell (RDSL) agreed to pay $352.6 million to non-US investors on Wednesday as it seeks to put behind it the reserves overbooking scandal that rocked the oil giant in 2004', accessed 25 August 2011 at http://www.reuters.com/article/2007/04/11/us-shell-settlement-idUSWLB753220070411.

Prakash, A. (2000), 'Responsible Care: an assessment', *Business & Society*, **39** (2), 183–209.

Prakash, A. and M. Potoski (2006), *The Voluntary Environmentalists: Green Clubs, ISO 14001, and Voluntary Environmental Regulations*, Cambridge: Cambridge University Press.

Prakash Sethi, S. (1994), *Multinational Corporations and the Impact of Public Advocacy on Corporate Strategy: Nestlé and the Infant Formula Controversy*, New York: Springer.

Prakash Sethi, S. (2011), *Globalization and Self-Regulation: The Crucial Role that Corporate Codes of Conduct Play in Global Business*, London: Palgrave Macmillan.

PR News (2002), 'Public relations in reputation rescue mode in accounting industry', **58** (28), 22 July, accessed 1 May 2012 at http://www.prnewsonline.com/news/5755.html.

Project Underground (2006), 'Shell in Nigeria', accessed 25 August 2011 at http://www.thirdworldtraveler.com/Africa/Shell_Nigeria.html.

Quelch, J., C-I. Knoop and R. Johnson (2011), 'Toyota recalls (A): hitting the skids', *Harvard Business School Case*, 9-511-016.

Rabinow, P. and W. Sullivan (1988), *Interpretive Social Science: A Second Look*, Berkeley, CA: University of California Press.

Radford, T. (1995), 'Marine scientists say sea dumping was best option', *The Guardian*, 21 June.

Ragas, M. (2013), 'Agenda building and agenda setting theory: which companies we think about and how we think about them', in Craig Carroll (ed.), *Handbook of Communication and Corporate Reputation*, London: Wiley Blackwell.

Ramus, C. and I. Monteil (2005), 'When are corporate environmental policies a form of greenwashing?', *Business and Society*, **44** (4), 377–414.

Randall, Tom (2012), 'How to clean five billion pounds of carpeting: Interface', accessed 8 January 2013 at http://www.bloomberg.com/news/articles/2012-06-04/how-to-clean-five-billion-pounds-of-carpeting-interface.

Rawcliffe, P. (1993), 'Eco-radicalism and green ideology', *Futures*, May.

The Ray C. Anderson Foundation (2012), 'Ray C. Anderson biography', accessed 30 November 2014 at http://www.raycanderson foundation.org/biography.

Reddy, S. (1995), 'No grounds for dumping: the decommissioning and abandonment of offshore oil and gas platforms', London: Greenpeace International, accessed 25 August 2011 at http://repub.eur.nl/res/pub/9404/ERS-2007-014-ORG.pdf.

Reingold, E. (1999), *Toyota: People, Ideas and the Challenge of the New*, London: Penguin.

Reputation Institute (2008), 'Global pulse survey', accessed 30 June 2009 at http://reputationinstitute.com/events/Global_Pulse_2008_Results.pdf.

Reputex (2008), 'Low carbon survey', accessed 2 May 2011 at http://worldisgreen.files.wordpress.com/2008/07/mr-reputex_announces_australias_best_low_carbon_companies_030708.pdf.

Reuters (2010), 'Prius recall puts Toyota troubles into overdrive', accessed 14 January 2011 at http://blogs.reuters.com/breakingviews/2010/02/09/prius-recall-puts-toyota-troubles-into-overdrive/.

Richardson, P. (2004), 'Corporate crime in a globalized economy: an examination of the corporate legal conundrum and positive prospects for peace', *Journal of Public and International Affairs*, **15**, 166–89.

Ricoeur, P. (1981), *Hermeneutics and the Human Sciences: Essays on Language, Action and Interpretation*, Cambridge: Cambridge University Press.

Rikowski, G. (2001), *The Battle in Seattle: Its Significance for Education*, London: The Tufnell Press.

Robèrt, K-H. (2008), *The Natural Step Story: Seeding a Quiet Revolution*, Gabriola Island, BC: New Catalyst Books.

Roberts, P. and G. Dowling (2002), 'Corporate reputation and sustained superior financial performance', *Strategic Management Journal*, **23** (12), 1077–93.

Robinson, G. (2013), *Global Warming-Alarmists, Skeptics and Deniers: A Geoscientist Looks at the Science of Climate Change*, Abbeville: Moonshine Cove Publishing.

Ronit, K. (2001), 'Institutions of private authority in global governance: linking territorial forms of self-regulation', *Administration and Society*, **33** (5), 555–78.

Rosebro, J. (2007), 'Automakers rally US citizens to oppose higher fuel economy standards', *Green Car Congress*, 27 May, accessed 28 May 2007 at http://www.greencarcongress.com/2007/05/automakers_rall. html.

Roszak, T. (1970), *The Making of a Counter Culture: Reflections on the Technocratic Society and its Youthful Opposition*, London: Faber.

Royal Dutch Shell (1995), 'Press release: clear thinking in troubled times', Shell Petroleum Development Company, 31 October, accessed 25 August 2011 at http://www.icai-online.org/xp_resources/icai//oil_ companies//roles_and_responsibility.pdf.

Royal Dutch Shell (1998), *Profits and Principles: Does There Have to be a Choice*, London: Royal Dutch Shell, accessed 25 August 2011 at http://sustainabilityreport.shell.com/2010/servicepages/previous/ files/shell_report_1998.pdf.

Royal Dutch Shell (2002), 'Meeting the energy challenge: The Shell Report', London: Royal Dutch Shell, accessed 25 August 2011 at http://sustainabilityreport.shell.com/2008/servicepages/downloads/files/ download2.php?file=shell_report_2002.pdf.

Royal Dutch Shell (2008), 'Brent Spar dossier', accessed 25 August 2011 at http://www-static.shell.com/static/gbr/downloads/e_and_p/brent_ spar_dossier.pdf.

Royal Dutch Shell (2010), 'Shell and Cosan: fuelling a lower-carbon future with biofuels', accessed 18 March 2014 at http://www. shell.com/media/news-and-media-releases/2011/shell-cosan-raizen-bio fuels.html.

Royal Dutch Shell (2011a), 'Human rights', accessed 8 May 2011 at http://www.shell.com/sustainability/transparency/human-rights.html.

Royal Dutch Shell (2011b), 'Shell at a glance', accessed 25 August 2011 at http://www.shell.com/home/content/aboutshell/at_a_glance/.

Royal Dutch Shell (2011c), 'Sustainability report', accessed 2 February 2014 at http://reports.shell.com/sustainability-report/2011/service pages/welcome.html.

Royal Dutch Shell (2011d), 'Sustainable development at Shell', accessed 24 February 2015 at https://www.shell.com.au/environment-society/ sustainable-development.html.

Royal Dutch Shell (2012), 'Sustainability report', accessed 2 February 2012 at http://reports.shell.com/sustainability-report/2012/service pages/welcome.html.

Royal Dutch Shell (2013), 'Sustainability report', accessed 2 September 2014 at http://reports.shell.com/sustainability-report/2013/service pages/welcome.html.

Royal Dutch Shell (2014), 'General business principles', accessed 30 January 2015 at http://s05.static-shell.com/content/dam/shell-new/ local/global-content-packages/corporate/sgbp-english.pdf.

Rubenstein, J. (2008), *Making and Selling Cars: Innovation and Change in the U.S. Automotive Industry*, Baltimore, MD: Johns Hopkins University Press.

Ruggie, J-G. (2002), 'The theory and practice of learning networks: corporate social responsibility and the Global Compact', *Journal of Corporate Citizenship*, **5**, January, 27–36.

Ruggie, J-G. (2004), 'Reconstituting the global public domain: issues, actors and practices', *European Journal of International Relations*, **10** (4), 499–531.

Safety Research and Strategy (2010), 'Toyota unintended acceleration complaints update', accessed 13 October 2010 at http://www. safetyresearch.net/2010/03/04/toyota-unintended-acceleration-complaints-update-2/.

Sage, G. (1999), 'Justice Do It! The Nike Transnational Advocacy Network: Organization, Collective Actions, and Outcomes', *Sociology of Sport Journal*, **16** (3), 206–35.

Saikal, A. (2009), *The Rise and Fall of the Shah: Iran from Autocracy to Religious Rule*, Princeton, NJ: Princeton University Press.

Sale, R. and E. Potapov (2009), *The Scramble for the Arctic: Ownership, Exploitation and Conflict in the Far North*, London: Frances Lincoln.

Sampson, A. (1973), *The Sovereign State: The Secret History of ITT*, London: Coronet.

Sampson, A. (1975), *The Seven Sisters: The Great Oil Companies and the World They Shaped*, New York: Viking Press.

Sasser, E., A. Prakash, B. Cashore and G. Auld (2006), 'Direct targeting as an NGO political strategy: examining private authority regimes in the forestry sector', *Business and Politics*, **8** (3), 1–32.

Scherer, A.G. and G. Palazzo (2010), *Handbook of Research on Global Corporate Citizenship*, Cheltenham, UK and Northampton, MA, USA: Edward Elgar Publishing.

Schermerhorn, J. (2012), *Exploring Management*, 3rd edn, New York: Wiley & Sons.

Schiavone, M. (2007), *Unions in Crisis? The Future of Organized Labor in America*, New York: Praeger.

Schlesinger, S. and S. Kinzer (2005), *Bitter Fruit: The Story of the American Coup in Guatemala*, Cambridge, MA: David Rockefeller Center on Latin American Studies.

Schmit, J. (2010), 'Regulators share blame in BP oil spill, lawmakers say', *USA Today*, 20 July, accessed 16 September at http://www.usatoday.com/money/industries/energy/2010-07-20-oil-spill-hearing_N.htm.

Schnietz, K. and M. Epstein (2005), 'Exploring the financial value of a reputation for corporate social responsibility during a crisis', *Corporate Reputation Review*, **7** (4), 327–45.

Scholte, J. Aart (1997), 'The globalization of world politics', in John Baylis and Steve Smith (eds), *The Globalization of World Politics: An Introduction to International Relations*, Oxford: Oxford University Press, pp. 13–30.

Schoon, N. (1997), 'David's great victory over Goliath', *The Independent*, 21 June, p. 19, accessed 25 August 2011 at http://www.independent.co.uk/news/uk/davids-great-victory-over-goliath-1587532.html.

Schwartz, F. (2002), *Nestlé: The Secrets of Food, Trust and Globalization*, Toronto: Key Porter Books.

Schwartz, P. and B. Gibb (1999), *When Good Companies Do Bad Things: Responsibility and Risk in an Age of Globalisation*, New York: Wiley & Sons.

Scott, J. (2005), 'Beyond the war of words: cautious resistance and calculated conformity', in Louise Amoore (ed.), *The Global Resistance Reader*, London: Routledge, pp. 392–410.

Scruton, R. (2007), *The Palgrave Macmillan Dictionary of Political Thought*, 3rd edn, London: Sage.

Securities and Exchange Commission (2012), 'What is a Ponzi Scheme?', accessed 30 January 2013 at http://www.sec.gov/answers/ponzi.htm.

Seeger, M. (2010), 'Image restoration and the Toyota recall', *Communication Currents*, **5** (2), accessed 15 April 2011 at http://www.natcom.org/CommCurrentsArticle.aspx?id=967.

Seeger, M. and R. Ulmer (2001), 'Virtuous responses to organizational crises: Aaron Feuerstein and Milt Cole', *Journal of Business Ethics*, **31** (4), 369–76.

Sell, S. (1999), 'Multinational corporations as agents of change: the globalization of intellectual property rights', in Claire Cutler, Virginia Haufler and Tony Porter (eds), *Private Authority and International Affairs*, New York: State University of New York Press, pp. 169–98.

Sessions, G. (1995), *Deep Ecology for the Twenty-First Century*, Boston, MA: Shambhala Publications.

The Shell Foundation (2011), 'About Us', accessed 25 August 2011 at http://www.shellfoundation.org/About-Us.aspx.

Shifferes, S. (2003), 'US names coalition of the willing', accessed 29 April 2011 at http://news.bbc.co.uk/2/hi/americas/2862343.stm.

Skeel, D. (2005), 'Corporate shaming revisited: an essay for Bill Klein', *Berkeley Business Law Journal*, **105**, 107–15.

Sluyterman, K. (2010), 'Royal Dutch Shell: company strategies for dealing with environmental issues', *Business History Review*, **84** (2), 203–26.

Smarzynska, B. and Shang-Jin Wei (2001), 'Pollution havens and foreign direct investment: dirty secret or popular myth?', *National Bureau of Economic Research*, Working Paper No. 8465, accessed 2 January 2004 at http://www.nber.org/papers/w8465.

Smil, V. (2008), 'Moore's curse and the great energy delusion', *The American: A Magazine of Ideas*, 19 November, accessed 15 November 2009 at http://www.vaclavsmil.com/wp-content/uploads/docs/smil-article-20081119-the_American.pdf.

Sobol, R. (1993), *Bending the Law: The Story of the Dalkon Shield Bankruptcy*, Chicago, IL: Chicago University Press.

Sontag, S. (2001), 'Talk of the town', *The New Yorker*, 24 September, accessed 29 May 2005 at http://www.newyorker.com/archive/2001/09/24/010924ta_talk_wtc.

Spagnoletti, B. and T. O'Callaghan (2011), 'Going undercover: the paradox of political risk insurance', *Asia-Pacific Journal of Risk and Insurance*, **5** (2).

Spagnoletti, B. and T. O'Callaghan (2013), 'Let there be light: alleviating energy poverty in Asia', *Energy Policy*, **63**, 726–37.

Spar, D. (1998), 'The spotlight and the bottom line: how multinationals export human rights', *Foreign Affairs*, **7** (2), 7–12.

Spar, D. and L. La Mure (2003), 'The power of activism: assessing the impact of NGOs on global business', *California Management Review*, **45** (3), 78–101.

Spear, S. and K. Bowen (1999), 'Decoding the DNA of the Toyota Production System', *Harvard Business Review*, September–October.

Starr, A. (2000), *Naming the Enemy: Anti-corporate Movements Confront Globalisation*, Sydney: Pluto Press.

Stauber, J. and S. Rampton (1995), *Toxic Sludge is Good for You: Lies, Damn Lies and the Public Relations Industry*, London: Robinson.

Stern, N. (2007), *The Economics of Climate Change: The Stern Review*, Cambridge: Cambridge University Press.

Stewart, D. (2010), 'Toyota and the end of Japan', *Newsweek*, 5 March, accessed 5 March 2010 at http://www.newsweek.com/id/234574.

Stewart, T. and A. Raman (2007), 'Lessons from Toyota's long drive', *Harvard Business Review*, July–August, pp. 74–83.

Strange, S. (1996), *The Retreat of the State: The Diffusion of Power in the World Economy*, Cambridge: Cambridge University Press.

Strasser, K. (2011), *Myths and Realities of Business Environmentalism: Good Works, Business or Greenwash?*, Cheltenham, USA and Northampton, MA, USA: Edward Elgar Publishing.

Stuart, H. (2003), 'The effect of corporate structure on corporate identity management', in John Balmer and Stephen Greyser (eds), *Revealing the Corporation: Perspectives on Identity, Image Reputation, Corporate Branding, and Corporate-Level Marketing*, London: Routledge, pp. 106–23.

Stubbs, W. and C. Cocklin (2006), 'An ecological modernist interpretation of sustainability: the case of Interface Inc.', *Business Strategy and the Environment*, **17**, 512–23.

Sullivan, A. (1989), 'Exxon tries to spread the blame around before Valdez claims go to trial', *Wall Street Journal*, 7 June, B8.

Suzuki, D. (1993), *Time to Change*, Toronto: Stoddart Publishing.

Taleb, N.N. (2010), *The Black Swan: The Impact of the Highly Improbable*, New York: Random House.

Tata, R. (2013), *How Detroit Became the Automotive Capitol of the World: The Story Behind the Founding of the U.S. Auto Industry*, Bloomington, IN: Author House.

Taylor, B. (2006), 'Shell shock: why do good companies do bad things?', *Corporate Governance: An International Review*, **14** (3), 181–93.

Taylor, C. (1992), *The Ethics of Authenticity*, Cambridge, MA: Harvard University Press.

Taylor, C. (2007), 'The age of authenticity', in *A Secular Age*, Cambridge, MA: Belknap Press, pp. 473–504.

Taylor, J.G. and P.J. Scharlin (2004), *Smart Alliance: How a Global Corporation and Environmental Activists Transformed a Tarnished Brand*, New Haven, CT: Yale University Press.

Thomas, K. (2009), 'Documents: Toyota boasted saving $100M on recall', 21 February, accessed 21 February 2009 at http://yahoo.com/s/ap/20100221/ap_on_be_ge/us_toyota_recall.

Thompson, P. and R. Macklin (2010), *The Big Fella: The Rise and Rise of BHP Billiton*, Sydney: Random House Australia.

Thomsen, S. and B. Rawson (1998), 'Purifying a tainted corporate image: Odwalla's response to an E. Coli poisoning', *Public Relations Quarterly*, **43** (3), 35–46.

Toffel, M., R. Eccles and C. Taylor (2012), 'InterfaceRAISE: sustainability consulting', *Harvard Business School*, 9-611-069, Boston, MA: Harvard Business School Publishing.

Tomlinson, J. (1999), *Globalisation and Culture*, London: Polity.

Toyoda, A. (2010), 'Toyota's plan to repair its public image', accessed 9 February 2010 at http://www.washingtonpost.com/wp-dyn/content/article/2010/02/08/AR2010020803078_pf.html.

Toyota Motor Corporation (2011a), 'Floor mat recall', accessed 3 May 2012 at http://www.toyota.com/recall/floormat.html.

Toyota Motor Corporation (2011b), 'Pedal recall', accessed 3 May 2012 at http://www.toyota.com/recall/pedal.html.

Toyota Motor Corporation (2012), 'Globalizing and localizing manufacturing', accessed 10 March 2013 at http://www.toyota-global.com/company/vision_philosophy/globalizing_and_localizing_manufacturing/.

The Union of Concerned Scientists (2007), 'Honda, Toyota beat Detroit in new automaker "green" rankings', accessed 4 October 2010 at http://www.ucsusa.org/clean-vehicles/fuel-efficiency/automaker-rankings-2007#.V049VDJJl9M.

United Nations (1973), 'Multinational corporations in world development', accessed 5 February 2008 at http://www.unhistory.org/briefing/17TNCs.pdf.

United Nations Conference on Trade and Development (UNCTAD) (2006), 'World investment report: FDI from developing and transition economies: implications for development', accessed 30 April 2011 at http://www.unctad.org/en/docs/wir2006_en.pdf.

United Nations Conference on Trade and Development (UNCTAD) (2007), 'World Investment Report 2007', accessed 5 January 2008 at http://unctad.org/en/pages/PublicationArchive.aspx?publicationid=724.

United Nations Global Compact (2011), *Annual Review of Business Policies & Actions to Advance Sustainability*, New York: The United Nations, accessed 30 April 2014 at http://www.sterci.com/lang/DE/downloads/2011_Global_Compact_Implementation_Survey.pdf.

Vachini, S., J. Doh and H. Teegen (2009), 'NGOs influence on MNEs social development strategies in varying institutional contexts: a transaction cost perspective', *International Business Review*, **18** (5), 446–56.

Van Riel, C., N. Stoeker and O.J.M. Maathius (1998), 'Measuring corporate images', *Corporate Reputation Review*, **1** (4), 318–26.

Vernon, R. (1971), *Sovereignty at Bay: The Multinational Spread of U.S. Enterprises*, New York: Basic Books.

Viacom Inc. (2012), Form 10K: Annual Report, accessed 28 May 2011 at http://ir.viacom.com/secfiling.cfm?filingID=1193125-12-471870&CIK =1339947.

Vidal, G. (2003), 'The erosion of the American dream: it's time to take action against our wars on the rest of the world', *Counterpunch*, 14 March, accessed 23 August 2011 at http://www.counterpunch.org/ 2003/03/14/the-erosion-of-the-american-dream/.

Vitello, P. (2011), 'Ray Anderson, businessman turned environmentalist, dies at 77', *New York Times*, 10 August, accessed 18 March 2012 at http://www.nytimes.com/2011/08/11/business/ray-anderson-a-carpet-innovator-dies-at-77.html?_r=0.

Vivoda, V. (2008), *The Return of the Obsolescing Bargain and the Decline of Big Oil: A Study of Bargaining in the Contemporary Oil Industry*, Saarbrücken: VDM Verlag.

Vivoda, V. (2009), 'Resource nationalism, bargaining and international oil companies: challenges and change in the new millennium', *New Political Economy*, **14** (4), 517–34.

VOA News (2010), 'Toyota faces tough job rebuilding reputation', accessed10 October 2012 at http://www.voanews.com/english/news/ economy-and-business/Toyota-Faces-Tough-Job-Rebuilding-Reputation-84388992.html.

Vogel, D. (2005), *The Market for Virtue: The Potential and Limits of Corporate Social Responsibility*, Washington, DC: Brookings Institution Press.

Vohs, K. and R. Baumeister (2010), *The Handbook of Self-Regulation: Research, Theory and Applications*, New York: Guilford Press.

Waddock, S. and S. Graves (1997), 'The corporate social performance–financial performance link', *Strategic Management Journal*, **18** (4), 303–19.

Waldman, P. (1998), 'Hand in glove: how Suharto's circle, mining firm did so well together', *Wall Street Journal*, 29 September, accessed 23 May 2005 at http://www.wsj.com/articles/SB907020100505646000.

Walker, R.B.J. (2005), 'Social movements/world politics', in Louise Amoore (ed.), *The Global Resistance Reader*, London: Routledge, pp. 136–49.

Wallace, H. (1995), 'Brent Spar – the scientific debate', London: Greenpeace International, accessed 25 August 2011 at http:// archive.greenpeace.org/comms/brent/bp01.html.

Walmart (2014), 'Annual Report', accessed 11 February 2015 at http:// www.corporatereport.com/walmart/2014/ar/_pdf/WMT2014Annual ReportFinancials.pdf.

Warren, R. (1993), 'Codes of ethics: bricks without straw', *Business Ethics: A European Review*, **2** (4), 185–91.

Wartick, S. (2002), 'Measuring corporate reputation: definition and data', *Business and Society*, **41** (4), 371–93.

Watson, McClain (2011), 'Doing well by doing good: Ray C. Anderson as evangelist for corporate sustainability', *Business Communication Quarterly*, **14** (1), 63–7.

Watson, T. (2007), 'Reputation and ethical behaviour in a crisis: predicting survival', *Journal of Communication Management*, **11** (4), 3371–84.

Watts, M. (2004) 'Resource curse? Governmentality, oil and power in the Niger Delta, Nigeria', *Geopolitics*, **14** (47), 50–71.

Wells, L. (1998), 'A wolf in sheep's clothing: why Unocal should be liable under U.S. law for human rights abuses in Burma', *Columbia Journal of Law & Social Problems*, **32** (1), 35–71.

Wells, L. and R. Ahmed (2007), *Making Foreign Investment Safe: Property Rights and National Sovereignty*, London: Oxford University Press.

Werre, M. (2003), 'Implementing corporate responsibility: the Chiquita case', *Journal of Business Ethics*, **44** (2/3), 247–60.

Wettstein, F. (2010), 'The duty to protect: corporate complicity, political responsibility and human rights advocacy', *Journal of Business Ethics*, **96** (1), 33–47.

Wicki, S. and J. van der Kaaij (2007), 'Is it true love between the octopus and the frog? How to avoid the authenticity gap', *Corporate Reputation Review*, **10** (4), 312–18.

Williams, S., H. Bradley and R. Devadason (2014), *Globalization and Work*, London: Polity Press.

Willis, C. and N. Hardcastle (eds) (2004), *The I Hate Corporate America Reader: How Big Companies from McDonald's to Microsoft are Destroying Our Way of Life*, Cambridge, MA: Da Capo Press.

Wilson, M. and R. Lombardi (2001), 'Globalisation and its discontents: the arrival of triple bottom line reporting', *Ivey Business Journal*, September/October, pp. 69–72.

Windsor, Duane (2001), 'Corporate citizenship: evolution and interpretation', in Jörg Andriof and Malcolm McIntosh (eds), *Perspectives on Corporate Citizenship*, Sheffield: Greenleaf Publishing, pp. 39–52.

Womack, J. (2006), 'Why Toyota won', *Wall Street Journal*, accessed 27 April 2012 at http://online.wsj.com/article/SB1139801759825 72192.html.

Womack, J., D. Jones and D. Roos (1990), *The Machine That Changed the World: The Story of Lean Production*, New York: Harper Perennial.

World Bank (1995), 'The Niger Delta: a stakeholder approach to environmental development', *Findings: African Region*, **57**, 1–5, accessed 25 August 2011 at http://www-wds.worldbank.org/external/default/WDSContentServer/WDSP/IB/2003/11/06/000090341_200311061309 55/Rendered/PDF/271580English0Findings0no10530.pdf.

World Commission on Environment and Development (1987), *Our Common Future*, Oxford: Oxford University Press.

World Health Organization (n.d.), 'Air quality and health', accessed 29 April 2011 at http://www.who.int/mediacentre/factsheets/fs313/en/index.html.

World Health Organization (2004), *World Report on Road Traffic Injury Prevention*, Geneva: World Health Organization, accessed 1 June 2005 at http://www.who.int/violence_injury_prevention/publications/road_traffic/world_report/en/index.html.

World Health Organization (2013), *Global Status Report on Road Safety 2013*, accessed 16 April 2014 at http://www.who.int/violence_injury_prevention/road_safety_status/2013/en/.

Yergin, D. (2009), *The Prize: The Epic Quest for Oil, Money & Power*, New York: The Free Press.

Young, O. (1992), *Arctic Politics: Conflict and Cooperation in the Circumpolar North*, London: Dartmouth.

YouTube (2010a), 'Toyota 911 call of family's fatal Lexus crash', accessed 4 May 2011 at http://www.youtube.com/watch?v=03m7fmnhO0I.

YouTube (2010b), 'Runaway car kills CHP officer', accessed 4 May 2011 at http://www.youtube.com/watch?v=gZWPItpu2bM.

Zadek, S. (2003), *The Civil Corporation: The New Economy of Corporate Citizenship*, Abingdon: Earthscan Publications.

Zyglidopoulos, S. (2002), 'The social and economic responsibilities of multinationals: evidence from the Brent Spar case', *Journal of Business Ethics*, **36** (10–12), 141–51.

Index